Y0-ACD-285

Human Settlement
Systems

Human Settlement Systems

International Perspectives on Structure, Change and Public Policy

Editor
Niles M. Hansen

Ballinger Publishing Company • Cambridge, Massachusetts
A Subsidiary of J.B. Lippincott Company

This book is printed on recycled paper.

Copyright © 1978 by International Institute for Applied Systems Analysis. All rights reserved. No part of this publication may be reproduced, stored in a retrieval system, or transmitted in any form or by any means, electronic mechanical photocopy, recording or otherwise, without the prior written consent of the publisher.

International Standard Book Number: 0–88410–176–2

Library of Congress Catalog Card Number: 77–9964

Printed in the United States of America

Library of Congress Cataloging in Publication Data

Main entry under title:

Human settlement systems.

   1. Cities and towns—Addresses, essays, lectures. 2. Human ecology—Addresses, essays, lectures. I. Hansen, Niles M.
HT151.H86   301.36   77–9964
ISBN 0–88410–176–2

Contents

List of Figures

List of Tables

Preface

This volume is an outgrowth of a conference on the dynamics of human settlement systems organized by the Human Settlements and Services Area of the International Institute for Applied Systems Analysis, Laxenburg, Austria. The IIASA member organizations are Academies of Science or equivalent institutions in Eastern and Western Europe, North America and Japan. The research activities of IIASA are directed toward finding solutions to problems that often result from the success of modern science and technology and that now require the joint efforts of East and West in order to find solutions.

The primary focus of research in the Human Settlements and Services Area is on people—how many there are, where they live and work, the kinds of work they do, their needs and demands for various facilities and services, and their impact on resources and environment. At this writing the Area's research activities are organized around four major tasks: modeling health care systems; migration and settlement; population, resources and growth; and human settlement systems: development processes and strategies, the task within which this study was undertaken.

Policy makers concerned with regional and urban problems should have a clear grasp of the factors that influence the evolution of human settlement systems. Yet despite increasing interest in human settlement issues, the relevant spatial-temporal processes still are very imperfectly understood. The purpose of this book is to give students, scholars and policy makers a thorough exposure to issues being debated at the frontiers of theory and policy. We hope that they will be able to make positive use of the empirical and theoretical insights found in these pages and that they will be stimulated to improve on remaining deficiencies.

I have divided the book into two parts, the first dealing primarily with Human Settlement Processes and the second dealing primarily with Systems Approaches to Human Settlements. The chapters in the first part deal systematically with processes and they generally are couched in the context of explicit or implicit theoretical orientations. Similarly, the chapters in the second part—which tend to be more directly concerned with models and theories—also are concerned with processes.

Chapter 3 is based largely on Thomas Falk's book *Urban Sweden* (Stockholm: The Economic Research Institute at the Stockholm School of Economics, 1976). However, wherever possible this chapter incorporates more recent data. Chapter 6 is a revised updated version of an earlier paper published in *Geographia Polonica, 32,* 1975. Chapter 12 originally appeared in *The Annals of Regional Science, 11,* 1976.

I am indebted to numerous IIASA colleagues for their administrative and technical support in preparing this volume. They include Roger Levien, Director; Andrei Bykov, Head of the Secretariat; Andrei Rogers, Chairman of the Human Settlements and Services Area; and Robert Duis, Head of Documents and Publications. I wish to acknowledge the generous cooperation of the IIASA Council representatives from the national member organizations. I especially appreciate the excellent secretarial assistance of Olivia Carydias. Jean Anderer, Ilse Becky, Anita Fildes, Angelika Loskot, Linda Samide, and Jim Thompson also were quite helpful. Part of the financial support for this study was provided by the Ford Foundation.

The views expressed herein are those of the respective authors and do not necessarily represent those of IIASA or the national member organizations supporting the Institute.

Human Settlement Systems

 *Chapter 1*

Preliminary Overview

Niles M. Hansen

INTRODUCTION

Patterns of human settlement vary significantly according to complex and interrelated historical, cultural, political, economic, geographic and demographic factors. During most of mankind's history population size and distribution have been conditioned in large measure by the interplay of economic and Malthusian processes. Famine, war and disease repeatedly have overwhelmed man's ability to control his natural and social environment. It was not until the nineteenth century that the systematic, practical application of advancing scientific knowledge permitted sustained population growth and rising living standards for large numbers of people in the Western world. Since the Second World War the progress of technology has accelerated on a world-wide scale but too often it has resulted in rapid population growth without significant improvement in the economic well-being of great masses of people in the developing countries. Although considerable attention has been given for some time to issues of aggregate population size and growth at the national and global levels, the systematic study of settlement patterns and their relation to human well-being is relatively recent.

One of the most persistent human settlement themes has been that of optimal city size. At least since the time of the ancient Greeks there has been speculation concerning the best population size for a city. In recent years the optimal city-size question has been raised with unprecedented frequency but the answer is as elusive as ever;

the relevant criteria are too many and too complex and the very notion of a relatively self-contained city has less and less meaning.

Political rulers (and even religious orders) have from time to time influenced settlement patterns through activities such as the creation of new towns or the encouragement of specific migration patterns. However, these efforts have rarely been related to a grand human settlement design. Of course, political capitals frequently have become hubs of national settlement systems. Broader considerations of the size and spacing of cities and of interrelations both among cities and between cities and rural areas have been shaped largely by market forces operating in a geographical context favoring one or another location, e.g. transhipment points. Often, too, the original reason for a city's early growth has played a relatively small role in its later growth. As in other aspects of life nothing succeeds like success. Thus, cities have grown simply because of the many advantages—termed "external economies of agglomeration" in the economics literature—they have offered households and businesses.

It also is alleged that the growth of large cities generates "external diseconomies of agglomeration" such as traffic congestion, crime, and air, water and noise pollution. There is now a large literature dealing with the question of whether these and related problems are caused *by* large city-size as such or whether they are problems *of* cities, in which case they should be dealt with by coming directly to grips with the sources of the problems (Hansen, 1975a; Richardson, 1973). Since World War Two there has been a widespread feeling in many developed and developing countries that some of their cities are too big (or in danger of becoming so) in the sense that the social costs of further growth exceed the social benefits. There also has been a growing feeling that assistance should be given to promote the development of economically lagging regions. These areas usually are rural and have a relatively high proportion of their employment in the primary sector (agriculture, fishing and extractive industries) but in some instances they are old industrial areas in need of modernization. Thus, as Rodwin (1970, p. 3) has pointed out,

> the conviction that urban growth does not take place the way it should is no longer the view of merely a few sensitive intellectuals and professional urbanists. It has become one of the dominant beliefs of the age. If somehow we could determine the best locations for urban growth, and could steer economic activities and families into those areas and away from less desirable ones, we would have powerful weapons for changing our environment. Instead of being stricken or overwhelmed by movements of population and economic activity, we could help communities and regions adjust more effectively to these changes.

Problems of large urban areas (including income and fiscal disparities between central cities and their suburbs), and other parts of any
given country are not independent of one another because the various areas are linked by flows of goods and services, energy, migration,
information, etc. Policies for specific types of cities or regions have
consequences for the whole country. Moreover, to the extent that a
national economy is open to the rest of the world—and most tendencies are in this direction—the international implications of settlement
and related policies also need to be taken into account.

POLICY-RELEVANT MODELS OF HUMAN
SETTLEMENT DEVELOPMENT

When numerous Western governments first became interested in
human settlement policies there was surprisingly little guidance available from the social sciences. In the mid-1960s, Friedmann and
Alonso (1964, p. 1) correctly maintained that "the conceptual structure necessary for intelligent making of policy is in its infancy. The
social sciences, principally economics and sociology, have been lag-
gard in taking notice of space; while geography, which has always
dealt with space, has lacked analytic power." Today the situation is
quite different, especially in the economics and geography disciplines.
With respect to economics, there has been a remarkable international
expansion of university programs, books and journals dealing with
urban and regional issues. This has been due in no small part to the
significant amounts of government funds that have become available
to support such activities. Meanwhile, geography has experienced a
quantitative-theoretical revolution that has moved it much closer in
many respects to economics. Due to the pioneering efforts of Walter
Isard, "regional science" has emerged as a distinctive field of research
on spatial issues; by and large, however, the scholars active in this
area are economists and geographers.

Consideration of all the theories with possible relevance to the
structure and evolution of human settlement systems is beyond the
scope of this chapter [for a recent instructive survey see Friedmann
(1975)]. Nevertheless, those which have had a significant impact on
spatial distribution policies clearly merit some attention.

Central Place Theory

Central place theory, based on the seminal works of Christaller
(1933) and Lösch (1940), has been the principal vehicle for attempting to explain the spatial distribution of urban places in terms of
their size and functions. Despite more recent refinements intended

to provide a better explanation of the typical spacing, size and hierarchy of settlements, the policy relevance of central place theory remains quite limited. Although the theory's assumptions have some relevance to spatial patterns of mercantile centers, they do not apply to most kinds of manufacturing activity. Moreover, because it is essentially static, central place theory in itself yields few insights into spatial development processes.

Growth Center Theory

In many respects growth center theory began in the mid-1950s as a reaction to static central place and location theories, as well as to the restrictive assumptions of the balanced and steady growth theories of economic development. Surveys of growth center theory are available elsewhere (Hansen, 1972, 1975b; Kuklinski, 1972; Moseley, 1974) but it should be emphasized here that the growth centers that are the object of public policy are not simply urban centers that already are growing rapidly—i.e., spontaneous growth centers. Indeed, one of the principal arguments for investments in induced growth centers is that population can thereby be diverted away from allegedly overcrowded metropolitan areas toward smaller cities. On the other hand, growth center theory quite explicitly recognizes the existence of economies of agglomeration. It maintains that the most efficient way to generate development in lagging regions is to concentrate projects in a relatively few places with genuine growth potential. Ideally, public investments in these places would initiate a kind of chain reaction of mutually induced public and private investments. (Some writers have made a distinction between growth poles, defined in terms of the expansion of interrelated economic sectors, and growth centers, defined in terms of geographic location. Because growth center policies rely on the concentration of sectoral activities within very specific geographic places, I use the terms "growth center" and "growth pole" interchangeably.) However, the benefits realized by a growth center approach are supposed to be regional in nature, and not just limited to the few select centers. In theory, economic expansion in the growth centers, or poles, is linked to similar expansion in their hinterlands by means of "spread effects," or "trickle down effects."

How well have growth center strategies worked in practice? With some exceptions in small countries they have not been very successful. They have suffered from a tendency toward proliferation of a large number of relatively small centers incapable of effectively performing the role attributed to them. There is increasing realization that viable growth center strategies require greater selectivity in choice of centers and of activities. However, it still is uncertain whether spread effects from induced growth centers can really raise income and employment opportunities in lagging or declining regions to levels comparable to those in more advanced regions. In some cases it is possible that the economic infrastructure bias that has accompanied growth center policies has done a disservice by shifting attention away from the critical health, education, and social problems that plague less developed regions.

Despite these difficulties the indications are that growth centers will continue to play a major role in human settlement strategies in both the developed and developing countries. For example, a recent major study of regional economic systems viewed from an anthropological perspective concludes that the solution to development problems "may rest on promoting several urban centers or 'growth poles' in the developing region or nation, which will individually concentrate capital but will also provide competition and markets for one another, thereby providing the necessary internal dynamic for sustained growth (Smith, 1976, p. 58)." And a prominent urban and regional economist maintains that the disenchantment of planners with the growth center approach is premature because effective spatial planning requires a fifteen-to-twenty year time horizon; his theoretical analysis "suggests that a well-located growth pole, promoted with vigor and appropriate economic conditions and resistant to political trimming, should pay off as a regional policy instrument if the planning horizon is long enough (Richardson, 1976, p. 8)." Political realities may make it difficult to implement a strategy based on only one or a few urban centers. A successful growth center strategy would have to be based on careful analysis of employment growth prospects, commuting, migration, and the location preferences of people in the context of actual opportunities available in alternative locations.

Hierarchical Diffusion
In the late 1960s several major strands of spatial analytic thought were synthesized in a general model of hierarchical diffusion. As described by Berry (1973a, pp. 8–9) this urban-oriented framework of economic activities in space has two major elements: (1) a system of cities arranged in a functional hierarchy and (2) corresponding areas of urban influence surrounding each of the cities in the system. Given this framework, the spatial extent of developmental spread effects radiating from a given urban center is proportional to the center's size and functions. "Impulses of economic change" are transmitted from higher to lower centers in the hierarchy so that

continuing innovation in large cities is critical for the development of the whole system. Areas of economic backwardness are found in the most inaccessible places, that is, between the least accessible lower-level towns in the urban hierarchy. Finally the growth potential of an area located between any two cities is a function of the intensity of interactions between the cities.

It was pointed out earlier that static central place and urban hierarchy schemes are not in themselves adequate for analyzing growth and change. The synthesis just outlined takes the central place framework as a kind of locational matrix or landscape within which dynamic processes take place. Growth center concepts also fit well within the general synthesis. One merely has to view induced growth centers as means for linking lagging regions more closely with the national scheme of hierarchical filtering and spread effects from urban centers to their hinterlands. Clearly, the synthesis has a great deal of inherent intellectual appeal and it has had some demonstrated applicability, especially in explaining industrial decentralization processes and the spatial-temporal diffusion of certain product innovations, e.g., television sets.

Having looked at the positive side, it must also be said that the model is not adequate for dealing with many important human settlements issues, even in Western urban-industrial countries. The failure of growth center policies to generate significant spread effects to lagging region hinterlands already has been mentioned. Although these policies may not have provided an adequate test of theory — because they used too many small centers and may not have used an adequate time horizon — the burden of proof nonetheless still rests with the believers in spread effects. In addition, there is more general evidence that interrelations among cities in national urban systems are more complex than the hierarchical filtering model would indicate.

Industrial Organization and Spatial Economic Linkages

The influence of organizational decision-making linkages on the development of settlement systems has recently received considerable attention (Goddard, 1975; Lasuén, 1973; Pred, 1975a, 1975b, 1976; Törnqvist, 1973). Pred, in particular, has systematically explored the role of large private and public organizations in the diffusion of growth-inducing innovations that affect city system development. He finds that large organizations are continuing to expand their economic dominance and that metropolitan interdependence is becoming increasingly complex because of the intraorganizational linkages of multilocational business organizations. The intricate web of economic interdependence contradicts simple central-place hierarchy depictions of city systems; empirical evidence indicates that growth-inducing innovation linkages run not only from large cities to smaller cities but also from large cities to even larger cities, from smaller to larger cities, and between cities of comparable size. Moreover, the most important nonlocal linkages are not those between a metropolis and its hinterland—as central place theory and growth center theory concerning spread effects would have it—but rather they are those between large metropolitan complexes.

Several important policy implications are indicated by Pred's studies. For example, planners should avoid growth center schemes that emphasize the manufacturing sector (total manufacturing jobs are declining and lagging regions tend to receive "trickle-down" low wage industrial plants) and supposed input-output linkages with nearby areas. However, it may be efficient to provide smaller and intermediate-size metropolitan complexes (say, in the 100,000 to 250,000 population range) with the infrastructure and services needed for the successful operation of high-level administrative and management functions. In Pred's (1975b, p. 139) view, the single most important policy question is "How can explicit and implicit organizational location decisions be influenced or controlled in order to help bring about greater regional equality in terms of per capita income, labor market alternatives, and public service accessibility?"

Pred's empirical findings rest heavily on data for the amount of employment in other metropolitan areas "controlled" by major industrial organizations from the metropolitan areas where the respective organizational headquarters are located. It is assumed that the number of growth-inducing innovations steered to a city from headquarters is roughly proportional to the number of employees in the organization in the given city. Clearly this assumption needs closer investigation, particularly by detailed case studies of the amount and kinds of investments made in various dispersed organizational units.

Nevertheless, from a policy perspective, the literature on information flows already makes it apparent that, as Pred (1976, p. 16) argues, "no regional-planning policy is likely to be either goal consistent or as successful as anticipated unless its formulation is preceded by studies establishing the peculiar underlying structure of growth-transmission interdependencies within the concerned regional and national system of cities." Moreover, it would be desirable if such research would attempt to incorporate more economic analysis than has been the case in the past. In particular, careful consideration should be given to the costs and benefits of efforts to create new interdependencies between selected small and medium-size metropolitan areas and other urban complexes within the system of cities.

CONCLUSIONS

Stöhr and Tödtling point out in Chapter 4 that although regional development policies have been partly successful in their quantitative aspects, they have tended to be unsatisfactory with respect to qualitative and structural aspects of settlement systems. It is further argued that these difficulties are related less to the resources devoted to regional development efforts than to an inadequate conceptual basis for regional policies.

Despite deficiencies in theories intended to provide insights into the structure and evolution of settlement systems, one clear gain has been made in recent years. This is the general recognition that policy-relevant analysis must take account of the interdependencies among the various elements of the spatial system being considered. As pointed out earlier, within countries the study of small towns and rural areas cannot be divorced from their relation to the urban system; similarly, the study of urban places must take account of demographic, economic and other flows between rural and urban areas and among urban areas. Although the determinants of migration have received major attention in the migration literature, Greenwood (1975, p. 421) emphasizes that these studies are "almost completely devoid of direct policy implications." Moreover, the logic and assumptions of migration models, like those underlying other models of movement, rarely are made explicit. In Chapter 9, Alonso attempts to develop a more general framework for tracing unrecognized implications of the forms of particular movement models; hopefully, this approach will "help to open new ideas or to discard old ones."

Discussions of human settlement issues increasingly have been influenced by environmental and quality of life concerns. Whether or to what extent it is possible to measure quality of life may be debatable but attempts to do so no doubt will continue. In Chapter 13, Nijkamp places problems of changes in settlement patterns and in mobility patterns in the broader context of the postwar evolution of welfare and quality of life. On the basis of a welfare model for residential choices and consequent commuting behavior he derives an aggregate assignment model of journey-to-work behavior. Particular attention is given to the analysis of quality of life indicators and to some statistical methods for dealing with them. Next the important notion of spatial spill-over effects is introduced and an interregional model of residential choice and commuting behavior is constructed. An attempt is made to develop a procedure, based on mixed entropy and behavioral assumptions, to disaggregate the interregional model at the interlocal level. The working of the model is clarified by reference to empirical findings from the Netherlands. The analytic part of the chapter is then related to policy proposals to achieve more integrated and coordinated settlement planning in The Netherlands.

Finally, national and subnational settlement systems often need to be studied in the light of increasing international economic integration, as in the case of the European Economic Community. In this regard the factors promoting or inhibiting the development of border regions need more careful examination (see Chapter 12). On the other hand, a great deal of progress has been made in placing systems studies of developing countries in an international context.

THE DEVELOPING COUNTRY CONTEXT

The structure of urbanization in developing countries usually differs from that in most Western countries in that the former tend to have a "primate" city (or a very few large cities) dominating the rest of the nation in terms of both size and influence. An influential paper by Lasuén (1973) analyzed this phenomenon in the context of international hierarchical diffusion processes. He argued that nations develop according to the degree to which they adopt innovations brought forward internationally; in other words, the international development process affects nations according to the way in which particular national urban processes react to it. In the developed countries the spread of innovations has been accelerated by the existence of multiplant firms because the filtering process works much faster in these firms than under conditions where single plant firms are prevalent. In developing countries the plant and the firm are generally identical; the spatial spread of innovations in developing countries is relatively slow because it is a result of a host of unrelated individual decisions. Lasuén maintains that the only feasible way developing countries can absorb successive innovation clusters more rapidly is to reduce technical and organizational lags by overriding national boundaries and planning multinational firms on a continental basis. He notes that even though the countries of the European Economic Community are ready to pool their markets, they have considerable difficulty in merging their firms into multinational enterprises. "As everybody is aware, the only really multi-national firms in the Common Market are the subsidiaries of the large multi-product multi-plant American conglomerates" (Lasuén, 1973, p. 187).

But how, under present institutional conditions, are the developing countries supposed to do better in this regard than the nations of Western Europe? Moreover, it is quite possible that the very efforts of multinational corporations to extend their operations in developing countries can have negative results from a developmental perspective; they are part of a process which leads to the accelerated growth of a subsystem oriented toward the demands of a small privileged section of the population (in Latin America, for example, 5 percent of the population accounts for over 50 percent of the demand for commodities) without changing the status of the workers and peasants.

The assumptions behind the notion that a strategy of economic polarization and dependent integration is equivalent to a development policy for developing countries has been criticized on four grounds. First, this approach erroneously assumes that there is no structural unity among social, economic and political phenomena. This in turn implies that a strategy aiming at social objectives can be reduced to purely economic terms; social and political considerations can simply be tacked on later. Second, it assumes that international relations take place in a harmonious context. Third, the State is an idealized, autonomous element in the social system; it is regarded as apart from any real power structure. Similarly, it is assumed that a neutral, rational bureaucracy exists. Thus application of the strategy would not bring about changes in the predominant political structures. Finally, the strategy assumes that polarization mechanisms can be reproduced independently at any level. What these criticisms add up to is a contention that a theory of regional development must be embedded in a theory of social change. Without denying that the main problems of development have an economic basis, it is impossible to compose a strategy of development through "economic engineering" alone (Corragio, 1975).

Perhaps the main criticism of the technical economics approach to development is that high aggregate growth rates and new power projects, ports, highways and other large infrastructure projects have been largely irrelevant to the mass poverty of rural societies. In keeping with this view is the notion that the developing countries have become overly dependent on the West because they have passed up opportunities in the agricultural and rural light industry sectors (Friedmann and Douglass, 1975). Imaginative thinking in this regard has emphasized greater direct involvement of local people in the development process and spatial organization in terms of functional economic areas. Johnson (1970, p. 419), for example, concludes that:

The goals of rational spatial policy should be the creation of truly functional economic areas, which will provide employment opportunities not merely in primary production (farming, mining, forestry, fishing) but in industry and in service activities, thus utilizing to the full the varied potential productivity of a work force. Furthermore, by creating a sense of "community" there can be a far better protection of regional ecology than is possible if "outside" enterprises without any local roots "mine" the natural resources and pollute the rivers and the air. The main goal of rational spatial policy should be to improve the quality of life in a community not only by providing tasks appropriate to interests and ability but by protecting the environment, by supplying the proper educational facilities, health measures and convenient recreational facilities. But beyond all these ends of enlightened policy should be a goal even more important: the creation of a cultural milieu that will release the largest possible amount of a community's creative power.

Johnson believes that there is nothing visionary or fanciful in these proposals because economists and geographers have the knowledge and tools to indicate appropriate policy guidelines. The real problem lies in the inability of archaic political systems to deal with contemporary socioeconomic difficulties.

So long as the developing countries merely continue to adopt innovations that originate in the developed countries it is difficult to imagine that disparities between them will be closed to any marked degree in the near future. However, this does not mean that per capita gross national product will not grow in developing countries or that interregional disparities within these countries will not diminish. Indeed, both cross-section and time series analyses indicate that there is a systematic relation between national development levels and regional inequality or geographic dispersion. Rising regional income disparities and increasing dualism are typical of early development stages, whereas regional convergence and a disappearance of severe dualism are typical of the more mature stages of national growth and development (Williamson, 1965; see also Gould, 1970). Moreover, as Mera points out in Chapter 7, "it appears quite probable that the maintenance of high growth of the economy is an effective way of reducing the rate of population concentration as well as reducing income disparities among regions once the economy reaches a certain stage;" and that "the Korean experience is particularly encouraging for currently-developing countries, because of the success in reversing worsening trends at a fairly early stage of development." But to the extent that this evolutionary type of process does not significantly improve the material conditions of poor people and create more *human* settlement systems in developing countries, revolutionary "solutions" are likely to have increasing appeal to many segments of the population.

SOCIALIST PLANNING AND HUMAN SETTLEMENTS

Berry (1973, pp. 154–155) remarks that, in contrast to Western experiences,

> the Communist Revolution of 1917 marked the beginning in Russia, and later in Eastern Europe, of yet another path in urban development. The revolutionaries had great faith in the power of the government to transform society for the betterment of man, in seizing the government not to restrict its power but rather to use it. They aspired to remould society through a state monopoly of the production of goods, of means of communications, of education, and of science.

Despite the ravages of the Second World War, the accomplishments the Soviets have made in transforming an essentially rural society into a modern, largely-urbanized nation are unquestionable. In 1926 the nation's population was 82 percent rural but by 1974 it was 60 percent urban. Today the Soviet Union has roughly the same number of cities with over 100,000 population as the United States. Thirteen cities have populations in excess of one million and approximately 10 others could easily reach this level in the near future. Although no data are available for regions corresponding to the Standard Metropolitan Statistical Areas of the United States, it has been estimated that at least 20 metropolitan areas have over one million inhabitants (Jensen, 1976, p. 35).

The objectives of urbanization planning in the Soviet Union, as in other Socialist countries, have been set forth in the following terms:

> harmony between economic development and urbanization; the existence of the objective prerequisites for regulating urbanization, mainly with the purpose of creating the best possible conditions for the life of the working people; the attainment of a high economic and social effect in the course of urbanization; the absence of antagonism of interests between town and countryside and between the towns themselves, and the successive planned union of town with countryside; the socialist drawing together of nations and nationalities in the process of urbanization; the absence of social and spatial segregation of the population in towns and agglomerations (Lappo, 1976, p. 197).

The egalitarianism that characterizes the cities of the Soviet Union and other Socialist countries stands in sharp contrast to the spatial social and economic disparities found in many metropolitan areas of the United States, the Third World, and increasingly even in Western Europe. However, it should not be assumed that the Socialist countries have a uniform approach to urban and regional development planning. Although long-term objectives are similar, the means for realizing them vary because of differing historical, geographic, demographic and other conditions. In fact, Socialist planning must even take account of such differences within countries. Thus, in Chapter 6 Dziewoński stresses very strongly that Polish national policies should be regionally adjusted and diversified. Similarly, in Chapter 5 Lüdemann and Heinzmann remark that "A basic principle of the location of the productive forces in Socialist countries is the even distribution of production over the whole country. The realization of this principle is the presupposition for being able to offer the people in all parts of the country good conditions for working and living." But they point out that:

> This principle does not mean, as sometimes wrongly interpreted, an even distribution of all branches of industry over the whole country, i.e. a regional balance in the degree of industrialization. Rather, it involves the formation of regional centers in all parts of the country and the concentration of industries in those locations where the economic conditions are best for them. For example, the systematic development of industrial agglomerations and the utilization of their economic powers is part of this principle, just as the creation of predominantly agricultural production complexes in certain areas. The formation of a regionally differentiated but highly developed economic base in all parts of the country according to different historical, natural, and demographic conditions is a universal problem faced by most countries, though in varying degree according to specific conditions. Such a regionally differentiated structure of the economic base brings about regionally differing starting points and objectives for the dynamics of the human settlement systems.

In the case of the German Democratic Republic, Lüdemann and Heinzmann illustrate some issues of regional economic development and settlement structure by examining structural shifts between northern and southern parts of the country.

SOVIET AND AMERICAN PERSPECTIVES ON URBANIZATION

Similar discussions have taken place in the Soviet Union and the United States concerning city-size questions and the national system of cities. During the 1960s considerable work was done in the Soviet

Union on the relationship between city-size and per capita costs of providing services and maintaining a clean environment. It was held that at some population-size threshold the costs of essential services would become economical but beyond a certain size they would tend to rise sharply. Thus there was a high level of interest in limiting the growth of large cities and in developing smaller urban places; these policies were also viewed as supporting the general objective of reducing differences between cities and rural areas (Jensen, 1976, p. 35). Similar concerns were widely in evidence in the United States at this time (Hansen, 1970, pp. 239–253). In both instances the greatest economies of scale were found in cities in the 50,000 to 400,000 population range; beyond this range significant diseconomies of scale were encountered in the public-services sector.

In the early 1970s, Perevedentsev and other Soviet economists argued that the economically optimal city is not that which requires the smallest per capita investment but rather the one which maximizes the difference between per capita expenditures and output. Therefore, in the perspective of national efficiency there were economic advantages to concentrating people and production in the largest cities. The economies of agglomeration found in large Soviet cities apparently have been great enough to override efforts to restrict their growth (Jensen, 1976, pp. 35–36). During the early 1970s Moscow, Kiev, Tashkent, Minsk and Odessa continued to grow at an accelerated pace. The absolute annual increase in population in large cities between 1970 and 1974 was 10 to 20 percent higher than the increase in the 1960s (Kochetkov, 1976, p.7).

In the United States, an influential paper by Alonso (1971) convincingly argued that the optimal size of a city will differ according to whether a national or a local viewpoint is assumed, but in neither case will it coincide with the point of minimum costs. Alonso concluded that it appears that the biggest cities are not too large from the standpoint of economic efficiency. Whatever the merits of this position, during the first part of the 1970s there was an unprecedented reversal of long-established urban trends in the United States. For every 100 persons who moved into a metropolitan area between 1970 and 1975, 131 moved out. (During the 1965–1970 period 94 persons moved out of metropolitan areas for every 100 who moved in.) Many of the largest metropolitan areas, e.g. New York, Chicago, Philadelphia, Cleveland, Seattle and Los Angeles, were actually losing population during the first part of the 1970s. One in every three metropolitan residents was living in a declining area by 1975. Conversely, from 1970 to 1975 three-fourths of all nonmetropolitan counties experienced population increases; many of these areas were quite distant from metropolitan influence and had been experiencing losses until recently (Morrison and Wheeler, 1976).

Current thinking in the Soviet Union appears to have shifted from a focus on individual cities and their size to a consideration of urban agglomerations and systems of cities. Alayev and Khorev (1976, p. 180) maintain that "the problem of regulating the process of urbanization under socialism should be tackled, above all, through balanced development of a rational territorial organization of the settlement network as a single whole across the country's territory, in accordance with the principles of the socialist location of productive forces." Khodzhaev and Khorev (1975) developed the notion of a "unified settlement system" whose essence is the transformation of settlement patterns into integrated regional systems that are socially and economically interlinked. Their size will depend on local conditions but the increasing mobility of people, goods and information gives rise to urban fields that are not limited to a clearly defined area. Similarly, Kochetkov (1976, p. 9) argues for the coordinated development of cities and settlements.

> This means the planned unification of cities and settlements of various sizes and basic production orientations into group systems of communities that have developed territorial production ties, common transportation and utilities infrastructures, unified networks of social, cultural and recreational facilities, geographical dimensions in which a center city having great national economic and cultural potential can be reached within one or two hours, and the common use of communal territory.

In light of such considerations increasing attention is being devoted to problems of regional economic development and of the division of the country into economic regions (Alampiyev, 1976), since "it has long been an axiom of socialist regional policy that economic regionalization and administrative districting should coincide (Alayev and Khorev, 1976, p. 175)." In Chapter 11, Korcelli reviews selected hypotheses and findings pertaining to regional and interregional dimensions of settlement systems and explores some of their planning implications. An examination of interrelations between the administrative hierarchy of Polish cities and the pattern of tertiary activities within the Polish national settlement provides empirical illustrations of some of the issues discussed.

DECENTRALIZATION AND THE EMERGENCE OF URBAN FIELDS

Broader spatial concepts also characterize much recent urban and regional analysis in the United States. Anticipating the changing nature of human settlement systems, Friedmann and Miller (1965, p. 313) wrote that

> Looking ahead to the next generation, we foresee a new scale of urban living that will extend far beyond existing metropolitan cores and penetrate deeply into the periphery. Relations of dominance and dependency will be transcended. The older established centers together with the intermetropolitan peripheries that envelop them, will constitute the new ecological unit of America's post-industrial society that will replace traditional concepts of the city and metropolis. This basic element of the emerging spatial order we shall call the "urban field."

The urban field, in this view, represents a fusion of metropolitan areas and nonmetropolitan peripheries into areas with a minimum population of 300,000 persons and extending outward for approximately one hundred miles, that is, a driving distance of about two hours. It will be noted that this spatial perspective is akin to that of Kochetkov for the "common use of communal territory" in the Soviet Union.

In 1970 Brian Berry (1970a, p. 49) wrote that he could envisage an inversion of American settlement patterns by the end of the century.

> I foresee the legal central cities assuming a new reality as the bases within which the nation's poor minorities can gain and exert political power and influence. I also foresee that gradients of distance-accretion will replace those of distance-decay. Persons of greater wealth and leisure will find homes and work among the more remote environments of hills, water and forest, while most will aspire to this as an ideal. This, of course, is another inversion; the environments historically least valued are rapidly becoming those most desired. The signs are already there to be noted.

Yet at the same time Berry (1970b, p. 10) was proposing—on the basis of data from the 1960s—that

> Proper regional strategies can contribute to self-sustaining urban growth and also to efficient allocation of resources by facilitating equalization of returns at the margin by easing migration out of the interstices and periphery under the condition that the migration stream is not directed at the big city ghettos. But these results will only be possible when regional economic development policies are explicitly urban in orientation, urban in content, urban in result. To try to keep people down on the farm or in the small town is to condemn regional policy to failure.

What is at issue here is not so much a contradiction as an under-estimation of the counterurbanization forces—discussed by Berry in Chapter 2—already at work. Whether and to what extent the counter-urbanization process in the United States is dampened by energy conservation measures or general economic recovery from the worst recession since the Great Depression remains to be seen. Neverthe-less, it is quite pertinent that pronounced decentralization tendencies have been noted in numerous industrially-advanced countries (Illeris, 1974; Drewett, Goddard and Spence, 1976; Robert, 1976; Vining and Kontuly, 1976; Falk, Chapter 3 of this volume). The evidence suggests that the cities in an urban system may pass through a sequential process wherein concentration and decentralization are dependent on the stage of the system's life cycle. This appears to be a promising direction for human settlement research in the coming years. Such research should contribute significantly to the effective formulation and evaluation of policies that attempt to direct urban and regional change in desired directions. But the notion of "desired directions" in turn implies that policy makers are—in some sense—trying to increase the aggregate level of welfare. In fact not a great deal is known about the relationships between people's satisfactions and location; clearly more attention should be given to understand-ing the preferences that policy makers presumably are trying to sat-isfy through urban and regional policies.

A SPATIAL FRAMEWORK FOR ANALYZING HUMAN SETTLEMENT SYSTEMS

It is encouraging that analyses of spatial-temporal development processes increasingly are being carried out in terms of functional economic areas, such as the Bureau of Economic Analysis (U.S. De-partment of Commerce) regions of the United States. In the BEA delineation process Standard Metropolitan Statistical Areas—which have a minimum population of 50,000 inhabitants—were chosen where possible as core units because of their obvious significance as trade and labor market centers. However, not all SMSAs were made core units. Some are part of larger metropolitan complexes, as in the New York area. Also, in relatively remote parts of the country cities with fewer than 50,000 inhabitants were selected as urban cores. Once the core units were identified, intervening counties were allo-cated to them on the basis of journey-to-work patterns and other economic linkages as well as relevant geographic features. In cases where commuting patterns overlapped, counties were included in the economic area containing the urban core with which there was the greatest commuting connection. Thus, insofar as possible each BEA region combines place of work and place of residence of employees; and even though each region produces goods and services for export, most of the services and a large amount of the goods required by the region's residents and firms are provided within the region. The 173 BEA regions constitute the spatial framework for Olsen's computer model of regional and interregional socioeconomic development. The model, which is presented in Chapter 10, interprets the economy of each BEA region as a labor market, measures all activity in terms of people as members of the population or as employees, and simultaneously forecasts the demands and supplies of labor in each BEA region at five-year intervals.

At this writing a study is being undertaken at the International Institute for Applied Systems Analysis (in collaboration with the University of Reading, England) to delineate functional urban regions for most countries of Western and Eastern Europe. These regions will be comparable to the BEA regions and similar regional delineations already made in Great Britain (Hall et al., 1973) and Japan (Glickman, 1976). Hopefully, analyses based on the data being organized in terms of these regions will lead to greater understanding of the structure and evolution of human settlement systems both nationally and internationally.

In the future it would be desirable to extend this kind of research to other countries, including those in the developing world. However, as Gilbert stresses in Chapter 8, the fact that the internal characteristics and development potentials of developing countries differ widely demands considerable flexibility in urban and regional planning methods. Moreover, it should not be blithely assumed that settlement policies that have been formulated in the context of developed countries will be useful in the poorer parts of the world. The evidence rather indicates that the masses of people in the informal sector too often have been neglected or perhaps even harmed by the application of large-scale, expensive plans.

REFERENCES

Alampiyev, P.M. (1976), "The New Tasks of Economic Geography," *The Current Digest of the Soviet Press, 28*, pp. 14–15.

Alayev, E. and B. Khorev (1976), "Formation of a Unified Settlement System in the USSR," *Soviet Geographical Studies*, Moscow, USSR Academy of Sciences, National Committee of Soviet Geographers.

Alonso, W. (1971), "The Economics of Urban Size," *Papers of the Regional Science Association, 26*, pp. 67–83.

Berry, B.J.L. (1970a), "The Geography of the United States in the Year 2000," *Transactions, 51*, pp. 21–53.

Berry, B.J.L. (1970b), "Labor Market Participation and Regional Potential," *Growth and Change, 1*, pp. 3–10.

Berry, B.J.L. (1973a), *Growth Centers in the American Urban System*, Vol. I, Cambridge, Mass., Ballinger.

Berry, B.J.L. (1973b), *The Human Consequences of Urbanisation*, London, Macmillan.

Cristaller, W. (1933), *Die zentralen Orte in Süddeutschland*, Jena, Gustav Fischer.

Corragio, J.L. (1975), "Polarization, Development, and Integration," in A.R. Kuklinski, Ed., *Regional Development and Planning*, Leyden, The Netherlands, Sijthoff, pp. 353–374.

Drewett, R., J. Goddard and N. Spence (1976), *British Cities: Urban Population and Employment Trends 1951–71*, London, Department of the Environment.

Friedmann, J. (1975), "Regional Development Planning: The Progress of a Decade," in J. Friedmann and W. Alonso, Eds., *Regional Policy: Readings in Theory and Application*, Cambridge, Mass., The MIT Press, pp. 791–808.

Friedmann, J. and W. Alonso, Eds. (1964), *Regional Development and Planning*, Cambridge, Mass., The MIT Press.

Friedmann, J. and M. Douglass (1975), "Agropolitan Development: Towards a New Strategy for Regional Planning in Asia," in *Growth Pole Strategy and Regional Development Planning in Asia*, Nagoya, Japan, United Nations Centre for Regional Development.

Friedmann, J. and J. Miller (1965), "The Urban Field," *Journal of the American Institute of Planners, 31*, pp. 312–319.

Glickman, N.J. (1976), "On the Japanese Urban System," *Journal of Regional Science, 16*, pp. 317–336.

Goddard, J.B. (1975), "Organizational Information Flows and the Urban System," in H. Swain and R.D. MacKinnon, Eds., *Issues in the Management of Urban Systems*, Laxenburg, Austria, International Institute for Applied Systems Analysis.

Gould, P.R. (1970), "Tanzania 1920–63: The Spatial Impress of the Modernization Process," *World Politics, 22*, pp. 149–170.

Greenwood, M.J. (1975), "Research on Internal Migration in the United States: A Survey," *Journal of Economic Literature, 13*, pp. 397–433.

Hall, P. *et al.* (1973), *The Containment of Urban England*, Vol. I, London, George Allen and Unwin.

Hansen, N.M. (1970), *Rural Poverty and the Urban Crisis*, Bloomington, Indiana University Press.

Hansen, N.M., Ed. (1972), *Growth Centers in Regional Economic Development*, New York, The Free Press.

Hansen, N.M. (1975a), *The Challenge of Urban Growth*, Lexington, Mass., D.C. Heath Lexington Books.

Hansen, N.M. (1975b), "An Evaluation of Growth Center Theory and Practice," *Environment and Planning*, 7, pp. 821–832.

Illeris, S. (1974), "The Urbanization of Denmark," unpublished manuscript, Copenhagen, National Agency for Physical Planning.

Jensen, R.G. (1976), "Urban Environments in the United States and the Soviet Union: Some Contrasts and Comparisons," in B.J.L. Berry, Ed., *Urbanization and Counter-Urbanization*, Beverly Hills, Calif., Sage Publication.

Johnson, E.A.J. (1970), *The Organization of Space in Developing Countries*, Cambridge, Harvard University Press.

Khodzhaev, D.G. and B.S. Khorev (1975), "The Concept of a Unified Settlement System and the Planned Control of Growth in the USSR," in A.R. Kuklinski, Ed., *Regional Development and Planning*, Leyden, Sijthoff, pp. 219–230.

Kochetkov, A. (1976), "The Socioeconomic Aspects of Urban Development," *The Current Digest of the Soviet Press*, 28, pp. 7–9.

Kuklinski, A.R., Ed. (1972), *Growth Poles and Growth Centres in Regional Planning*, Paris and The Hague, Mouton.

Lappo, G. (1976), "Geographical Aspects of Urbanisation Studies," *Soviet Geographical Studies*, Moscow, USSR Academy of Sciences, National Committee of Soviet Geographers.

Lasuén, J.R. (1973), "Urbanization and Development—the Temporal Interaction between Geographical and Sectoral Clusters," *Urban Studies*, 10, pp. 163–188.

Lösch, A. (1940), *Die räumliche Ordnung der Wirtschaft*, Jena, Gustav Fischer.

Morrison, P. and J.P. Wheeler (1976), "Rural Renaissance in America? The Revival of Population Growth in Remote Areas," *Population Bulletin*, 31, Washington, D.C., Population Reference Bureau.

Moseley, M.J. (1974), *Growth Centres in Spatial Planning*, Oxford, Pergamon Press.

Pred, A.R. (1975a), "Diffusion, Organizational Spatial Structure and City-System Development," *Economic Geography*, 51, pp. 252–268.

Pred, A.R. (1975b), "On the Spatial Structure of Organizations and the Complexity of Metropolitan Interdependence," *Papers of the Regional Science Association*, 35, pp. 115–142.

Pred, A.R. (1976), *The Interurban Transmission of Growth in Advanced Economies: Empirical Findings Versus Regional Planning Assumptions*, Laxenburg, Austria, International Institute for Applied Systems Analysis, Research Report 76–4, March.

Richardson, H.W. (1973), *The Economics of Urban Size*, Lexington, Mass., D.C. Heath Lexington Books.

Richardson, H.W. (1976), "Growth Pole Spillovers: the Dynamics of Backwash and Spread," *Regional Studies*, 10, pp. 1–9.

Robert, J. (1976), "Prospective Study on Physical Planning and the Environment in the Megalopolis in Formation in Northwest Europe," *Urban Ecology*, 1, pp. 331–411.

Rodwin, L. (1970), *Nations and Cities*, Boston, Houghton Mifflin.

Smith, C.A. (1976), "Regional Economic Systems: Linking Geographical Models and Socioeconomic Problems," in C.A. Smith, Ed., *Regional Analysis*, Vol. I, New York, Academic Press, pp. 3–63.

Törnqvist, G. (1973), "Contact Requirements and Travel Facilities," in A. Pred and G. Törnqvist, Eds., *Systems of Cities and Information Flows: Two Essays*, Lund, Sweden, University of Lund, Department of Geography, Studies in Geography, Series B, No. 38, pp. 85–121.

Vining, D.R., Jr., and T. Kontuly (1976), "Population Dispersal from Metropolitan Regions," unpublished paper, Philadelphia, University of Pennsylvania Regional Science Department.

Williamson, J.G. (1965), "Regional Inequality and the Process of National Development: A Description of the Patterns," *Economic Development and Cultural Change, 13*, Part II, pp. 3–45.

✳ *Part I*

Human Settlement Processes

✳ *Chapter 2*

The Counterurbanization Process: How General?

Brian J.L. Berry

INTRODUCTION

It is only twenty years since, in the exuberance of that period, the Committee on Urbanization of the Social Science Research Council convened in New York and set as its task the identification of the universals of structure and process that, transcending any idiosyncracies of time and space, would provide a value-free basis for a general theory of urbanization. Without such a general theory, it was felt, the social sciences could advance no particular claims as sciences in the strict sense. Yet the search was futile: much like that of Marco Polo, as recorded by Italo Calvina in *Invisible Cities:*

"From now on, I'll describe the cities to you," the Khan had said, "in your journeys you will see if they exist."

But the cities visited by Marco Polo were always different from those thought of by the emperor.

"And yet I have constructed in my mind a model city from which all possible cities can be deduced." Kublai said. "It contains everything corresponding to the norm. Since the cities that exist diverge in varying degree from the norm, I need only foresee the exceptions to the norm and calculate the most probable combinations."

"I have also thought of a model city from which I can deduce all the others," Marco answered. "It is a city made only of exceptions, exclusions, incongruities, contradictions. If such a city is the most improbable, by reducing the number of abnormal elements, we increase the probability that the city really exists. So I have only to subtract exceptions from my

25

model, and in whatever direction I proceed, I will arrive at one of the cities which, always as an exception, exists. But I cannot force my operation beyond a certain limit: I would achieve cities too probable to be real.

The mistake of the committee was to assume that urban theory—indeed *any* social theory—could be value-free. Urbanization is a complex behavioral phenomenon, both the outcome of myriad decisions and actions, individual and collective, private and public, and the context within which such decisions and actions are formulated and take place. Indeed, one of the most fundamental axioms of social theory is that structure influences behavior only when filtered through screens of cognition and is itself, at any instant, simply the state of processes that are composed of repetitive or sequential behaviors.

Extending the axiom with a generalization from systems theory, such processes may incorporate either negative or positive feedback. Negative feedback is by intent system-maintaining, when actors react to problems and try to solve them, or seek by skillful regulation to attempt to avoid them in the future; if successful, such negative feedback ensures routinized behaviors and rhythmic processes that preserve structure. Positive feedback, on the other hand, enhances change; if incremental it promotes structural evolution, but on occasion it results in hierarchical jumps to new levels of system complexity that require transformed structures if they are to be functional.

Process, structure, cognition, behavior, process. . . . The sequence cannot be value-free because values are the essence of cognitive screens and perceptual filters; what we believe is what we see, and what we believe is what we have learned growing up in a particular culture, including the political and ideological premises of that culture. But beliefs can shift, and along with them behavior, and in turn processes and structure. It is one such set of shifts, which I term the counterurbanization process, that is the theory of the body of this chapter.

SETTING: A VALUE-SPECIFIC TAXONOMY OF URBANIZATION PROCESSES

But first, we should review the value-specific taxonomy of urbanization processes, which provides the setting within which it is possible to evaluate the nature and consequences of behavior change. The first perspective is that of liberal capitalism, according to which market-directed economic growth is valued as an end in itself, urban agglomeration and economic development have been assumed to go hand in hand, and there is a basic acceptance of the likelihood of temporary perturbations and structural bottlenecks arising as a consequence of growth. Public intervention is seen as appropriate as a mechanism for solving these adjustment problems, thus preserving and enhancing the role of the market. Hence, a publicly supported private developmental style characterizes the American scene, involving bargaining and negotiation among major interest groups and special interest group politics as business as usual. The outcome of this pluralistic give and take is the protection of developmental interests by reactive or regulatory actions. What is ensured thereby is that the American future is most likely to be a continuation of present trends, changing only as a result of developments arising from the entrepreneurial planning of American corporations, or from perceptual shifts that produce broad behavioral changes in the population at large. Yet such changes do occur, which is the reason for this study.

Contrasting with the American model are hierarchical social and political systems, where the governing class is accustomed to govern, where other classes are accustomed to acquiesce, and where private interests have relatively less power. In such societies, it has apparently been easier to develop urban and regional growth policies at the national level than in the case of systems under the sway of the market. Indeed, progressive changes in system structure can be produced by collective action if use of the land is effectively regulated in conformity to a plan that codifies some public concept of the desirable future and welcomes private profit-seeking development only to the extent that it conforms to the plan. The developmental outcome in such circumstances involves the aspirations of private developers and individual citizens involved in the development process on the one hand, and the images of the planners built into the Master Plan on the other. It is the resolution of these two sets of forces that ultimately shapes the urban scene. In much of Europe, the planners' images of the desirable future have been essentially conservative, aiming to project into future structure their belief that centrality is an immutable necessity for urban order, leading to an attempted preservation of urban forms that are fast vanishing in North America. Thus, the utopian image that becomes embedded in the specific plan, and the efficacy with which the public counterpoint functions to constrain private interests, are the key elements. Yet there, too, there has been the change of direction that, in the American scene, we label "counterurbanization."

Nowhere has the imagery of the social reformers been more apparent than in Soviet planning for the 'city of socialist man'. Reflecting reactions against the human consequences of nineteenth-century industrial urbanization, the objective in the socialist states has been to achieve social justice and to eliminate spatial inequalities. Yet ironically, broader economic growth objectives have apparently dominated in the Soviet Union, producing greater urban concentration, and enhancing centrality.

It has, indeed, been in Maoist China and in revolutionary Cambodia that a radical alternative settlement pattern has been most aggressively pursued. In China, big cities—essentially the colonialist treaty ports—were felt to have been reactionary in the past, potentially revisionist in the future, and alienating at all times. Thus, their growth has been controlled by an unprecedented policy which limits their size and which channels new industrial investment into new or smaller cities in previously remote or backward areas, or into rural communes, which are to be made industrially as self-sufficient as possible without acquiring the morally corrupting and alienating qualities of big cities, nor their damaging effects on the environment. City-dwellers, especially white collar workers, must spend a month or more every year, whatever their status, in productive physical labor in the countryside, where they may regain 'correct' values. The distinctions between mental and manual labor, city and countryside, 'experts' or bureaucrats and peasants or workers are to be eliminated. The benefits and the experience of industrialization and modernization are to be diffused uniformly over the landscape and to all of the people, while the destructive, de-humanizing, corrupting aspects of overconcentration in cities are to be avoided.

THE COUNTERURBANIZATION
CONUNDRUM REVISITED

The conundrum that I now want to address is as follows. Only ten years ago, there was a fundamental belief about the inseparability of urbanization and economic growth in the United States, and elsewhere. The proper role of urban and regional policy was perceived to be removing structural bottlenecks to further growth, solving adjustment problems, and ensuring that certain minimal standards of welfare were provided for the most disadvantaged. Yet today that link has been severed. Economic growth continues, albeit at a slower pace, but classical processes of urban concentration appear to have ended. Indeed, a turning point appears to have been reached in the American urban experience. Counterurbanization has replaced urbanization as the dominant force changing the nation's settlement patterns.

In Britain, too, the dominant trend is accelerating decentralization. By the 1960s relative decline of the central cities had been turned into an absolute loss of population (although "natural" change in the system has been dramatically affected by the New and Expanded Town legislation).

Similarly, urbanization in Australia and Canada appears to have entered a new period. Growth rates are beginning to decline and their distribution across the two urban systems is changing. Internal migration streams have shifted away from the dominant major metropolitan areas in each country toward medium sized cities and to small centers just outside the metropolitan regions.

Clear differences are appearing between the West and East as far as city sizes are concerned. In the West the small towns have been the most successful ones, especially in the German-speaking countries. Ironically, it has been the East that has been most successful to date in maintaining the traditional European concept or the city core as the center of urban life and economic activity, despite the Marxist goal of eliminating spatial inequities by blending urban and rural lifestyles into new settlement patterns. Thus, in the Soviet Union a positive attitude toward the city and city life has prevailed, and what has transpired has been that the city has become the expression of the ideals of socialist society, in sharp contrast to rural living which is to be gradually transformed by the infusion of urban life styles.

And then there are the complexities of the developing countries. In Brazil, for example, urban growth is very much related to the whole process of Brazilian development: the concentration of economic power in an important urban-industrial focus, Sao Paulo, and spilling out for about 200 km from it. There has been mushrooming of the biggest places, emergence of medium-sized towns, asymmetry in growth between the south and the northeast, and accelerating diffusion of economic development into new places—in all, a very classical process.

On the other hand, urbanization in much of Africa is almost entirely a twentieth century phenomenon and quintessentially the product of European colonialism and economic exploitation. Thus it cannot be understood apart from the more pervasive process of underdevelopment, initiated during the period of European colonial contact. Many of the contemporary problems and issues of change and policy derive from this "false start," and each of the countries must, to some extent, reorder its urban system and its cities to reflect the new goals of independence, distributive justice, and cultural integrity. Policies designed to alter the present realities are at the core of governmental deliberations everywhere.

The extreme is in China where the peasant communism of Mao Tse Tung has found a different solution to Marxist ideas. Not only industrial urbanization but also industrial ruralization are held out as a means of eliminating the antagonism between city and country and of leading to new forms of collective life. Yet the continuous Chinese experience with urbanization is perhaps longer than that of any other society. The Maoist design is not being imposed upon a *tabula rasa*; the Chinese past helps explain why current development has been so successful. The two major revolutionary goals, as identified by Chairman Mao, are (as noted before) the elimination of the twin and closely interrelated distinctions between mental and manual labor and between city and countryside.

Underlying much of the foregoing is a common response to the laissez-faire industrial urbanization that produced the big cities of the nineteenth century—large, dense agglomerations of socially heterogeneous immigrants. In the cities, economic opportunities multiplied, and traditional peasants were transformed into modern men. But the cities were poorly built and inadequately serviced, suffering from epidemic disease, poverty and inequality, anomie, alienation and social disorganization. There was a shared revulsion, but there have been many attempted solutions—by private builders providing a suburban haven to which the upwardly mobile could escape where free enterprise prevails, and by various social reformers seeking more radical planned solutions for those who could not. From these reactions have emerged several types of counterurbanization, each an expression of contemporary urbanization policy: the individualistic decentralization that has culminated in the decreasing size, decreasing density and increasing homogeneity of cities and the more ruralized life styles of the more liberal capitalist states; planned new towns as counterpoints to speculative private interest in the welfare states of Western Europe; the Soviets' search for a new settlement pattern for mankind, the *city* of socialist man in which traditional antagonisms between city and country are no more; and Mao's ruralized society.

These forms of counterurbanization have been joined with attempts at decolonization in the Third and Fourth Worlds. As the new industrial powers grew in size and influence, they reached overseas for guaranteed supplies of raw materials and monopoly markets, producing direct political control of much of the rest of the globe. Colonial development was centered in primate cities, and resulted in patterned socioeconomic inequality traceable to the exploitative practices through which national and international institutions are linked in the interest of surplus extraction and capital accumulation. Even after political independence was achieved, most Third and Fourth World countries were faced with inherited neocolonial institutions and sociospatial inequalities, and, learning from both Eastern and Western examples, many have proposed counterurbanization policies of deliberate decentralization or explicit ruralization as solutions to their ills.

The result is as described by Lloyd Rodwin in 1970. "Before World War II," he said, "almost no one wanted the central government to determine how cities should grow." But, he continued, "radical changes in technology and in analytical and planning methods now make significant changes in the urban system not only feasible, but to some extent manipulable," and, because of this, "today, national governments throughout the world are adopting or are being implored to adopt urban growth strategies."

Rodwin put his finger on two important bases of today's near-universal desire in some manner to counter urbanization: the planning method and the political process, linked as they are ideologically in terms of world view, which involves both the perception of urban problems and the specification of goals to be achieved, and practically in terms of the power to implement the means thought likely to achieve the ends. Societies differ in their planning capabilities, and this introduces one important element of differentiation. But more importantly, cultural differences have produced divergent goals, divergent planning methods, divergent plans, and now divergent paths being followed by urban and counterurban development in the world today.

COUNTERURBANIZATION IN THE UNITED STATES

The archetypal form of counterurbanization remains that which has emerged in recent years under market-directed circumstances in the United States. Since changes in the U.S. are often taken to be a bellwether of changes that are likely to follow elsewhere, either in lockstep or in planned opposition, I will thus devote the balance of this paper to the American scene. The questions to be addressed are these: What changes have taken place? Why?

Let us look first at a quick summary of the changes in perception of national growth and distribution trends in the past decade, prepared by Ralph R. Widner, Director of the Academy for Contemporary Problems, Columbus, Ohio.

As They Were Perceived in 1965	*As They Are Perceived in 1976*

1. Population Shifts

A. Substantial population increase must be accommodated.	A. Dramatic decline in birth and fertility.
B. Education and other systems must be expanded to accommodate war baby generation.	B. War baby generation expands labor force growth through ± 1982, also increases growth in household formation.
C. Metro areas swamped by influx of rural migrants.	C. Net rural out-migrations have ended.
D. Population growth of largest metros irreversible.	D. Large industrial metros losing population.
E. Nonmetro areas emptying out.	E. Many nonmetros must accommodate population growth.
F. Net migrations out of South to North and West.	F. Net migrations out of North, Midwest to South, Southwest. Western growth rates slowing.

2. Economic Shifts

A. Full employment to be attained through active fiscal, monetary policy.	A. U.S. growth will be constrained by international dependency, increased costs. Lower growth rate. Emphasis should shift away from consumption in favor of capital formation.
B. Industrial development basis for area development.	B. Production employment no longer prime sources of employment. Emphasis should be on advanced manufacturing, tertiary, and quarternary sectors.
C. Need to attract manufacturing into lagging regions.	C. Manufacturing growing rapidly in South, declining in industrial Northeast, Midwest. Rural manufacturing growing, metropolitan industrial centers declining.
D. Production and service employment metropolitan-centered.	D. Production and some service employment decentralizing and diffusing, less metropolitan-centered.

As They Were Perceived in 1965	*As They Are Perceived in 1976*

2. Economic Shift *(cont'd.)*

E. Productivity can be improved through technology in production, better training.	E. Productivity declining because of increasing concentration of service employment, sluggish modernization of production.

3. Resource Shifts

A. Cheap energy/resources.	A. Expensive energy/resources.
B. Assured supply of energy/resources.	B. Interruptable supply.
C. Economic growth based upon intensive energy consumption.	C. Curtail, control consumption.
D. Resource-based regional economies most vulnerable to economic distress.	D. Resource-based regional economies have major comparative advantages over energy-importing (and non-agricultural) regions.

4. Regional Shifts

A. South, West, and "rim" lagging regions should be brought to regional parity.	A. South, West approaching parity; Northeast and Midwest now lagging.
B. Production employment should be more evenly distributed.	B. Production employment losses hurting old industrial heartland.
C. Advanced services will remain major function of primate cities.	C. Advanced services decentralizing out of primate cities to new regional capitals.
D. Federal expenditure policy should aid South, West to reach parity.	D. Northeast, Midwest Federal "Balance of Payments" problem aggravates loss of private investment. Federal expenditure policy should be changed.
E. Public works (water, sewer, transport, etc.) can aid lagging regions to acquire comparative advantages for development.	E. Public works no longer key need in lagging regions.
F. Tax incentives, subsidies can help attract production employment into lagging regions.	F. Incentives and subsidies of marginal (or dubious) relevance to structural or territorial problem.

Dominating all of these demographic and settlement trends is the continuation of a long-term decline in the rate of national population increase. The population of the United States continues to grow, but at a steadily decreasing pace; during the 1950s the national population grew by 19.0 percent, during the 1960s, by 13.3 percent, and if current growth rates continue through the close of this decade, the national population will have increased by 8.4 percent during the 1970s.

There are several demographic components, viz., birth and death rates and immigration levels, which together account for current low-level population increases. The current annual death rate, after falling continuously throughout the twentieth century, stabilized after 1950 at about 9.4 deaths per thousand population before dropping again to a current level of 8.9 deaths per thousand. Meanwhile, following the anomaly of the post-World War II baby boom, the birth rate has continued to fall. It was 19.4 per thousand in 1940, rose to 24.9 per thousand in 1955, but has declined continuously since, dropping to 14.7 per thousand by 1975, the lowest level in American history. When all women are taken into account, the eventual number of births expected per woman averages to 2.1 children for today's younger age cohorts, i.e., barely at the replacement level required for a stable population. Of the total population increase of 1.73 million in 1975, 1.24 million was from natural increase (an excess of births over deaths); immigration from other countries accounted for the remaining 494,000 (which includes 130,000 Vietnamese refugees).

These trends have caused the Bureau of the Census to issue new population projection series I, II, and III to replace earlier estimates (Series A–D). Each assumes that annual net immigration will continue at 400,000 per year and that a slight reduction will occur in future mortality rates. The three projections differ only in their assumptions about future fertility, from a high of 2.7 lifetime births per woman in Series I, to 2.1 for Series II, to a low of 1.7 in Series III. These three projections suggest that the nation's population in the year 2000 will increase from its present 214.5 million to somewhere between a low of 245 million and high of 287 million. These projections are significantly lower than those made in the late 1960s because of a lowering of the expected lifetime fertility rates. Total population projections for the year 2000 at that time ranged from a low of 283 million (Series D) to a high of 361 million (Series A), or as much as 25 percent above current estimates.

Superimposed upon this long-term decline in population growth there are, of course, the continuing consequences of earlier fluctuations in birth rates, for example, the sharp rise in the number of births following World War II, and the fall thereafter to an all-time low. The population of individuals aged 18 to 24 and 25 to 34, age-groups now occupied by members of the postwar "boom," has grown 13 and 23 percent respectively since 1970. The aging of these large cohorts will continue to play a primary role in raising the average age of the nation's population and in changing housing needs and locational preferences.

Major changes in the populations of other age-groups during the first half of the 1970s include a decline in the number of youths and an ever increasing number of elderly. The lower birth rates of the latter 1960s have produced a decline of 8 percent in the number of children aged 13 and under, while the declining mortality rate has served to increase the size of the 65 and over age-group by 12 percent. Continued declines in the birth rate, coupled with the death rate remaining either constant or dropping slightly, will produce a population that contains proportionately more elderly persons year by year. The median age of the population, which dropped from 30.2 years in 1950 to a low of 27.9 years in 1970 has already begun to rise and as of 1975, stood at 28.8 years.

Alongside these shifts in the demographic structure of the nation's population are changes in the overall structure of marital relations. As the large birth cohorts of the late 1940s and early 1950s move through young adult ages, marriage rates are declining, median age at first marriage is increasing, divorce rates are increasing (from 35 per 1,000 in 1960 to 47 per 1,000 in 1970), more young unmarried adults are maintaining their own homes, and more children are living at home with a single parent. Since 1970, the largest increase among family groups has been in those headed by a woman who had no husband living with her; half of this increase was accounted for by women who were divorced. The combination of falling birth rates and changing household composition is reflected in the sharp decline in the average number of persons per household.

These national demographic trends—lowered birth rates, increasing numbers of elderly, changes in family structure—carry with them not only long-term consequences but also immediate consequences for the 1970s. Although current low birth rates imply lowered future household formation, the number of new households formed since 1970—about 7.7 million—represents an increase of 10.8 percent over the number of household units at the beginning of the decade. Most households in 1975, as earlier, were maintained by two or more related family members (primary families) but a growing proportion are maintained by persons who live alone or with nonrelatives only (primary individuals). Since 1970 the proportion of primary family households has decreased from 81 to 78 percent, with an accompanying increase of households headed by primary individuals from 19 to 22 percent. By 1975, 20 percent of all households were single persons living alone.

Although households headed by primary individuals still account for less than one-quarter of the total number of households, they have accounted for half of the increase in new household formations since 1970. With national trends toward increased numbers of individuals delaying entry into marriage, higher divorce rates, and both greater numbers and larger proportions of the elderly maintaining their own households, the size of households will continue to decline with resultant consequences for housing requirements as well as labor markets and public services.

Accompanying these national shifts are changes at the regional and interregional level. Signs of a reversal of the long-term pattern of metropolitan growth rates exceeding those of nonmetropolitan areas first appeared during the 1960s. During this time, several nonmetropolitan regions experienced a turnaround from population decline to modest increase and it appeared that at least in some of these areas, outmigration had peaked during the previous decade. The metropolitan population growth of 22 million persons during the 1960s resulted in part (one-third) from growth through the addition of new land area, while the remaining two-thirds was derived from population increases within the 1960 boundaries. Of the growth within these earlier boundaries, three-quarters was due to natural increase, and of the remaining quarter, a larger proportion resulted from inmigration from overseas than from the inmigration of former rural area residents. Thus, only a small proportion of the increase in America's metropolitan population during the 1960s can be attributed to rural outmigration.

Nonetheless, while the nation's total population increased 13.3 percent during the 1960s, the number of individuals residing in metropolitan areas increased 16.6 percent, or 8½ times the rate of nonmetropolitan areas. Since 1970, however, a reversal has occurred, resulting in the growth rates for nonmetropolitan areas exceeding those of metropolitan locations. Nationwide statistics for the first half of the 1970s indicate that population has increased 6.3 percent in nonmetropolitan areas and only 3.6 percent in metropolitan places.

When the nation's metropolitan areas are divided between their central cities and surrounding suburbs, an even more dramatic pattern is evident. The lower metropolitan area population growth of the 1970s has resulted from a combination of the depopulation of the central cities and a slackening of the suburban boom. Since 1970, central cities have experienced an absolute population loss of nearly two million persons, or 3 percent of the total number of residents at the beginning of the present decade. Net outmigration from the central cities to the suburbs and to nonmetropolitan areas during this same period exceeds seven million persons, for a central city population loss of 11.2 percent.

What is new, of course, is the current nationwide trend of *absolute* central city population decline; the *proportion* of metropolitan residents living in the central city rather than the suburbs reached a peak during the 1920s and has declined continually since. In 1920, central city dwellers accounted for 66 percent of America's metropolitan residents, with the remaining 34 percent being suburban residents. By 1960 metropolitan residents were about equally divided between central cities and suburbs; by 1975 central city residents accounted for only 43 percent of the nation's metropolitan population.

Absolute losses of population in certain central cities did occur prior to 1970; however gains in the remaining central cities always more than offset these losses to create overall central city growth. The decade of the 1950s saw 56 central cities lose population while the national total of central city residents increased 11.6 percent. During the 1960s, central city population increased 6.5 percent, but the number of central cities which lost population increased to 95, or 39 percent of all central cities in the nation. Altogether, the central cities of 47 of the nation's metropolitan areas lost population continuously throughout the twenty-year period from 1950 through 1970. With an aggregate central city population decline of 3.1 percent between 1970 and 1975, the number of central cities experiencing losses may be expected to increase.

While central city population losses during the 1950s and 1960s occurred in a relatively large number of metropolitan areas, they were in large measure confined to the industrial heartland cities of the North Central and Northeast regions of the country. During the 1950s, 81 percent of the central cities that lost population were located in this northern region extending from the Midwest through New England. This concentration of declining central cities in the North lessened somewhat during the 1960s, when its share of the total number of the central cities dropped to 74 percent; however, of the nation's central cities that lost population during both decades, 90 percent were located in this northern region. Large northern cities that lost population during both the 1950s and 1960s include Baltimore, Boston, Buffalo, Chicago, Cincinnati, Cleveland, Detroit, Minneapolis, Philadelphia, Pittsburgh, and St. Louis.

In the 1970s, the greatest concentration of central cities losing residents continues to lie within this northern region. In the South, the central city portions of metropolitan areas containing over one million total residents lost population, while the central cities of metropolitan areas of less than one million increased, resulting in an insignificant decrease in the total number of central city residents. In the West, the number of residents in metropolitan places of all sizes increased, with the largest gains occurring in the central cities of areas with less than one million total residents.

The experience of nonmetropolitan America has been the opposite of the foregoing. From the 1940s through the 1950s, outmigration from the nation's rural areas continued apace. Certain rural areas reached a turning point where they were no longer losing residents during the 1960s, but it was not until the 1970s that nonmetropolitan areas as a whole shifted to the status not only of retaining residents, but also of gaining population through net inmigration from metropolitan areas.

The number of individuals residing in the nation's nonmetropolitan areas during the 1960s grew by 6.8 percent, a rate of increase that was only half the national average. During the first half of this decade, however, the nonmetropolitan population increase of 6.3 percent was above the national average of 4.4 percent and well above the increase of 3.6 percent for metropolitan areas.

More significant for nonmetropolitan areas than their current faster growth rate is the turnaround that has occurred in migration between the nonmetropolitan and metropolitan portions of the nation. The increased mechanization of farming since World War II has lead to a decrease in the size of the farm population along with rural outmigration. During the 1950s, nonmetropolitan areas lost over five million persons. This high level of outmigration continued into the 1960s as the nation's farm population has declined at an annual rate of only 1.8 percent and has now reached an all time low of 8.9 million, or only 4.1 percent of the nation's total population. With fewer outmigrants and greater numbers of inmigrants, nonmetropolitan areas have experienced a net inmigration of approximately two million persons since 1970, thus reversing the trend of population loss that existed since the 1940s.

While not all nonmetropolitan areas are sharing in this new pattern of growth, it is true that net migration reversal has occurred in almost every nonmetropolitan subregion of the country. Actual population increases in the four major regions of the country vary from a low of 1.8 percent in the North Central region to 5.1 and 5.4 percent respectively in the Northeast and South, and a high of 11.6 percent in the West. Intraregionally, overall population decline continues in those nonmetropolitan counties that contain the smallest settlements, i.e. those with less than 2,500 residents. This is especially true in the Northeast, where such areas lost 31.9 percent of their 1970 population between 1970 and 1975. However, sparsely settled areas in the South have grown by 11.6 percent. Even though the West has experienced the highest overall nonmetropolitan growth, the South has been the region of the country with the most widespread nonmetropolitan gains, with population increases in counties with both smaller and larger-sized urban centers.

Generally, those nonmetropolitan areas located immediately adjacent to metropolitan centers (accounting for 51.5 percent of all nonmetropolitan residents) have experienced the highest nonmetropolitan growth rates during the 1970s: a 4.7 percent increase through 1973 for adjacent counties compared with 3.7 percent for nonadjacent counties. Nonmetropolitan areas that have a high level of integration of their residents into metropolitan labor markets, in particular, have experienced larger recent growth rates. Through 1974, population has increased 9.1 percent in those nonmetropolitan areas where 20 percent or more of the residents commute to a metropolitan place for work, but only 4.8 percent in those areas where less than 3 percent of the residents commute to metropolitan places for employment. Yet even this latter rate is higher than the average growth rate of metropolitan places during this same period.

The subregions of nonmetropolitan America that underwent turn-arounds from population decline during the 1960s to growth during the 1970s are quite diverse. In the South, a region extending from the Ozarks through eastern Texas and containing a predominantly white population underwent a shift during the 1960s from reliance upon agricultural employment to development of manufacturing, as well as benefitting from newly developed recreational areas. The Upper Great Lakes area bordering the southern coast of Lake Superior is a second nonmetropolitan region that experienced growth throughout the 1960s and 1970s—again primarily as the result of manufacturing decentralization and the development of recreational facilities and retirement communities. The nonmetropolitan areas of the Blue Ridge-Piedmont, Florida, the Southwest, and the northern Pacific Coast regions all experienced growth in both the 1960s and 1970s as the result of either decentralization of manufacturing, recreational-retirement developments, the opening up of new resources, or the expansion of improved transportation facilities (the interstate highway system) which enable persons to reside in rural areas but participate in metropolitan labor markets.

During the 1970s, the nonmetropolitan growth rate has not only exceeded the 1960s level, but has also spread to a greater number of the nation's rural subregions. For example, a new growth axis now cuts through central Maine along the route of the interstate highway. While only those six rural areas discussed in the previous paragraph experienced net inmigration during the 1960s, there is now only one rural subregion that continues to lose population through net outmigration. That subregion is the old tobacco and cotton belt extending from the North Carolina Cape to the delta area of the Mississippi River. This subregion, which contains a large rural black population, has not benefitted significantly from the decentralization of manufacturing, and its residents continue to migrate to the cities of the North.

Drawing together the evidence, the major shifts thus appear to be these:

1. Rapid growth of the South, which is experiencing net inmigration from all other regions. Significantly, the long-term trend of net outmigration by blacks from the South to the North has been reversed during the first half of the 1970s. During the five-year period from 1965–1970 the black population of the South decreased by 216,000 due to outmigration, but since then it has gained 14,000 blacks from other regions of the country. During the first half of the 1970s, immigration by blacks to the South has increased 86.4 percent and outmigration has decreased 23.8 percent, compared to the last half of the 1960s.

2. The growth of the West continues to be the highest in the country, but the most rapid growth within that region has shifted from the coastal states to those of the mountain area.

3. The net flow of migrants out of the Northeast and North Central regions during the first half of the 1970s is almost double that of the last five years of the 1960s. This increase has resulted primarily from a 34.1 percent rise in the level of migration from the North to the South coupled with a 17.3 percent decrease in migration from the South to the North.

4. Since 1970, the metropolitan areas of the United States have grown more slowly than the nation as a whole, and substantially less rapidly than nonmetropolitan America, a development that stands in sharp contrast to all preceding decades back to the early 19th century.

5. On a net basis, metropolitan areas are now losing migrants to nonmetropolitan territory, although they still show slight population increases due to natural increase and immigration from abroad.

6. The overall decline in metropolitan area growth is largely accounted for by the largest metropolitan areas, particularly those located in the Northeast and North Central regions. Through 1974 the eight metropolitan areas exceeding three million population added only 285,000 residents to a 1970 population base of 56 million, while their central cities declined in population absolutely. All central cities of the nation's SMSAs grew at an average annual rate of 0.6 percent between 1960 and 1970, but have declined at an average annual rate of 0.4 percent since 1970 (annexations excluded). Much of the decrease is attributable to the post-1970 decline in the number of white central city residents, which has occurred at a rate of one percent per annum.

7. Metropolitan decline is not universal. Rapid growth has taken place in smaller metropolitan areas, particularly in Florida, the South, and the West and ex-urban counties located immediately outside metropolitan areas as currently defined, but with substantially daily commuting to metropolitan areas.

8. Particularly impressive are the reversals in migration trends in the largest metropolitan areas and in the furthermost peripheral counties; the metropolitan regions with populations exceeding three million gained between 1960 and 1970 but have lost residents since 1970; the nation's peripheral nonmetropolitan counties lost migrants between 1960 and 1970 but have gained migrants since 1970. The balance of migration flows has been reversed.

9. High growth rates prevail in certain nonmetropolitan areas, especially those with manufacturing, centers of higher education, resources for recreational development, and retirement centers. The long-term shift out of agricultural employment has also tapered off, adding to rural population retention.

The evidence is clear. An increasing number of U.S. central cities and a widening ring of their older suburbs must now learn to cope with population decline, especially within the nation's largest metropolitan areas. Half-way through the decade, the central cities of U.S. metropolitan areas already have lost 3.1 percent of their 1970 residential population. During the same period, suburban areas have grown by 9.3 percent more residents than central cities, an increase of 15 percent in five years. Suburban areas are now the home of 38.9 percent of the nation's population, as compared with 29.2 percent for central cities and 32.0 percent for nonmetropolitan areas, which are growing once again.

In short, a turning point has been reached in the American urban experience. Counterurbanization has replaced urbanization as the dominant force shaping the nation's settlement patterns. To those who wrote about nineteenth and early twentieth-century industrial urbanization, the essence was size, density, and heterogeneity. "Urbanization is a process of population concentration," wrote Hope Tisdale in 1942. "It implies a movement from a state of less concentration to a state of more concentration." But as we have just seen, since 1970 American metropolitan regions have grown less rapidly than the nation, and have actually lost population to nonmetropolitan territory.

Because migration has been selective of particular social and economic groups, very specific subgroups have been left behind.

The process of counterurbanization therefore has as its essence decreasing size, decreasing density, and decreasing heterogeneity. To mimic Tisdale: *counterurbanization is a process of population deconcentration; it implies a movement from a state of more concentration to a state of less concentration.* There are some who argue that the trends are a temporary perturbation, a product of the current recession that will vanish when the health of the economy improves. But such an attitude is hardly credible; twentieth-century trends have all pointed in the same direction—*creation of nothing less than an urban civilization without cities*, at least in the classical sense. As early as 1902, H.G. Wells wrote that the "railway-begotten giant cities" he knew were "in all probability . . . destined to such a process of dissection and diffusion as to amount almost to obliteration . . . within a measurable further space of years. These coming cities . . . will present a new and entirely different phase of human distribution. . . . The city will diffuse itself until it has taken up considerable areas and many of the characteristics of what is now country . . . The country will take itself many of the qualities of the city. The old antithesis . . . will cease, the boundary lines will altogether disappear." Similarly, Adna Weber suggested in his remarkable 1899 study that "the most encouraging feature of the whole situation is the tendency . . . towards the development of suburban towns (which) denotes a diminution in the *intensity* of concentration. . . . The rise of the suburbs it is, which furnishes the solid basis of hope that the evils of city life, so far as they result from over-crowding, may in large part be removed. If concentration of population seems desired to continue, it will be a modified concentration which offers the advantages of both city and country life." Later Frank Lloyd Wright argued that "Broadacre City" was the most desirable settlement pattern for mankind, and Lewis Mumford called for a new reintegration of men and nature in dispersed urban regions, to cite but a few cases.

Throughout the twentieth century all trends have pointed in the directions suggested by these writers. Every public opinion survey has indicated that population preferences are for smaller places and lower densities, with richer environmental amenities (Sundquist, 1975). The trend has been one leading unremittingly towards the reversal of the processes of population concentration unleashed by technologies of the industrial revolution, a reversal finally achieved after 1970.

Viewed more generally, though, what has finally been achieved in the 1970s is not something new, but something old—the reassertion of fundamental predispositions of the American culture that, because they are antithetical to the urban concentration that was produced by large-scale industry and primitive intraurban transportation, have resulted in many of the contradictions and conflicts of recent decades.

It was 200 years ago that Hector de Crèvecoeur outlined these fundamental values in his *Letters from an American Farmer.* "Who, then, is this new man, the American?" he asked, and his answer was a description of basic American culture traits. Foremost among these was *a love of newness.* Second was the overwhelming desire to be *near to nature. Freedom to move* was essential if goals were to be realized, and *individualism* was basic to the self-made man's pursuit of his goals, yet *violence* was the accompaniment if not the condition of success—the competitive urge, the struggle to succeed, the fight to win. Finally, de Crèvecoeur perceived a great *melting pot* of peoples, and a manifest *sense of destiny.*

There has been no more evocative description of the consequences of the love of newness for American metropolitan structure than Homer Hoyt's discussion of *The Structure and Growth of Residential Neighborhoods in American Cities,* published in 1939. Hoyt said that

the erection of new dwellings on the periphery . . . sets in motion forces tending to draw population from older houses and to cause all groups to move up a step, leaving the oldest and cheapest houses to be occupied by the poorest families or to be vacated. The constant competition of new areas is itself a cause of neighborhood shifts. Every building boom, with its crop of structures equipped with the latest modern devices, pushes all existing structures a notch down in the scale of desirability. . . . The high grade areas tend to preempt the most desirable residential land . . . intermediate rental groups tend to occupy the sectors in each city that are adjacent to the high rent area. . . . Occupants of houses in the low rent categories tend to move out in bands from the center of the city by filtering up. . . . There is a constant outward movement of neighborhoods because as neighborhoods become older they tend to be less desirable. A neighborhood composed of new houses in the latest modern style . . . is at its apex. . . . Physical deterioration of structures and the aging of families . . . constantly lessen the vital powers of the neighborhood. . . . The steady process of deterioration is hastened by obsolescence; a new and more modern type of structure relegates all existing structures to lower ranks of desirability.

Hoyt's perceptions cut right to the core of much of that which has transpired, for the accompaniment of the process of counterurbanization is urban decay.

The love of newness joins with the desire to be near nature. H.G. Wells' 1902 forecasts should be recalled.

Many of our railway-begotten giant cities are destined to such a process of dissection and diffusion as to amount almost to obliteration . . . within a measurable further space of years. . . . These coming cities . . . will present a new and entirely different phase of human distribution. . . . The social history of the middle and later thirds of the nineteenth century . . . all over the civilized world has been the history of a gigantic rush of population into the magic radius of—for most people—four miles, to suffer there physical and moral disaster . . . far more appalling than any famine or pestilence that ever swept the world . . . But new forces . . . bring with them. . . . The distinct promise of a centrifugal application that may finally be equal to the complete reduction of all our present congestions . . . What will be the forces acting upon the prosperous household? The passion for nature and that craving for a little private *imperium* are the chief centrifugal inducements. . . . The city will diffuse itself until it has taken up considerable areas and many of the characteristics of what is now country. . . . We may call . . . these coming town provinces 'urban regions'.

To occupy this new frontier, close to nature, and to keep on adjusting to succeeding waves of growth has demanded freedom to move. Americans are the world's most mobile people. Forty million Americans change residence each year; Americans change residence an average of 14 times in a lifetime. The typical American's life might be characterized as a prolonged odyssey. Marriage, childbearing, military service, higher education, changes from one employer to another or shifts from one plant or office location to another with the same employer, divorce, retirement—all may bring a change in residence and locale, not to speak of upward social mobility which may impel people to move for other reasons as well. Now as in the past Americans continue to migrate for reasons that are connected to the working of national economic and social systems. The quick exploitation of new resources or knowledge requires the abandonment of old enterprises along with the development of the new, and migration is also an *assortive* mechanism, filtering and sifting the population as its members undergo social mobility. Yet again, there is an antiphonal note. Filtering in housing markets, for example, is a process that has positive welfare consequences if new construction exceeds the rate necessary to house normal growth and produces an excess housing supply at the point where the filtering originates; if such new construction exerts a downward pressure on the rents and prices of existing housing, permitting lower income families to obtain better housing bargains relative to their existing housing quarters; if the upward mobility is apart from any changes caused by rising incomes and/or declining rent/income ratios and if a decline in quality is not necessarily forced by reductions in maintenance and repair to the extent that rents and prices are forced down; and finally if a mechanism exists to remove the worst housing from the market without adversely affecting rents and prices of housing at the lowest level. Part of the reason for urban decay is that the last two conditions have not been met: deterioration has accelerated in many older neighborhoods, and abandonment has become contagious, frequently adversely affecting access by low-income residents to the better-quality housing available locally.

Contrary to the views of most radicals, however, urban expansion and urban decay are not caused by a single-minded conspiracy among large-scale institutions and investors. They result instead from myriad decisions made individually, within a tradition of privatism. This tradition has been called by Sam Bass Warner (1968) "the most important element of American culture for understanding the development of cities. It has meant that the cities of the United States depended for their wages, employment, and general prosperity on the aggregate successes and failures of thousands of individual enterprises, not upon community action. It has also meant that the physical forms of American cities, their lots, houses, factories and streets have been the outcome of a real estate market of profit-seeking builders, land speculators, and large investors. And it has meant that the local politics of American cities have depended for their actors, and for a good deal of their subject matter, on the changing focus of men's private economic activities." Privatism has prevailed throughout America's history, and a consequence is a preference for governmental fragmentation and for interest-group politics under presumed conditions of democratic pluralism. Antithetically, it has also meant that, as we have noted earlier, American city planning has been curative rather than future-oriented, reactive rather than going somewhere.

While achievement in the mainstream has involved an individual fight to succeed, violence also is a pervasive underpinning of American life if only because fights have to have more than one participant. Acrimonious confrontations mark the fights to control turf within cities, while for the underclass abandoned in deteriorating ghettos, crime and violence is a way of life. President Johnson's *Commission on Crimes of Violence* reported that if present trends continue

> we can expect further social fragmentation of the urban environment, greater segregation of different racial groups and economic classes . . . and the polarization of attitudes on a variety of issues. It is logical to expect the establishment of the 'defensive city' consisting of an economically declining central business district in the inner city protected by people shopping or working in buildings during daylight hours and 'sealed off' by police during night-time hours. Highrise apartments and residential 'compounds' will be fortified cells for upper-, and middle-, and high income populations living in prime locations . . . suburban neighborhoods, geographically removed from the central city, will be 'safe areas,' protected by racial and economic homogeneity . . .

In the expanding frontiers of suburban America, upwardly-mobile individuals from a variety of backgrounds have been readily integrated into the achievement-oriented mainstream of society. When the heterogeneity of American cities was caused primarily by the influx of successive immigrant waves, the policy of encouraging such assimilation was taken for granted ideologically. But even in the suburbs, what poured out of the melting pot rapidly crystallized into a complex mosaic of sharply-differentiated communities of achievers counterposed against those who have been unable or unwilling to move out of the cities. Thus, for many, the national ideal of integration remains inaccessible—in particular, to the unassimilable blacks, browns and reds, for whom segregation within the central cities remains the rule as battle lines are drawn along neighborhood boundaries and at the gates of the schools. For others, integration is undesirable—perceived destructive of self-identity by the unassimilated ethnics, and to be avoided by members of new communities including those, for example, seeking a return to simpler ways in rural communes.

Yet alongside individualized withdrawal to the periphery there remains the continuing feeling that Americans should no longer be willing simply to *react* to problems, or to *act* in a privatised mode, but should—collectively—go *somewhere*, to achieve goals, to "win" the "wars" on poverty, underprivilege, and urban decay—to perfect

America and Americans. One version is a favorite of planning professionals. How many recall the call of the National Resources Committee of 1937, repeated many times since?—". . . If the city fails, America fails. The Nation cannot flourish without its urban-industrial centers . . . City planning, county planning, rural planning, State planning, regional planning, must be linked together in the strategy of American national planning and policy, to the end that our national and local resources may best be conserved and developed for our human use . . . the Committee is of the opinion that the realistic answer to the question of a desirable urban environment lies . . . in the judicious reshaping of the urban community and region by systematic development and redevelopment in accordance with forward looking and intelligent plans."

And thus the counterurbanization conundrum reappears: social trends move one way, and the planners want them to move in an opposite direction. Is it true that elsewhere, too, this oppositional quality prevails?

REFERENCES

Alexandersson, Gunnar and Thomas Falk (1974), "Changes in the Urban Pattern of Sweden 1960–1970: The beginning of a return to small urban places?" *Geoforum*, 8:87–92.

Beale, Calvin L. *The Revival of Population Growth in Nonmetropolitan America.* ERS–605. Washington, D.C.: Economic Research Service, U.S. Department of Agriculture, 1975.

Berry, Brian J.L. (1970), "The Geography of the United States in the Year 2000," *Transactions of the Institute of British Geographers*, 51:21–53.

_____ (1973), *The Human Consequences of Urbanisation.* Basingstoke: Macmillian and New York: St. Martin's Press.

_____ (1975), "The Decline of the Aging Metropolis: Cultural Bases and Social Process," paper prepared for a conference at the Center for Urban Policy Research Rutgers University, and forthcoming in the Proceedings.

_____ and Quentin Gillard (1976), *The Changing Shape of Metropolitan America: Commuting Patterns, Urban Fields And Decentralization Processes, 1960–1970.* Cambridge, Mass.: Ballinger Publishing Co.

Brown, David L. *Socioeconomic Characteristics of Growing and Declining Nonmetropolitan Counties, 1970.* Washington, D.C.: Economic Research Service, U.S. Department of Agriculture, 1975.

De Crèvecoeur, J. Hector St. John (1782), *Letters from an American Farmer.* London: Thomas Davies.

Forstall, Richard L. "Trends in Metropolitan and Nonmetropolitan Population Growth Since 1970." Revision of paper delivered at the Conference on

Population Distribution, sponsored by the Center for Population Research, National Institute of Health, 29−31 January 1975, Washington, D.C.

Forstall, Richard L. (1975), "Trends in Metropolitan and Nonmetropolitan Population Growth Since 1970." Washington, D.C.: Population Division, U.S. Bureau of the Census.

Fuguitt, Glenn V. and Calvin L. Beale. "The New Pattern of Nonmetropolitan Change." CDE Working Paper 75−22. Madison: Center for Demography and Ecology, University of Wisconsin, 1975.

Hines, Fred K., David L. Brown, and John M. Zimmer (1975). *Social and Economic Characteristics of the Population in Metro and Nonmetro Counties, 1970.* Washington, D.C.: Economic Research Service, U.S. Department of Agriculture.

Holleb, Doris B. (1975), "Moving Towards Megacity: Urbanization and Population Trends," Chicago: Center for Urban Studies, University of Chicago.

Hoyt, Homer (1939), *The Structure and Growth of Residential Neighborhoods in American Cities.* Washington, D.C.: Federal Housing Administration.

Long, Larry H. (1975), "How the Racial Composition of Cities Changes." *Land Economics*, LI: 258−267.

Morrison, P. (1975), "The Current Demographic Context of National Growth and Development," Santa Monica. The Rand Corporation unpublished manuscript.

Rodwin, L. (1970). *Nations and Cities.* Boston, Houghton Mifflin.

Ross, Heather L. and Isabel V. Sawhill (1975), *Time of Transition: The Growth of Families Headed by Women.* Washington, D.C.: Urban Institute.

Sundquist, J.L. (1975), *Dispersing Population*, Washington, D.C.: Brookings Institution.

Taeuber, Conrad and Irene B. Taeuber. *The Changing Population of the United States.* Washington, D.C.: U.S. Government Printing Office, 1957.

Tisdale, H. (1942), "The Process of Urbanization." *Social Forces*, XX, 311−316.

U.S. Bureau of the Census. *Current Population Reports.* Series P−20, No. 285. "Mobility of the Population of the United States: March 1970 to March 1975." Washington, D.C.: U.S. Government Printing Office, 1975.

U.S. Bureau of the Census. *Current Population Reports.* Series P−20, No. 292. "Population Profile of the United States: 1975." Washington, D.C.: U.S. Government Printing Office, 1976.

U.S. Bureau of the Census. *Current Population Reports.* Series P−23, No. 55. "Social and Economic Characteristics of the Metropolitan and Nonmetropolitan Population: 1974 and 1970." Washington, D.C.: U.S. Government Printing Office, 1975.

U.S. Bureau of the Census. *Current Population Reports.* Series P−25, No. 601. "Projections of the Population of the United States: 1975 to 2050," Washington, D.C.: U.S. Government Printing Office, 1975.

U.S. Bureau of the Census. *Historical Statistics of the United States: Colonial times to 1970.* Washington, D.C.: U.S. Government Printing Office, 1975.

U.S. Domestic Council (1976), *Report on National Growth and Develop-*

ment. Biennial Report to the Congress: 1972—1976. Washington, D.C.: U.S. Government Printing Office.

U.S. Office of Management and Budget (1975), *Standard Metropolitan Statistical Areas.* Revised Edition. Washington, D.C.: U.S. Government Printing Office.

Warner, S.B., Jr. (1968), *The Private City.* Philadelphia, University of Pennsylvania Press.

Watson, J. Wreford (1970—71), "Image Geography: The Myth of America in the American Scene," *The Advancement of Science*, 27:1—9.

Weber, Adna F. (1899), *The Growth of Cities in the Nineteenth Century.* New York: The Macmillian Co.

Wells, H.G. (1902), *Anticipations. The Reaction of Mechanical and Scientific Progress on Human Life and Thought.* London: Harper and Row.

※ *Chapter 3*

Urban Development in Sweden 1960–1975: Population Dispersal in Progress

Thomas Falk

INTRODUCTION

During the 1960s and the early 1970s there was a lively discussion in Sweden about the role of the metropolitan areas in the urbanization process. The debate disclosed our limited knowledge of the spatial anatomy of urban Sweden; it became obvious that a better understanding of the pattern of population change both in metropolitan and in nonmetropolitan areas was needed.

This study challenges the notion of a concentration of population in the metropolitan regions (which strongly influenced regional planning and development policy in the 1960s), and discerns the beginning of population dispersal towards smaller urban places. Although based entirely on Swedish material, the results presented here reflect a general development which is likely to be characteristic of most industrial countries in the West.

The evidence suggests a two-way redistribution of the population in Sweden. At various levels of generalization, tendencies towards an interregional deconcentration from the metropolitan areas are observed. Further, the significance of the relative location of urban places is established: proximity to medium-sized and large agglomerations influences the growth rates of smaller urban places. Within such local subsystems of interconnected places (urban regions), each comprising an urban core and surrounding satellites, *intraregional* deconcentration is evident: satellites generally reported higher growth rates than the cores.

The inquiry is mainly confined to the period 1960–1970. However, during the final stages of this study, the first data from the 1975 census became available (some of the figures are preliminary). Whenever possible the analysis is therefore extended to include the period 1970–1975. A study of changes in the urban population distribution, with such a short period in focus, may seem to offer limited scope for a penetrating analysis. But the circumstances governing this choice were of a statistical nature. The attainment of the objectives demanded detailed and fully comparable data which Sweden actually lacked until 1960.

ABOUT THE STATISTICS

Prior to 1960, urban statistics in Sweden varied considerably in quality and reliability [1]. This applies particularly to the figures regarding *nonadministrative* urban places, where frequent changes in the definitions and a lack of formalized delimitation procedures hamper a comparison of data between censuses. A first step towards the achievement of greater reliability was taken in the 1950 census. The distinction between *administrative* and *nonadministrative* urban places was then dropped and all urban places were delimited in accordance with a residential building density criterion only. But the important improvement came in the 1960 census, when a system of formalized delimitation on physical maps was introduced. Since then Sweden has subscribed to a common Nordic definition of *localities* that follows the recommendations of the United Nations [2].

Accordingly, the Swedish census recognizes as a locality (*tätort*) any agglomeration with a population of 200 or more, if the distance between the houses does not normally exceed 200 meters [3]. All sorts of buildings are considered (uninhabited houses, working places, summer cottages, etc.), but only the *resident* (de jure) population is reported.

The entire population living in localities comprises the *urban population*; the residual—the people in sparsely populated areas (*glesbygd*)—make up the *rural population*. No other distinction between urban and rural is currently drawn in Sweden.

The unequivocal urban place definition in use since 1960, and the carefully prepared delimitation procedures, have together ensured continuity in the urban statistics and provided a degree of comparability unparalleled in the history of the Swedish census. Conditions have never been more suitable for unbiased comparisons of the population of individual places between censuses. Despite minor irregularities, the census material for the period 1960–1975 has been accepted in its entirety; it is assumed that the data are sufficiently reliable and comparable for the present purpose.

URBAN DEVELOPMENT PRIOR TO 1960

Any discussion of urban development in Sweden before 1960 has to use data in which there are considerable margins of error. These margins are most pronounced in the case of the smaller urban places. Over the years the proportion of such places has been consistently high, but they have accounted for a fairly small proportion of the urban population. It can therefore be maintained that a discussion based on aggregated data will capture the main characteristics of urban development since 1800 reasonably well. But the material cannot support excessively detailed analysis, and any conclusions drawn from data concerning periods prior to 1960 should not be pushed too far.

Urban and rural development since 1800 is outlined in Figure 3-1. The urban data were derived from several statistical sources; for each year, the rural population represents the residual of the urban. It should be noted that the urban data for the period 1800-1880 concern only the population reported for towns [5].

Despite the often sparse data, the tendencies are very clear. Before 1880 the urban population was small. In 1880 it accounted for less than 20 percent of the total population, and in the preceding decades for considerably less than that. Both the urban and the rural components increased until the 1880s, when the rural population began to fall—a decline that has continued ever since. For a long time rural depopulation concerned southern Sweden only; northern areas did not generally report a rural decline before the 1930s. Throughout the period 1800-1975, the urban population has increased steadily. Since 1840 the urban population has grown at a faster rate than the total population and by 1935 about half the population lived in urban places. In 1970 some 6.6 million urban dwellers accounted for 81.4 percent of the population. With 82.7 percent of the population (6.8 million) reported as urban in 1975, the rural-urban redistribution in Sweden is now likely to be near its completion.

The system of urban places has been remarkably stable. When the urban places reported in the 1920-1975 censuses were classified into nine size-groups (as in Table 3-4), each size group showed relatively small changes in its share of the urban population and of the number of places. Also, the urban system embraces a large proportion of small and medium-sized places—a proportion that has been more or less constant during the 55-year period. Places with populations

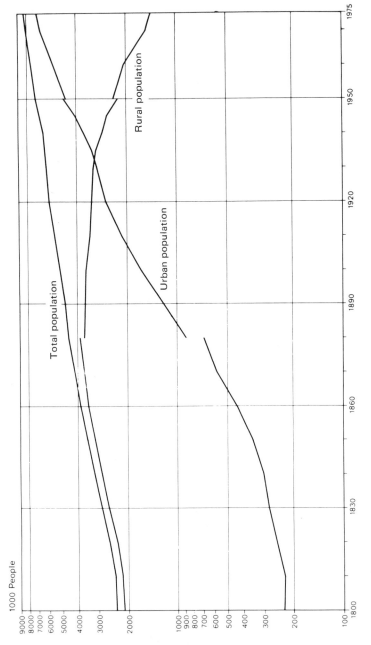

Figure 3–1.   Urban, Rural, and Total Population 1800–1975.

Sources: William-Olsson (1938), SCB (1955), Fo (1960:I), FoB (1965:I), FoB (1970:I), FoB (1960–1970), FoB (1975:III) [4].

below 500 have accounted for between 40 and 50 percent but, on an average, this size-group has represented less than 5 percent of the urban population. Urban places with fewer than 2,000 inhabitants have accounted for about four-fifths of the places, but for less than a fifth or a sixth of the population.

During the period 1920–1970 the urban growth rate has remained fairly stable, with a deviation that was low in the 1920s and high in the 1940s. However, a drastic retardation was reported for the early 1970s; between 1970 and 1975 the increase was only a low 3.3 percent. The rural population declined at a rather homogeneous rate in the three decades between 1930 and 1960. Rural depopulation accelerated during the 1960s, but slowed down considerably in the period 1970–1975, reaching a total of 1.4 million by 1975 (Table 3–1).

THE ROLE OF THE METROPOLITAN AREAS IN THE URBANIZATION PROCESS

During the 1960s and the early 1970s a discussion took place among urban planners, politicians, economists, geographers, and other social scientists in Sweden about the role of the metropolitan areas in the urbanization process. On the one hand it was contended that the population of Sweden was becoming concentrated in the three big-city regions (Stockholm, Göteborg, Malmö), and especially in the Stockholm metropolitan area. On the other hand it was maintained that the population development of the metropolitan areas was on a

Table 3–1. Percentage Urban Population Growth and Rural Population Decrease 1920–1975.

	Urban Growth	Rural Decrease
	Percent	Percent
1920–1930	11.5	2.1
1930–1940	20.3	11.8
1940–1950	30.1	14.6
1950–1960	17.0	14.3
1960–1970	20.6	26.5
1960–1965	10.3	14.2
1965–1970	9.3	14.3
1970–1975	3.3	5.5

Sources: SCB (1955), FoB (1960–1970), FoB (1975:III).

par with the average for all urban places in Sweden. This discussion will not be reviewed in any great detail here. Only some fundamental aspects of the argument will be highlighted. We will focus particularly on a problem of measurement—namely, how the geographical redistribution of the population should be measured. Let us first outline the main features of population development in Sweden between 1960 and 1970 in aggregated terms.

Population Development in Sweden
1960–1970. A Broad Outline by Regions

Sweden has a skewed population distribution [6]. In 1970 the Stockholm/Södertälje, the Göteborg, and the Malmö/Lund/Trelleborg A-regions together accounted for 32 percent of the total population. As will be seen later, this fundamental feature of the regional population distribution of Sweden is very much a historical legacy, and its origins can be traced back at least to the mid-19th century. Whereas all regions except two had an increasing urban population during the 1960s, more than a third of the regions—particularly in the northern two-thirds of Sweden—reported a total population loss. The decrease in these regions reflects the characteristic north-south drift of the population, which was accentuated after World War II as a result of the employment decline in forestry and agriculture. The three big-city regions each had a total population increase of more than twice the national average rate of 7.8 percent. However, in the case of urban development, the picture is strikingly different. Stockholm/Södertälje and Göteborg each exhibited an urban population growth that lay close to the 20.6 percent average for all urban places (19.0 and 22.0 percent respectively), while Malmö/Lund/Trelleborg was somewhat above the average (25.7 percent). Without exception, all regions exhibited a depopulation of their rural areas.

Besides the three big-city regions, another two regions had a *degree of urbanization* (i.e. the proportion of the total population living in urban places) above 90 percent. The lowest degree of urbanization was slightly below 50 percent. The ratio increased in all regions during the decade, but the change was minimal in the metropolitan areas. Even though most regions in the eastern portion of Central Sweden had exceeded 80 percent by 1970, a further increase in the urban proportion must still be expected for a majority of regions.

Interregional comparisons of the total population change on the one hand, and of the urban population change on the other, appear to lead to different conclusions about the growth of the metropolitan areas. The total growth rate in these regions was twice the national average; but their urban population increase more-or-less paralleled the average urban growth rate in Sweden. As we shall see, the controversy about metropolitan growth resolves into the question of whether the geographical redistribution of the population should be measured in terms of the *total* population or of the *urban* population. Let us examine these two approaches.

The Components of Population Change

The argument that the population was being concentrated in the three big-city regions, and especially in the Stockholm metropolitan area, was based on comparisons of the total population development in administrative regions (municipalities, A-regions, or counties). A typical and frequently recurring example of this argument is presented in Table 3–2. Here the total populations of the counties of Stockholm, Göteborg & Bohus, and Malmöhus, and of six other groups of counties, are compared over time [7].

The table has commonly been interpreted as follows. The Stockholm region has more or less doubled its share of the Swedish population since the turn of the century. Even though the Göteborg region increased its share considerably, this increase is modest com-

Table 3–2. **Total Population by Groups of Counties 1870–1970.**
(Percentage Distribution.)

Counties	1870	1900	1930	1960	1970
Stockholm	6.4	9.3	12.5	17.1	18.3
Göteborg & Bohus	5.6	6.6	7.5	8.4	8.9
Malmöhus	7.6	8.0	8.3	8.4	8.9
Uppsala, Södermanland, Östergötland, Örebro, Västmanland	18.5	17.8	16.5	16.6	17.1
Jönköping, Kronoberg, Kalmar, Gotland, Blekinge, Kristianstad	23.3	19.6	17.6	15.0	14.7
Halland, Älvsborg, Skaraborg	15.6	12.9	11.4	10.5	10.6
Värmland, Kopparberg, Gävleborg	13.9	13.8	13.1	11.6	10.6
Västernorrland, Jämtland	4.9	6.7	6.7	5.7	4.9
Västerbotten, Norrbotten	4.0	5.4	6.6	6.7	6.0
Sweden	100.0	100.0	100.0	100.0	100.0

Sources: SOU (1970:3), FoB (1970:I).

pared with that of Stockholm. The Malmö region has maintained a more or less constant share, but a small increase is noticeable during the 1960s. The counties of Uppsala, Södermanland, Östergötland, Örebro, and Västmanland constitute a stable region, while the rest of central and southern Sweden shows decreasing shares. Until recently the counties in northern Sweden maintained their shares, and for a long time northernmost Sweden even reported increasing shares [8].

In a series of articles, William-Olsson has argued against this interpretation [9]. He does not dispute that the county of Stockholm has greatly increased its share of the national population since 1900, but contends that this could with equal justification also be reported for many other areas in Sweden, namely the growing *urban places.* Each administrative region comprises urban places and rural areas in varying proportions. A fundamental feature of Swedish population development has long been an overall concentration of the population in urban places; any comparisons of analytical aggregates would only partly account for the rural-urban migratory movement. The net influx of people into a region's urban places from the rural areas of other regions affects the total population figure of the region concerned, whereas the rural-urban migration *within* the regions does not. In other words, since the rural population is declining rather uniformly throughout the country and the urban population is expanding, the ratio of the two components greatly affects the growth rate of the total population in an administrative region.

Take for example a region delimited in such a way that it consists of *one* large urban place and a surrounding rural area. Assume that the urban place grows more populous solely because of an influx from its own rural area. The total population figure in this region will not be affected since the rural loss is counterbalanced by a corresponding gain in the urban place. Thus, the total population in this region will not increase its share of the national population; obviously the expanding urban place will do so. William-Olsson therefore concludes that whether or not a region can report an increasing share of the national population will depend largely on the way it has been delimited.

In a comparison of the total population developments in different administrative regions, intraregional migration from rural areas to urban places remains concealed. Since each administrative region has a different degree of urbanization, and since the total population consists of two components (an increasing urban population and a decreasing rural population), William-Olsson contends that comparisons of regional totals are in fact comparisons of noncomparable magnitudes. If changes in the geographical distribution of the population are to be correctly interpreted, a distinction must be made between urban and rural components. An analysis based on a subdivision of the country into urban places and rural areas would be much more revealing than comparisons of arbitrarily delimited administrative regions. Hence, urban and rural population developments should be analyzed separately. This is especially important in the case of metropolitan areas which are more or less totally urban in character. (As noted above, each of the three metropolitan A-regions had a degree of urbanization above 90 percent in 1970, and Stockholm/Södertälje had a ratio of 97 percent.) Thus, the urban population development in the metropolitan areas should be compared with developments in other urban places in Sweden. Focusing on Greater Stockholm, William-Olsson shows that this area has maintained a constant share (around 20 percent) of the Swedish urban population since 1880. This, he claimed, disproves the alleged concentration of population in this region.

In a situation with a declining rural and an expanding urban population, the urban gain (U_r) must be greater than the total population change (T_r) in both absolute and relative terms. In each decade since 1920 the urban population in Sweden increased considerably faster than the total population and, taking the 1960s as an example, we find the absolute urban increment to be almost twice as large as that of the total population.

It is clear that U_r may increase even if T_r is zero or negative. In this case the urban gain is maintained solely by the net migration from rural areas within the region and by the natural increase. If T_r declines while U_r increases (or is stationary), the rural decline is not fully counterbalanced by a corresponding urban gain; the region will thus show a net loss of population. Obviously, the rural-urban redistribution is a function of both migratory movements and of differences between the rural and urban components in terms of births and deaths. But Swedish statistics do not permit a breakdown of the regional population change into these components. The census provides stock data and comparisons over time yield only the net outcome of population changes between censuses. If we take migration as an example, we can see clearly that comparisons of population change based on a *holistic* approach (i.e., on total population development) will not fully recognize all migratory movement. The rural-urban migration within administrative regions will be ignored. *An urban increment due to migration from rural areas will affect the total population change differently, depending on whether the migrants' place of origin is within the region or in the rural areas of some other region.*

These aspects of regional population development have important practical implications. If, for example, funds for residential housing are allocated to regions on the basis of their total population development, then the supply and the demand for housing will almost certainly fail to match. In a situation where the rural population declines homogeneously and the urban population increases, a varying degree of urbanization in each region will affect the relation between the total and the urban population change. (By definition, urban and total population change must be identical when one hundred percent of the population is reported as urban.) As the degree of urbanization increases in regions reporting urban gains, the proportion of the urban increment that is counterbalanced by a rural loss will decrease. The lower the proportion of the urban increment that is matched by a corresponding rural loss, the higher the proportion of the regional urban gain which affects the total population figure. Regions with a high total growth rate tend to have a low proportion of their urban increment counterbalanced by a rural loss, and vice versa. For example, only a minute share of the urban increment in the metropolitan A-regions was accounted for by a corresponding rural loss.

The shortcomings of interregional comparisons of population change on a total population basis have been clearly demonstrated here. Since each region has a different degree of urbanization, comparisons of regional totals conceal the rural-urban redistribution within the regions. Hence, to reveal the role of the metropolitan areas in the urbanization process, the urban population development of these areas should be viewed in relation to the development of all urban places, not to the total population.

The Growth of the Metropolitan Areas

We now return to population developments in the groups of counties discussed in Table 3−2. The table has been recalculated so that the urban development is discernible. The three metropolitan counties of Stockholm, Göteborg & Bohus, and Malmöhus achieved a high degree of urbanization earlier than any other group of counties—in the case of Stockholm, the index was above 50 percent as early as 1870.

Table 3−3, in which the urban population by groups of counties has been related to the national urban population, provides a completely different picture of the growth of the big-city regions than that presented in Table 3−2. Having initially accounted for a larger share of the urban population, the county of Stockholm has maintained a more-or-less constant share. Since 1900, the county of Göteborg & Bohus has reported a decreasing share; so has Malmöhus,

Table 3–3. Urban Population by Groups of Counties 1870–1970.
(Percentage Distribution.)

Counties	1870*	1900*	1930	1960	1970
Stockholm	26.4	28.6	21.9	22.0	21.7
Göteborg & Bohus	12.2	13.2	11.6	10.0	9.8
Malmöhus	11.4	11.8	10.9	9.3	9.5
Uppsala, Södermanland, Östergötland, Örebro, Västmanland	16.9	15.8	15.8	16.8	17.5
Jönköping, Kronoberg, Kalmar, Gotland, Blekinge, Kristianstad	14.7	11.5	12.9	12.8	13.1
Halland, Älvsborg, Skaraborg	7.1	7.3	8.4	8.6	9.2
Värmland, Kopparberg, Gävleborg	7.6	7.2	10.2	10.6	9.9
Västernorrland, Jämtland	2.2	2.9	4.6	4.4	4.1
Västerbotten, Norrbotten	1.4	1.7	3.8	5.4	5.3
Sweden	100.0	100.0	100.0	100.0	100.0

*Towns only.
Sources: SCB (1955), Fo (1930:I), FoB (1965:II), FoB (1970:II), FoB (1960–1970).

except for 1970 when a small increase was again recorded. The remaining groups of counties have generally increased their shares of the urban population since 1900, but counties in the northern half of Sweden reported falling shares in the 1960s.

If the rural-urban redistribution within the administrative regions is allowed for, then the alleged concentration of the population to the three big-city regions—and especially to the Greater Stockholm area—cannot be corroborated. The concentration-in-the-big-city notion was basic to regional planning and policy during the 1960s and the early 1970s; as demonstrated, this notion was largely based on a dubious interpretation of the statistics.

In fact, the skewed population distribution of today is a legacy of the past. At an early stage, the metropolitan counties acquired a dominant position as population centers, but their initial weight was not augmented over the years. These areas developed more or less *pari passu* with the total urban system in Sweden [10]. This is clearly demonstrated by Figure 3–2. The urban population in the three metropolitan counties accounted for 50 percent of the town population

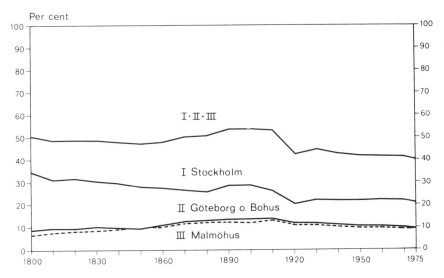

Figure 3–2. Urban Population in the Counties of Stockholm, Göteborg & Bohus, and Malmöhus. Percentage share of the national urban population 1800–1975. Prior to 1920 data concern towns only.

Sources: SCB (1880), SCB (1955), Fo (1920:II), Fo (1930:I), Fo (1940:I), Fo (1950:I), FoB (1965:II), FoB (1970:II), FoB (1960–1970), FoB (1975:III).

in 1800 (the earliest year for which urban statistics are available), and about 40 percent of the urban population in 1975. The county of Stockholm reported a 35 percent share of the urban population in 1800; both Göteborg & Bohus and Malmöhus accounted for less than 10 percent. While Stockholm reported steadily decreasing shares in the preindustrial period, Göteborg & Bohus and Malmöhus increased their shares somewhat. This continued after 1850, and these counties reached a peak of about 13 percent in 1910. By 1975 the two counties had fallen back and held just below 10 percent each. The influence of industrialization on population development in the Stockholm region is clearly indicated by an increasing share between 1880 and 1900. After a dip in 1920, the urban population in the county of Stockholm has since accounted for an average of 22 percent of the national urban population.

Greater Stockholm

So far, metropolitan development has been broadly outlined in terms of urban population change within counties. This section concludes with a closer look at Greater Stockholm and its development since 1920. Figure 3–3 shows urban development in Greater Stockholm and in Sweden as a whole. Greater Stockholm is here defined as the municipality of Stockholm and the southern and northern suburban municipalities within the Regional Planning Area as of 1 January 1971.

In 1920 Greater Stockholm had a degree of urbanization as high as 91.2 percent; by 1970 it had reached 98 percent. The urban population in Greater Stockholm increased almost twice as fast as the national average between 1920 and 1930 (Table 3–1). Apart from this period, the area has developed more-or-less at the same rate as the national urban population, keeping a constant share of some 20 percent of the urban population in Sweden. The most pronounced deviation from the national urban growth between 1920 and 1970 occurred during the 1940s and the 1960s. Between 1940 and 1945 the increase in Greater Stockholm was somewhat above average; in the following five-year period it was somewhat below. During the 1960s Stockholm increased by 16.0 percent, and the national urban population by 20.6 percent. Greater Stockholm's share thus dropped from 20.6 percent in 1960 to 19.8 percent in 1970.

In the early 1970s, the below-average growth of the region became more pronounced; with a 0.4 percent increase between 1970 and 1975, Greater Stockholm's share of the national urban population was down to 19.2 percent in 1975. During the intercensal years, Greater Stockholm became the first metropolitan region to report an absolute population decline. After two successive years of depopulation (1971 and 1972) a small increase was recorded again [11]. (A development towards zero population growth was also indicated for the Göteborg and Malmö metropolitan regions between 1971 and 1973 [12].) As discussed below, the metropolitan regions have reported a strong suburbanization, and exceptionally high growth rates were found in urban places surrounding the metropolitan cores. But the material concerning Greater Stockholm for the early 1970s indicates a spillover into the world beyond suburbia, to exurbia. The region's rural population recorded a 16 percent *increase* (4,100 people) between 1970 and 1975 as compared with a consistent decline during the sixties; the degree of urbanization was actually lowered from 98.0 to 97.8 percent.

The retarded population development in Greater Stockholm during the 1960s was highlighted in a study by Ahnström (1976), who investigated the industrial development of the Capital region since 1950 by computing location quotients (LQ) [13]. Most activities reported falling LQs but Ahnström's most striking find was the declining LQ for activities believed to be particularly big-city oriented. For example, in 1950 Greater Stockholm had three times the

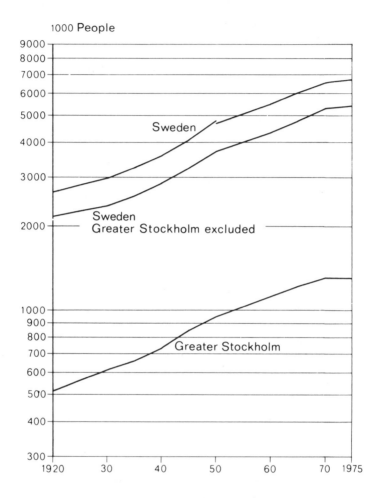

Figure 3–3. Urban Population 1920–1975, Sweden and Greater Stockholm. Greater Stockholm is defined as the municipality of Stockholm and the southern and northern suburban municipalities within the Regional Planning Area as of 1 January 1971, except for the municipality of Upplands-Bro and the parishes of Sigtuna, Sankt Olof, Sankt Per, and Haga in the municipality of Sigtuna. For the extension of The Regional Planning Area and a list of the southern and northern suburban municipalities see *Statistisk Årsbok för Stockholm 1971*, pp. 316 f.

Sources: SCB (1955), Fo (1920:I), Fo (1930:I), Fo (1935:I), Fo (1940:I), Fo (1945:I), Fo (1950:I), FoB (1960–1970), FoB (1975:III).

national average employment in *business services* but by 1970 this *LQ* had dropped to less than two and a half.

Manufacturing industry stagnated and was gradually decentralized from Greater Stockholm in the decades following World War II. Ahnström shows an *LQ* of 0.89 for manufacturing in Greater Stockholm for both 1950 and 1960. In 1965 the *LQ* had fallen to 0.71 and by 1970 it had reached a low 0.64. Greater Stockholm's proportion of the total number of job opportunities in manufacturing decreased from 14.1 percent in 1965 to 13.7 percent in 1970 [14]. Between 1963 and 1970 about 150 manufacturing establishments were relocated across a county border. Half of these establishments originated in the county of Stockholm. Location changes in manufacturing between 1963 and 1970 resulted in a net decrease in employment of 27,000 people; more than half of this decrease was accounted for by the three metropolitan counties [15].

URBAN DEVELOPMENT 1960–1970

We now turn to a detailed analysis of urban development in Sweden between 1960 and 1970.

For an unbiased study of the population development in urban places, a *cohort of permanent places* was prepared. Included were those urban places which had been reported in each of the 1960, 1965, and 1970 censuses. Excluded were places entering the statistics after 1960 and places dropped from the statistics after that year. Urban places which had been amalgamated by an areal extension of built-up areas after 1960 were treated as one agglomeration throughout the ten-year period. The cohort of permanent places thus established comprises 1,569 urban places, or 98.8 percent of the urban population in 1970. The average growth rate of the cohort during the decade was somewhat lower than that of the total urban population: 19.9 and 20.6 percent, respectively.

Development by Size-Groups of Urban Places

A rather consistent pattern of urban growth was reported for various periods between 1920 and 1960: smaller size-groups recorded growth rates below the national average; medium-sized and larger urban places exhibited growth close to the average [16]. But during the 1960s Sweden registered a pattern of urban change that contrasts with those reported for the previous periods.

Table 3–4A demonstrates that, with the exception of the very smallest places, agglomerations with fewer than 10,000 inhabitants increased considerably faster than the national average for the sixties

Table 3-4.   Urban Population, Percentage Change 1960-1970 by Size of Urban Place (1960). Cohort of Urban Places Existing in 1960, 1965, and 1970.

Size (inhabitants)	A. Sweden Total			B. Metropolitan Areas*			C. Sweden Total (Metropolitan Areas Excluded)		
	Percentage Change			Percentage Change			Percentage Change		
	1960-1970	1960-1965	1965-1970	1960-1970	1960-1965	1965-1970	1960-1970	1960-1965	1965-1970
200- 499	18.7	6.9	11.0	87.1	27.6	46.7	13.9	5.4	8.1
500- 999	38.3	15.5	19.7	207.4	78.0	72.8	19.4	8.5	10.0
1000- 1999	33.3	14.1	16.8	111.7	39.4	51.9	26.0	11.8	12.8
2000- 4999	32.6	15.0	15.3	109.6	46.1	43.4	21.3	10.4	9.9
5000- 9999	32.6	15.7	14.6	95.7	38.6	41.2	23.1	12.2	9.7
10000-19999	24.4	13.7	9.4	55.9	28.3	21.5	21.3	12.3	8.1
20000-49999	26.0	13.2	11.3	51.5	25.8	20.4	20.4	10.4	9.0
50000-99999	16.2	7.9	7.7	-	-	-	16.2	7.9	7.7
100000-	4.5	4.1	0.3	4.5	4.1	0.3	-	-	-
Cohort Total:	19.9	10.1	8.9						

*The Stockholm/Södertälje A-region, the Göteborg A-region, and the Malmö/Lund/Trelleborg A-region.
Source: FoB (1960-1970).

(above 30 percent). Medium-sized agglomerations (10,000–49,999) were also somewhat above the national average (24 and 26 percent) while larger urban places showed a retardation of population growth. A further change in the urban pattern was observed; whereas places with fewer than 5,000 inhabitants reported higher growth rates during the second half of the sixties than in the period 1960–1965, the opposite applied to places above this size. During the decade, places with fewer than 10,000 inhabitants accounted for over 50 percent of the absolute urban increment. The beginning of a population dispersal towards smaller urban places was discernible.

It must be emphasized that the low figure (4.5 percent) for Stockholm, Göteborg, and Malmö (size-group 100,000 and above) concerns the metropolitan *cores* only. The 1960s was a decade of strong suburbanization and exceptionally high growth rates were recorded in urban places around the three largest agglomerations. In each metropolitan region the core reported a low growth rate in comparison with the suburbs (Table 3–4B) [17]. During the decade a substantial intraregional redistribution of the population was recorded for these areas. In the case of Stockholm, a *redistribution loss* of nearly 200,000 in the core (which increased by 0.2 percent in the sixties) was not fully counterbalanced by a redistribution gain of 180,000 in the suburbs (an increase of 107.8 percent) [18]. The region experienced an urban redistribution loss of 18,000 people in the sixties (Table 3–5). The Stockholm metropolitan core actually decreased by 1.8 percent between 1965 and 1970; in absolute figures the loss amounted to 17,800 people.

After the exclusion of metropolitan regions from the analysis, the development of remaining places (Table 3–4C) followed the urban average fairly closely.

This is as far as the analysis by size groups can take us. The conclusion must obviously be that at this level of generalization, the three metropolitan areas played a dominating role in the shaping of the urban patterns by size-groups which are shown in Table 3–4A. The picture given here of the growth of urban places in nonmetropolitan areas (Table 3–4C) was substantially altered when the material was further disaggregated down to the level of individual places. The subsequent discussion will reveal several places reporting rapid growth rates as well as areas with a strong suburbanization outside the metropolitan regions.

Development by Individual Places
The analysis of individual agglomerations is based on the maps in Figure 3–4. The left-hand map (A) shows the urban population in

Table 3–5. Metropolitan Growth 1960–1970.

A-region	Population 1970		Percentage Change 1960–70			Regional Redistribution 1960–70 (gains/losses)*		
	Core	Suburbs	Region	Core	Suburbs	Region	Core	Suburbs
Stockholm/ Södertälje	972,700	427,600	19.0	0.2	107.8	-18,400	-197,900	179,500
Göteborg	486,700	159,300	22.0	8.8	93.8	7,500	-52,700	60,200
Malmö/Lund/ Trelleborg	264,600	143,400	25.7	14.2	54.6	16,600	-14,900	31,500

* Gains and losses relative to equal growth in all regions (see text).
Source: FoB (1960–1970).

1970 (proportionate symbols). Place names were inserted for agglomerations with more than 30,000 inhabitants [19]. The right-hand map (B) shows the redistribution gains and losses. This map divides places into two categories: those with a below average growth rate (including those experiencing an actual decrease) and those with an above average growth rate.

Although, at first glance, places in the environs of the three largest agglomerations are the most conspicuous on the maps, a large number of other places also exhibited rapid growth rates. Consider, for example, several of the larger agglomerations on the coast of northern Sweden, places in areas around Lakes Mälaren, Vättern, and Vänern and places in central southern Sweden.

Places which actually decreased in size were largely confined to northern Sweden—especially in the interior. The great majority of agglomerations reporting depopulation were small. Only 19 places larger than 2,000 inhabitants had population losses in the sixties; 11 of these places were situated in the northern half of the country.

A fundamental feature of the maps are the fast-growing places around medium-sized and large nonmetropolitan agglomerations. The maps clearly indicate the existence of local subsystems of interconnected places, each comprising an urban core and surrounding satellites. We may call such a subsystem an *urban region*.

A study of the map series thus suggests that a closer look at the *relative location* of places is required. Proximity to large agglomerations influenced the growth rates of smaller and medium-sized urban places. The maps indicate that agglomerations within urban regions often registered higher growth rates than places outside, and that satellites generally showed higher growth rates than the core areas. In order to examine these phenomena the data were again rearranged. The material was aggregated according to the relative location of urban places to permit a study of urban regions.

Relative Location of Places—Urban Regions

Our findings suggested that the urban region comprises a core and surrounding satellites. The threshold size of such a core is not well defined. The analysis was performed for three definitions of regions according to the size of the core. The following population thresholds for urban cores were chosen: (1) 30,000, (2) 20,000, and (3) 15,000 [20]. The urban regions were delimited with an average commuting distance used as a radius. The limit was drawn 25 km from the center of each core; all urban places within this radius were included. During the sixties, 30 km was generally regarded as the maximum distance tolerated for travel to work [21]. A straight-

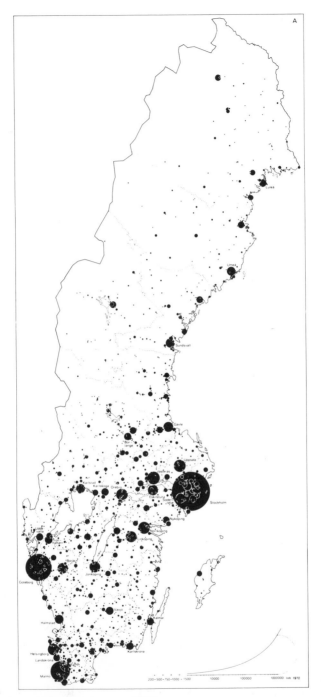

Figure 3–4A. Urban Population 1970.

Source: FoB (1960–1970).

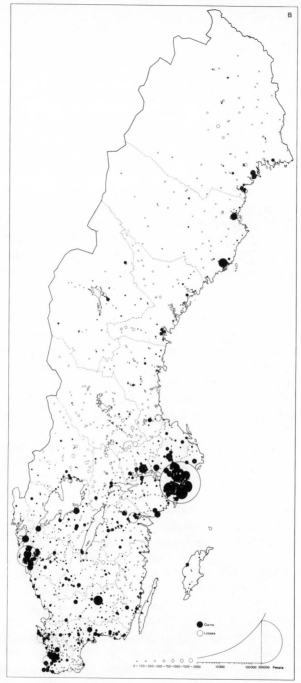

Figure 3–4B. Redistribution of the Urban Population 1960–1970. Gains and losses relative to equal growth in all places (see text).

Source: FoB (1960–1970).

line distance of 25 km was used as an operational approximation of a road distance of 30 km [22]. For the three largest agglomerations, Stockholm, Göteborg, and Malmö, a more generous limit was allowed: recognizing the higher efficiency of local transport systems in these areas, all satellites within a radius of 40 km were included. Urban places within overlapping areas were assigned to the closest core. Each region was checked against physical maps. Places were omitted if interspersed bodies of water considerably hampered accessibility.

Altogether 63 regions with a core of at least 15,000 inhabitants each were delimited. (A total of 44 regions had a core of at least 20,000, and 30 regions a core of 30,000 people or more.) Urban regions accounted for the main part of the urban population in Sweden. More than 80 percent of the urban population in 1970 was found in urban regions with a core of at least 15,000 inhabitants. On average satellites accounted for just above a quarter of the regional total.

Proximity to larger urban places strongly influenced growth rates of small urban places and the rise of new agglomerations. Three quarters of the new places in the sixties were located within urban regions. Only a third of the places that were dropped from the statistics in the same period were found within the limits of urban regions. Small and medium-sized places generally reported far more rapid growth rates in urban regions than in residual areas (the country outside the urban regions).

The regions of Stockholm, Göteborg, and Malmö reported high growth rates for small and medium-sized agglomerations. After the exclusion of metropolitan areas from the analysis, considerably higher growth rates were still recorded for small and medium-sized places in urban regions than in the residual areas.

No region reported depopulation during the 1960s (even though a few satellites did). An *interregional* redistribution of population was apparent: the regions of Stockholm, Göteborg, and Malmö reported growth rates below the national average in spite of the rapid growth of the satellites. With regard to Malmö, two adjacent regions, Lund (which increased 52.5 percent) and Trelleborg (38.8 percent), were largely responsible for the growth of 25.7 percent in the Malmö/Lund/Trelleborg A-region. Apart from Lund and Trelleborg, another 15 regions showed growth rates of 30 percent or more [23]. A total of 30 regions registered growth rates below the national average.

An *intraregional* deconcentration occurred during the sixties: on average, satellites grew some five times more rapidly than the cores. In the 30 regions with a core of at least 30,000 inhabitants, faster growth of the core was reported in five cases only. In no less than 20 regions, satellites grew more than twice as rapidly as the cores.

When the threshold for the core was lowered to 20,000 inhabitants, another four regions reported a slower growth rate for satellites than for the core, and with the threshold set at 15,000 people, 22 regions reported a higher growth rate in the core.

In summary then, the evidence presented here suggests a two-way redistribution of the population in the sixties: At various levels of generalization, tendencies towards an *interregional* deconcentration from the metropolitan areas was observed. The notion of a concentration of population in metropolitan regions, which was basic to much regional policy and planning in the 1960s, finds no support here. Although suburban places within the metropolitan regions registered unsurpassed growth rates, the regions on the whole showed a rate of increase below, or close to, the urban average. Considerably faster growth rates were found in numerous nonmetropolitan areas.

Small and medium-sized agglomerations in proximity to a larger urban core often reported rapid growth rates. Within such local subsystems of places (urban regions) an *intraregional* deconcentration was evident: satellites generally reported higher growth rates than the cores.

URBAN DEVELOPMENT 1970—1975

The early 1970s probably marked the beginning of a reversal in the population trends hitherto experienced in this century. A small increase in the urbanization index, from 81.4 to 82.7 percent between 1970 and 1975, a low urban growth rate (3.3 percent), and an equally low rural decrease (5.5 percent) in the period, indicate that one of the most conspicuous social and economic developments of the last hundred years is now running out of steam. This was not unexpected, since the population redistribution from rural to urban habitation is a finite process, concomitant with the change from an agrarian to an industrial society.

The dispersing urban population tendencies reported for the sixties were accentuated in the early 1970s. The metropolitan regions continued to register low growth rates, and considerably below-average growth rates were reported for Stockholm and Göteborg (see also Figure 3—3) [24]. Metropolitan suburban growth was still high (Table 3—6B). More interesting, however, is that smaller urban places outside these regions registered high growth rates, some three or four times the national average (Table 3—6C). Most striking is the retardation or reversal of population increases in many large and

Table 3–6. Urban Population, Percentage Change 1970–1975 by Size of Urban Place (1970). Cohort of Urban Places Existing in 1970 and 1975.

Size (inhabitants)	A. Sweden Total	B. Metropolitan Areas*	C. Sweden Total (Metropolitan Areas Excluded)
200– 499	11.5	33.8	9.6
500– 999	13.2	34.5	11.1
1000– 1999	16.4	64.6	12.3
2000– 4999	13.6	30.0	10.6
5000– 9999	6.2	15.6	4.0
10000–19999	4.2	16.6	1.7
20000–49999	1.7	3.2	1.5
50000–99999	–0.8	3.3	–1.3
100,000–	–5.0	–5.0	—
Cohort Total:	2.8		

*The Stockholm/Södertälje A-region, the Göteborg A-region and the Malmö/Lund/Trelleborg A-region.
Source: Population and Housing Census 1975, preliminary data.

medium-sized urban places. Each of the metropolitan cores reported absolute population losses, and of Sweden's 47 remaining places with a population of 20,000 or more, no less than 20 reported an absolute population decline.

A total of 64 urban regions with a core of at least 15,000 inhabitants in 1975 were delimited as described above. No fewer than 41 regions reported above-average growth rates, whereas an absolute population decline occurred in 8 regions. The intraregional redistribution was further accelerated in the period 1970–1975. In more than 85 percent of the regions, satellites grew more rapidly than the cores (and in 51 cases more than twice as rapidly). Although the cores reported an above-average growth in 21 regions, almost 50 percent of them registered absolute population losses. In more than 75 percent of the regions, satellites reported above-average growth rates and in almost a third of the regions, growth rates above 25 percent were recorded for the satellites.

CONCLUSION

Interregional Redistribution
If the geographical arrangement of the population is assumed to be determined by economic forces (this is at least true of industrial societies), the interregional redistribution of the population is a result of structural changes in the economy. We may therefore postulate that, in the long run, urban places will survive only if job opportunities are available in them or within acceptable commuting distance. An explanation of interregional shifts of the population must ultimately be based on an explanation of the structural changes in the economy as a whole. Such an explanation is an undertaking beyond the scope of this study. We must therefore leave the explanation of interregional population shifts to future research. An urgent task in such a research program would be to unravel the role of the metropolitan areas in the Swedish economy. Some promising directions for such research are discussed below.

It is likely that the regional development policy enacted by the Swedish Parliament in 1964 and extended in 1970 and 1972 [25] did not come early enough to have any impact on population development in the metropolitan areas during the 1960s. If the policy measures did exert some influence on this development, the effects must only have been marginal reinforcements of a structural change which was already under way. The below-average growth of Greater Stockholm in the 1960s must thus be regarded as a spontaneous development. We may then ask what caused this phenomenon. An appropriate approach would involve a study of metropolitan areas as undesirable environments, both in terms of noise, pollution, etc. and in terms of increasing costs arising from such things as high labor turnover, the high cost of meeting increasing demand for floorspace, or decreasing transferability within the regions due to congestion.

The influence of the regional development program on Greater Stockholm's population decline in 1972 and 1973 is a problem still to be investigated. However, an obvious nonpolicy factor which might have tipped the scales towards depopulation was the economic recession in the early seventies, which resulted in low immigration. By the same token the upswing in the business cycle should be credited for the population increase reported again for Greater Stockholm in 1974.

William-Olsson (1941) found the impetus for Stockholm's growth to be a set of pyramidally-organized specific city-forming functions: central government and private administrative functions, wholesaling, financing, and high-level cultural activities whose prime locational requirements were easy accessibility. With the stated aim of curbing the population increase in Metropolitan Stockholm, Parliament enacted schemes in 1971 and 1973 for relocating Government offices employing some 10,000 civil servants. An obvious direction of research would be to determine to what extent Greater Stockholm will be affected by this dispersal of specific city-forming functions.

Intraregional Redistribution

To a large extent intraregional population shifts are the result of changes in *residential preferences*. In this closing section some factors behind the observed development are discussed.

Slower growth rates in the urban cores could result from an increasing standard of living in terms of per capita demands for urban space (larger homes, more space for roads and other public uses, etc.). An increase of population in the satellites is a reflection of the desire for residence in the attractive surroundings of a smaller community, away from noise, pollution, congestion, and other environmental drawbacks characteristic of many urban core areas. The residential preference materializes as an increased demand for single-family housing; there was a drastic decline in the proportion of apartments in the total output of dwelling units constructed in and after the late 1960s. Since land near urban cores was mostly preempted for other land uses, single-family houses had to be sought in the satellites.

The emerging residential pattern in Sweden is highly dependent on a high standard of private transportation. Improved technology for the transfer of goods, people and information is mainly responsible for the increased spatial mobility and contact accessibility of the population. A fundamental feature of urbanization is thus the constantly widening conception of urban places; the need for physical proximity between urban functions, places of work, and places of residence has gradually diminished. Improved transport technology made possible an outward extension of urban built-up areas. In Sweden increased spatial mobility, especially the expansion of private car ownership, has facilitated a concentration of service outlets and a dispersed residential pattern.

The number of passenger cars in Sweden almost doubled in the sixties and reached about 2.29 million in 1970 (or 283 cars per thousand inhabitants) [26]. The family car was more common in the small and medium-sized urban places than in the largest centers.

An analysis of *journey to work* patterns in 1970 reveals a great daily mobility of the population. It resolves into two basic patterns of commuting. First, there is a radial pattern of commuting, between satellites and urban cores. A second pattern is found outside the urban regions, where people travel between urban places, and between rural areas and urban places. In 1970 almost three-quarters of the economically active population travelled to work in one way or the other by public or private transport; no less than 54 percent of these people used private cars [27].

Obviously apartment buildings are predominant in larger urban places. Smaller urban places mostly reported high proportions of one- and two-family houses. Residential units comprising one-family houses increased by 64 percent between 1960 and 1970. The number of apartments increased by only 32 percent.

Thus, in our local subsystems of interconnected places, satellites are predominantly places of residence comprising mostly single-family houses. The satellite populations rely on the cores for work and services; private car ownership seems to be imperative [28].

NOTES TO CHAPTER 3

1. See Falk (1976). *Administrative urban places* refers to agglomerations granted a municipal status (communities with local government functions), e.g. towns and cities; *nonadministrative urban places* refers to settlements without such status.

2. See, e.g., United Nations (1959, 1967).

3. "According to this definition all groups of houses having at least 200 inhabitants are counted as localities as long as the distance between the houses does not normally exceed 200 meters. The distance may however be permitted to exceed 200 meters in the case of groups of houses within the sphere of influence of a major community. On the other hand the maximum distance between the houses may be put at

less than 200 meters when this is called for by the character of the settlement, that is to say in small localities where no distinct centres are apparent and in cases where the boundary between locality and sparsely populated area is ill-defined. Areas used for public purposes such as parks, sports grounds, churchyards, wharfs, etc. are not to be regarded as a break in the settlement. The localities are demarcated irrespective of the administrative divisions." (FoB, 1970: II, p. 5).

4. References made to FoB (1960—1970) concern the material prepared for the analysis of the urban development in Sweden 1960—1970 contained in the following publications: Fo (1960:VI), FoB (1965:II), FoB (1965:IV), FoB (1970:II), SCB (1972 b, c), SCB (1973 a, b).

5. Material prepared by William-Olsson (1938, 1941) was used for the period 1880—1910, while the following years were covered by census material. The shift in 1880 in the urban curve (and by definition also in the rural) was caused by the switch to William-Olsson's population data for urban places. The similar break in 1950 reflects the change in the urban place delimitation procedures introduced in that year.

6. The analysis is based on the *A-regions* which are employed by the Central Bureau of Statistics. For statistical purposes the municipalities have been amalgamated to form 70 statistical areas (A-regions), each region including at least one major urban center. The subdivision employed here includes changes as of 1 January 1973. See SCB (1972 a).

7. The table is quoted from SOU (1970:3), table 1.2.1, which is a report from the *Expert Group of Regional Studies* within the Ministry of Labor. Figures for 1970 have here been substituted for the original 1965 and 1968 figures. The table also appeared in Hägerstrand (1966). The same approach can be found in a number of reports, see, e.g., Falk (1976, p. 114) for references. Sweden is subdivided into 24 administrative provinces (*län*), here referred to as *counties*. Each county has an administrative board headed by a provincial governor.

8. See SOU (1970:3) and Hägerstrand (1966).

9. *Kommunal tidskrift* 1968:6, 1970:19 and 20; *Svenska Dagbladet* 1970: November 8, 1971: January 14, July 21, July 23, and October 11, 1972: February 25; *Dagens Nyheter* 1970: February 7; *Industria* 1969:5.

10. Cf., e.g., Friedmann (1973): "Rudimentary patterns of urbanization and regional social structure, established quite early in a country's history, tend to maintain themselves over long periods of time. Subsequent flows of controlling decisions, innovation diffusion, migration, and economic location will tend to reinforce this pattern. The most probable future pattern will therefore resemble that of the past. Planned changes may require decades and even generations of counter-intuitive effort to alter this structural pattern in a significant way." (p. 238). The argument was illustrated by an analysis of the geographical distribution of the population in the United States. The relative proportions of major regions changed very little between 1850 and 1960.

11. *Source:* SSK (1975). The figures concern the total population for the area. Since the degree of urbanization in Greater Stockholm was around 98 percent, data should be comparable with those above. The decline in 1971—1972 was 2,700; in 1972—1973 the region lost 1,500 people.

12. SOU (1974:82, pp. 104 f.). See *ibid.* p. 67 for definition of Greater Göteborg and Greater Malmö.

13. To determine whether a region has more or less than its share of a specific activity, the location quotient (LQ), a simple ratio of ratios, may be computed. Let us illustrate with the case of manufacturing.

$$LQ = \frac{M_r}{T_r} \Big/ \frac{M_t}{T_t}$$

where M_r = region's employment in manufacturing

T_r = region's employment in all activities

M_t = national employment in manufacturing

T_t = national employment in all activities

If the region's percentage employment in manufacturing is greater than the corresponding ratio for the nation, the region has more than its share of this activity. An LQ of 2 thus means that the region has twice the national average employed in manufacturing and $LQ = 1$ indicates an employment on a par with the national average.

14. The corresponding figures for Greater Göteborg and Greater Malmö also decreased, from 8.3 to 8.1 and from 5.1 to 4.8, respectively. See SOU (1974:82, pp. 190 f.).

15. Ibid., p. 141.

16. See Falk (1976, pp. 99 ff.).

17. Here, the metropolitan areas of Stockholm, Göteborg and Malmö have been defined as the Stockholm/Södertälje A-region, the Göteborg A-region, and the Malmö/Lund/Trelleborg A-region, respectively.

18. By calculating how many urban dwellers regions should have in 1970 to have grown in the sixties at the rate of the national urban population, *gains* or *losses* in relation to the national average can easily be expressed in absolute terms. For the 1960s the redistribution figure (R) is obtained by the multiplication of the region's urban population figure in 1960 by the national urban growth rate for the sixties; the product is then compared with the figure actually reported for the region in 1970.

$$R = A_1 - A_0 \cdot \frac{B_1}{B_0}$$

where R = redistribution gain/loss

A_0 = region's urban population at the beginning of period

A_1 = region's urban population at the end of period

B_0 = national urban population at the beginning of period

B_1 = national urban population at the end of period

A positive value of R (redistribution gain) indicates that the region has increased its share of the national urban population, and a negative (redistribution loss) the opposite; thus, the value zero indicates a development on a par with the national urban population. Obviously the sum of redistribution gains and losses is zero.

It must be emphasized that the redistribution figures are not measures of net migrations among regions. A redistribution loss of 1,000 people does not mean that the region actually lost 1,000 people by out-migration. It simply means that the urban population in the region would have been 1,000 people more if the region's urban population had grown at the same rate as the national average.

19. With the exception of three Stockholm suburbs: Sollentuna, Roslags-Näsby, and Handen.

20. Although larger than 15,000 population, the suburbs of Märsta, Upplands-Väsby, Sollentuna, Roslags-Näsby, Lidingö, Bollmora, and Handen were included in the Stockholm region; Tumba was included in the Södertälje region, and Oxelösund in the Nyköping region. Frösön and Östersund together formed a core of 36,300 inhabitants.

21. See e.g. Kindahl (1965).

22. The central point of each urban place was assigned coordinates with an accuracy of one kilometer within the national grid system. The source was the register of coordinates prepared by Micklander and Torstensson (1964) in connection with the 1960 census which was later revised by Micklander for 1965 and 1970. (This edition was generously made available for this study by the *Expert Group of Regional Studies* within the Ministry of Labor.)

23. Umeå, Piteå, and Luleå on the coast of Norrland; Södertälje, Uppsala, Enköping, and Västerås surrounding Stockholm; Finspång, Lidköping, Skövde, and Mariestad in central Sweden; Växjö and Karlshamn in the south; Varberg and Alingsås in the south-west.

24. This section is partly based on preliminary data.

Between 1970 and 1975 the Stockholm/Södertälje A-region registered an urban increase of 0.9 percent. Corresponding figures for the Göteborg A-region and the Malmö/Lund/Trelleborg A-region were 1.5 and 3.3 percent respectively.

25. See, e.g., Planning Sweden (1973) for an outline in English of this policy.

26. *Statistisk årsbok för Sverige 1965*, table 32. *Statistisk årsbok för Sverige 1975*, table 170.

27. SOU (1974:1).

28. See, e.g., Hägerstrand (1972) and Mårtensson (1974) who show that lack of public transport facilities in settlement systems of this kind sometimes makes a privately-owned car almost imperative.

REFERENCES

Ahnström, L. 1976. Västeuropas ekonomisk-sociala geografi: Näringsgrensutvecklingen i Sverige och Storstockholm 1950−1970. *Ekonomiska Forskningsinstitutet vid Handelshögskolan i Stockholm, Working paper* (forthcoming).

Falk, T. 1976. *Urban Sweden: Changes in the Distribution of Population— the 1960s in Focus.* Stockholm: The Economic Research Institute at the Stockholm School of Economics.

Fo 1920:II. *Folkräkningen den 31 december 1920:II. Befolkningsagglome-*

rationer, trosbekännelse, stamskillnad, utrikes födelseort, främmande statsborgarskap, lyten mm. Stockholm: Kungl. Statistiska centralbyrån, 1925.

Fo 1930:I *Folkräkningen den 31 december 1930:I.* Areal, folkmängd och hushåll inom särskilda förvaltningsområden mm. Befolkningsagglomerationer. Stockholm: Statistiska centralbyrån, 1935.

Fo 1935:I. *Särskilda folkräkningen 1935:I.* Allmänna folkräkningen den 31 december 1935: Folkmängden kommunvis efter kön, civilstånd och större åldersgrupper. Befolkningsagglomerationer. Obefintliga. (*Recensement de la Population en 1935:I.* La population au 31 décembre 1935 dans les divisions communales par sexe, par état civil et par groupes d'âge. Agglomérations de caractère urbain à la campagne. "Introuvables.") Stockholm: Statistiska centralbyrån, 1937.

Fo 1940:I. *Folkräkningen den 31 december 1940:I.* Areal och folkmängd inom särskilda förvaltningsområden mm. Befolkningsagglomerationer. (*Recensement de la Population en 1940:I.* Superficie et population dans les différentes divisions administratives etc. Agglomérations de population de caractère urbain à la campagne.) Stockholm: Statistiska centralbyrån, 1942.

Fo 1945:I. *Folkräkningen den 31 december 1945:I.* Areal och folkmängd inom särskilda förvaltningsområden mm. Befolkningsagglomerationer. (*Recensement de la Population en 1945:I.* Superficie et population dans les différentes divisions administratives etc. Agglomérations de population de caractère urbain à la campagne.) Stockholm: Statistiska centralbyrån 1947.

Fo 1950:I. *Folkräkningen den 31 december 1950:I.* Areal och folkmängd inom särskilda förvaltningsområden mm. Tätorter. (*Census of the Population in 1950:I.* Area and population in different administrative divisions etc. Population clusters.) Stockholm: Statistiska centralbyrån, 1952.

Fo 1960:I. *Folkräkningen den 1 november 1960:I.* Folkmängd inom kommuner och församlingar efter kön, ålder, civilstånd mm. (*Census of the Population in 1960:I.* Population in communities and parishes by sex, age and marital status etc.) Stockholm: Statistiska centralbyrån, 1961.

Fo 1960:VI. *Folkräkningen den 1 november 1960:VI.* Förvärvsarbetande befolkning efter näringsgren och yrkesställning mm. inom kommuner, församlingar och tätorter. (*Census of the Population in 1960:VI.* Economically active population by industry and status etc. in communes, parishes and localities.) Stockholm: Statistiska centralbyrån, 1963.

FoB 1965:I. *Folk- och bostadsräkningen den 1 november 1965:I.* Folkmängd inom kommuner och församlingar samt kommunblock efter kön, ålder, civilstånd mm. (*Population and Housing Census in 1965:I.* Population in communes, parishes and co-operating communes by sex, age and marital status etc.) Stockholm: Statistiska centralbyrån, 1966.

FoB 1965:II. *Folk- och bostadsräkningen den 1 november 1965:II.* Folkmängd inom tätorter efter kön, ålder och civilstånd. (*Population and Housing Census in 1965:II.* Population in localities by sex, age and marital status.) Stockholm: Statistiska centralbyrån, 1967.

FoB 1965:IV. *Folk- och bostadsräkningen den 1 november 1965:IV.* Förvärvsarbetande befolkning efter näringsgren och yrkesställning mm. inom kommunblock, kommuner, församlingar och tätorter. (*Population and Housing Census in 1965:IV.* Economically active population by industry and status etc.

in co-operating communes, communes, parishes and localities.) Stockholm: Statistiska centralbyrån, 1967.

FoB 1970:I. *Folk- och bostadsräkningen 1970:1.* Befolkning i kommuner och församlingar mm. (*Population and Housing Census 1970:I.* Population in communes and parishes, etc.) Stockholm: Statistiska centralbyrån, 1972.

FoB 1970:II. *Folk- och bostadsräkningen 1970:2.* Befolkning i tätorter. (*Population and Housing Census 1970:2.* Population in localities.) Stockholm: Statistiska centralbyrån, 1972.

FoB 1960–1970. See footnote 4.

FoB 1975:III. *Folk- och bostadsräkningen 1975 del 3:2.* Folkmängd i tätorter. (*Population and Housing Census 1975 Part 3:2.* Population in localities.) Stockholm: Statistiska centralbyrån, 1976.

Friedmann, J. 1973. *Urbanization, Planning, and National Development.* Beverly Hills & London: Sage publications.

Hägerstrand, T. 1966. Regionala utvecklingstendenser och problem. Urbaniseringen. In *Svensk ekonomi 1966–1970 med utblick mot 1980: 1965 års långtidsutredning, huvudrapport,* pp. 273–290. Stockholm: SOU 1966:1.

Hägerstrand, T. 1972. Tätortsgrupper som regionsamhällen: Tillgången till förvärvsarbete och tjänster utanför de större städerna. In *Regioner att leva i: Elva forskare om regionalpolitik och välstånd. En rapport från ERU,* pp. 141–173. Stockholm: Allmänna förlaget.

Kindahl, J. 1965. De anställdas dagliga resor till arbetet. Studium av arbetskraftsundersökningen i maj 1964. *Arbetsmarknadsstyrelsen: Meddelanden från utredningsbyrån,* No. 18.

Mårtensson, S. 1974. Drag i hushållens levnadsvillkor. In *Ortsbundna levnadsvillkor. Bilagedel I till Orter i regional samverkan,* pp. 233–264. Stockholm SOU 1974:2.

Micklander, Å. & Torstensson, I. 1964. *Koordinatregister över Sveriges församlingar och tätorter.* Uppsala: Geografiska institutionen.

Planning Sweden. 1973. Regional development planning and management of land and water resources. A summary published by the Ministry of Labour and Housing and the Ministry of Physical Planning and Local Government. Stockholm: Allmänna förlaget.

SCB 1880. *Bidrag till Sveriges officiella statistik. A. Befolkningsstatistik, Ny följd XXII:2.* Statistiska centralbyråns underdåniga berättelse för 1880, andra afdelningen. Stockholm: 1883.

SCB 1955. *Historisk statistik för Sverige I.* Befolkning 1720–1950. (*Historical Statistics of Sweden I.* Population 1720–1950.) Stockholm: Statistiska centralbyrån.

SCB 1972 a. *Folkmängd 31 dec 1972 enligt indelningen 1 jan 1973.* Del 2. Kommunblock, judiciella och kyrkliga indelningar mm. (*Population Dec. 31, 1972 According to the Subdivisions Jan. 1, 1973.* Part 2. Co-operating communes, judicial districts and ecclesiastical divisions.) Stockholm: Statistiska centralbyrån, 1973.

SCB 1972 b. Folk- och bostadsräkningen 1970: Hushåll och lägenheter i kommuner och tätorter inom vissa län. I. Kalmar, Gotlands, Blekinge, Jämtlands, Västerbottens och Norrbottens län. Preliminära uppgifter. (Population and Housing Census in 1970: households and dwellings in communes and localities. First estimates.) *Statistiska Meddelanden*, Be 1972:9. Stockholm: Statistiska centralbyrån.

SCB 1972 c. Folk- och bostadsräkningen 1970: Hushåll och lägenheter i kommuner och tätorter inom vissa län. II. Södermanlands, Kronobergs, Kristianstads, Värmlands, Örebro och Kopparbergs län. Preliminära uppgifter. (Population and Housing Census in 1970: households and dwellings in communes and localities. First estimates.) *Statistiska Meddelanden*, Be 1972:12. Stockholm: Statistiska centralbyrån.

SCB 1973 a. Folk- och bostadsräkningen 1970: Hushåll och lägenheter i kommuner och tätorter inom vissa län. III. Uppsala, Östergötlands, Jönköpings, Skaraborgs, Västmanlands, Gävleborgs och Västernorrlands län. Preliminära uppgifter. (Population and Housing Census in 1970: households and dwellings in communes and localities. Preliminary data.) *Statistiska Meddelanden*. Be 1973:2. Stockholm: Statistiska centralbyrån.

SCB 1973 b. Folk- och bostadsräkningen 1970: Hushåll och lägenheter i kommuner och tätorter inom vissa län. Stockholms, Malmöhus, Hallands, Göteborgs och Bohus samt Älvsborgs län. Preliminära uppgifter. (Population and Housing Census in 1970: households and dwellings in communes and localities. Preliminary data.) *Statistiska Meddelanden*. Be 1973:6. Stockholm: Statistiska centralbyrån.

SOU 1970:3. *Balanserad regional utveckling: Delbetänkande avgivet av expertgruppen för regional utredningsverksamhet (ERU).* Stockholm: SOU 1970:3.

SOU 1974:1. *Orter i regional samverkan: Betänkande av expertgruppen för regional utredningsverksamhet (ERU).* Stockholm: SOU 1974:1.

SOU 1974:82. *Samverkan för regional utveckling: Betänkande av utredningen om regionalpolitiska styrmedel.* Stockholm: SOU 1974:82.

SSK 1975. Områdesindelning och folkmängd i Stockholms län. *Stockholms statistiska kontor.* Folk- och bostadsräkningen 1975. Rapport No. 2. Stockholm 1975.

Statistisk årsbok för Sverige 1965. (Statistical Abstract of Sweden 1965.) Stockholm: Statistiska centralbyrån, 1965.

Statistisk årbok för Sverige 1975. (Statistical Abstract of Sweden 1975.) Stockholm: Statistiska centralbyrån, 1975.

United Nations 1959. Handbook of Population Census Methods, Volume III: Demographic and Social Characteristics of the Population. *Studies in Methods*, Series F, No. 5, Rev. 1. New York: Statistical Office of the United Nations.

United Nations 1967. Principles and Recommendations for the 1970 Population Censuses. *Statistical Papers*, Series M, No. 44. New York: Department of Economic and Social Affairs. Statistical Office of the United Nations.

Wallner, H. 1971. The new land data bank in Sweden. In *Information Systems for Regional Development—A Seminar*, eds. T. Hägerstrand & A.R. Kuklinski, pp. 81–103. Lund: Lund Studies in Geography, Ser. B., Human Geography, No. 37.

William-Olsson, W. 1938. Utvecklingen av tätorter och landsbygd i Sverige 1880–1935. *Ymer*, Årg. 58, No. 2–4, pp. 243–280.

William-Olsson, W. 1941. *Stockholms framtida utveckling.* Stockholm: Norstedts.

✳ *Chapter 4*

An Evaluation of Regional Policies—Experiences in Market and Mixed Economies

Walter Stöhr
Franz Tödtling

INTRODUCTION

In a recent paper the authors made a critical evaluation of present regional development doctrine with regard to equity considerations in market and mixed economies (Stöhr and Tödtling, 1976). The present paper contains an evaluation of concrete regional development trends and policy instruments for less developed areas in a number of market and mixed economies and tries to interpret their success or failure in the light of regional economics and regional development theory.

Explicit policies for regional development have now been undertaken for about half a century ever since major regional programs such as the Ruhrsiedlungsverband in Germany, the Special Areas Policy in Great Britain and TVA in the USA were initiated. These programs were essentially oriented towards the solution of problems of individual regions or of specific types of regions. Since the 1950s, broader policies for regional development evolved, most of which were oriented towards reducing spatial disparities of living levels at the national level.

Spatial disparities in living levels had increasingly become a policy issue, both for objective and for subjective reasons. Objectively, because integration permitted formerly contained flows (of production

Editor's Note: This chapter is an abbreviated version of a longer study. The omitted sections were for the most part summaries of research results already published elsewhere. However, the references cited in the original paper are retained here in their entirety because of their obvious usefulness to students of regional development and human settlement policies. The longer version of this study is available from the authors as IIR–Discussion Paper No. 1 (1977).

factors, commodities, information, organizational linkages etc.) to move over much wider areas. This led to a change in the spatial pattern of activities and living levels by which some regions gained while others lost. Subjectively it became a policy issue, because with increasing scales of interaction and information exchange, existing spatial differences in living levels came to be perceived much stronger by local and regional communities than they had been before. These facts are valid for market and mixed economies as well as for planned economies.

In market and mixed economies, these flows and the choices of activity locations are essentially left to the individual decision-maker. Only when the divergence between private and social costs of such individual decisions surpasses a magnitude considered tolerable in economic, social or political terms, does policy intervention take place, either by promoting development in regions which lag behind the national average, or by controlling it in areas of extremely rapid growth accompanied by severe problems of agglomeration and congestion.

The actual effectiveness of these measures to avoid major divergences between private and social costs is still largely unknown. Much of what has been considered a success of regional development policies in the past decades may in reality have been due mainly to the market mechanism, which in periods of rapid economic expansion has produced "spill-overs" from congested to less developed areas (OECD, Working Party, 1976). It is nearly impossible to separate the influence of these two factors neatly because, like in most complex social science situations, it can rarely be defined *ex post* by empirical tests of how the system would have behaved without certain of these factors. Conclusions can therefore only be drawn from indirect statistical inference or from theoretical considerations. The present paper combines the results of a number of available statistical analyses (section II) with theoretical interpretation undertaken in section III. One of the contentions made in this paper in fact is that traditional regional policy instruments recently practiced in most market and mixed economies have essentially only accentuated existing market trends but not attacked the basic parameters underlying spatial inequalities in living levels.

A major evaluation of regional development policies has been in the air for at least the past decade. More recently it has been prompted by a number of facts: (1) spatial disparities in living levels have by far not decreased to the extent regional policy had hoped for; in many cases they have even increased (as have international disparities); (2) there are signs of increasing dissatisfaction of regional communities (often ethnically defined) with the degree to which they are able to define and realize their own objectives of development; (3) the recent reduction in the rate of overall economic growth and its foreseeable limitations indicate that with future resource limitations it may become increasingly difficult to mobilize sufficient funds to reduce spatial disparities of living levels with traditional policy instruments; (4) the reduction in overall economic growth is likely to reduce or even invert the "automatic" spill-over processes from congested to less developed areas and thereby increase the absolute magnitude of the regional problem in the foreseeable future; (5) the world-wide limitations of natural resources may require for regional (as well as for national and international) policies a much stronger emphasis on optimum resource utilization and conservation instead of the strong demand orientation which has predominated so far.

Essentially three types of evaluations of regional development policies have been made:

(a) Informal general evaluations of the experiences of regional polcies have been undertaken in great number with varying degrees of systematization for the past ten years, ever since Friedmann's (1966) work on Venezuela. Abundant case studies have been compiled in continental and national surveys such as those in the Regional Planning Series of the United Nations Research Institute For Social Development, edited by Kuklinski, and in Kuklinski's more recent books (1975 and 1977). There exist few systematic comparative studies of different national experiences of regional development policies, however, such as that organized by Hansen (1974).

(b) Formal macro-evaluations of regional policies have been made in the past three years to simulate the operation of regional systems and to estimate the effects of regional policies. These have either been formulated as complex (usually econometric) theory-based models (Klaassen and Venter 1974, Courbis 1975, Thoss 1976, Bölting 1976, etc.), as heuristic statistical analyses (Moore and Rhodes 1975, Berentsen 1976, etc.) or as more narrowly defined impact studies (Dawson and Ulrich 1975, etc.). Those formal approaches which use complex models in most cases face difficult operational and data problems and have therefore hardly been applied yet. Those which are more narrowly conceived usually shed light only on a small number of economic variables (e.g. aggregate regional investment, production, employment/unemployment, regional per capital income, net or gross migration, balance of payments, or rate of inflation) and remain on highly aggregated regional, state or provincial levels. Instrument variables evaluated are mainly of an economic type, such as investment incentives, building grants, depreciation allowances, employment premiums, public infrastructure investment, growth center policies, development controls, etc.

(c) Formal or informal micro-evaluations of regional policies have increasingly been undertaken in the past five years to analyze the effects of regional planning instruments (such as the above-mentioned ones) at the level of individual plants or types of plants and to evaluate their effects on local labor markets and local socio-economic conditions. They usually try to capture a broad scale of variables, including qualitative and structural ones (qualification structure and stability of new plants and new jobs, wage levels and their differentials, organizational linkages, control mechanisms and functional characteristics of new plants, changes in regional wage bargaining positions, etc.) and to disaggregate these variables to relatively small geographic, economic or demographic units.

The macro-studies (b) mentioned have the advantage of showing broad regional trends (usually in a national setting) and the respective policy implications for a few important economic variables using mainly rigorous analytical techniques. They usually, however, neglect qualitative and structural characteristics and changes in economic, social or political disparities at lower levels.

The micro-studies (c), on the other hand, are able to provide detailed insights into the effects of specific policy instruments and projects and analyze not only the quantitative but also important qualitative and structural transformations of small-scale communities. They are usually descriptive and use less sophisticated analytical techniques, and their ideographic findings usually are more difficult to generalize because they often depend on specific regional conditions.

In the present paper we have tried to synthesize the major findings of various macro-studies and a large number of micro-studies and to interrelate them, not in a formal quantitative way (which would have been impossible because of methodological and data differences of the various studies) but rather by applying some basic concepts of regional economics and regional development theory (section III) to them. We have particularly tried to fill in—on the basis of available theory—some explanatory variables which are difficult to operationalize in formal analysis on a larger scale, but which for that reason seem no less important in their effects on the well-being of regional populations. Examples of such explanatory variables are regionally differentiated external economies (essentially non-measurable), "leakages" via intra-organizational linkages (particularly of multiregional firms), changes in regional import and export propensities and the terms of trade, regional income and employment multipliers, power relations in space, etc. As it would have been impossible to undertake primary empirical research on the broad questions involved, only secondary information was used. In order to reach a fair degree of representativeness of the often ideographic results of available case studies, undertaken from different viewpoints and with different methodologies, it seemed necessary to use as large a sample of macro- and micro-studies as could be obtained.

At the end of the paper we present some hypotheses on alternative regional development policies which in the long run may prove to be more effective in reducing spatial disparities of living levels, particularly under conditions of reduced rates of overall economic growth.

THE EMPIRICAL SETTING

The following section attempts to pull together some empirical evidence of the performance of regional systems and of past regional policies in market and mixed economies. Country references were limited by the availability of relevant case studies.

A further limitation with regard to the topic of the present paper was that most authors found it difficult to distinguish clearly between autonomous and policy-induced trends of spatial development. Most case studies therefore evaluate the cumulative result of both. The policy effects have not in all cases been calculated in quantitative terms (e.g. by spatial or temporal correlation) and in some instances were estimated by rather subjective criteria. A third limitation is that most of the indicators used in these case studies refer to material indicators of living levels or what Allardt (1973) would call conditions of "having" (changes in income and employment trends, migration, and spatial linkages of the input-output type; in a few cases broader socio-economic variables were aggregated by factor analysis). Evaluations of indicators of non-material conditions (of "loving" and of "being" in Allardt's terms) are hardly available in spatially disaggregated form and by no means on a similarly broad comparative international basis.

The studies which have been used in the following section have been selected and analysed with a view towards getting information on both the quantitative aspects of spatial development trends (mainly in terms of numbers of created jobs, level of regional unemployment, etc.) and the qualitative and structural aspects of these trends (sectoral composition and level of technology of new activities, control and ownership relations, organizational characteristics of new plants, qualification of jobs, wage levels, cyclical and structural stability, etc.).

Although the quantitative and qualitative aspects are interrelated and not clearly separable, a grouping of the analysed studies according to each of these two criteria seemed useful because the respective studies usually also referred to different aggregation levels and used different indicators and methodologies.*

A. Quantitative Aspects of Interregional and Regional Development Trends

In this section we have tried to synthesize studies which contain information on the performance of indicators such as "jobs created," "reduction of regional unemployment," "income disparities," "net outmigration," etc. These sources have been grouped into studies which investigate the behaviour of regional systems in response to both regional policy instruments and "market trends" ("overall trends") and studies which try to relate inter- and intraregional trends to specific types of strategies or instruments (such as growth center policies, transport investment to improve interregional accessibility, investment incentives, etc.).

We shall try to summarize first the most important findings concerning the *overall trends of interregional and intraregional disparities.* The main conclusions seem to be:**

• In most of the countries analysed there is no clear indication of a major convergence of regional per capita income or other indicators of material living levels. This seems the case particularly in countries with sizeable regional problems (Italy, France, Brazil). For most countries it is difficult to say to which extent the trend is due to the "autonomous" forces of the market mechanism or to explicit policies of spatial development.

• From more detailed analyses available for some countries it seems that spatial development policies in general were not able to

*While the "quantitative" aspects of regional trends usually were studied on the basis of the total regional system of a country or of one region (case study) the basic units for the studies of the qualitative aspects are usually smaller (firms, specific employment strata, etc.).

**These conclusions are a further development of those presented in Stöhr and Tödtling (1976).

change spatial inequalities in material living levels significantly. In cases where this was possible at one scale (e.g. at the interregional one), it was usually accompanied by an increase in disparities at other scales (e.g. at the intra-regional or inter-personal ones). Such shifts in disparities from one geographical scale to another could be observed particularly where policies of "concentrated regional development" were applied, usually combined with sectorially unbalanced development (mainly industry) and a strong emphasis on overall efficiency (Brazil and Spain, and to a lesser extent France and Italy).

- In most countries where a reduction of spatial material disparities at least in some respects seems to have taken place (Austria, Japan, West Germany, USA, Canada, Great Britain) either spatial material disparities in other indicators increased (Great Britain, Canada), initial regional inequalities have been relatively small (Austria, West Germany), spatial development policies were fuzzy and little articulated (Austria, USA) or were considered to have had little effect upon the reduction of spatial disparities (Japan). The reduction in spatial disparities were then either attributed to market forces (West Germany) or to specific national geographical or historical conditions (Austria). There is some indication that this partial quantitative success of the establishment of jobs in peripheral areas has been slowing down recently due to the reduction of national and international economic expansion (West Germany, cf. Flore, 1976).

- There are no broader comparative analyses available on the impact of spatial development policies on non-material indicators of living conditions (such as Allardt's conditions of "loving" and of "being").

Concerning the impact of *specific policy instruments and strategies of regional policy*, studies have been selected which refer to "growth center policies," transport investment to improve interregional accessibility and to investment incentives and development controls.

The major findings of the studies on *growth center-hinterland effects* (we concentrated on these spread effects rather than on the development of the growth centers themselves) can be summarized as follows:

- Spread effects from growth centers were usually smaller than expected, or less than backwash-effects and therefore had a negative net result on the hinterland. They were narrowly limited in geographical extent, usually restricted to the commuting area, often as a function of the size of the center (Morrill, 1974).

● Increases in income of lower order centers or rural areas create strong income multipliers in higher order centers but not the other way around (Nichols 1969, Moseley 1973 a, 1973 b and 1974), i.e. they move upward rather than downward within the urban hierarchy.

● In the context of policies for broad spatial development it is difficult to justify growth-center policies for lagging areas due to their lack of spread effects from the growth center to a broader hinterland or downward in the urban hierarchy (Hansen 1975 a, Nichols 1969, Moseley 1973 a, 1973 b and 1974).

With regard to the improvement of *interregional accessibility* some of the most important results of the studies selected are:

● The improvement of interregional accessibility seems to contribute more to the relative rate of development of the "core regions" than to that of "peripheral regions." This is particularly the case in developing countries (Pedersen, 1975 b and Gauthier, 1968, for Latin-America and the Sao Paulo Region respectively).

● Initial production and settlement systems of small-scale, rather intensive production units and interaction patterns in peripheral areas become superseded by large-scale units and interaction patterns. This seems particularly pronounced in developing countries. For example, in Brazilian peripheral areas improvements in accessibility to core-regions caused a great number of settlers and farmers to be displaced by large-scale core-region based enterprises, introducing usually very extensive resource utilisation (Becker, 1976).

● The impact of interregional highway investment on absolute levels of development in peripheral areas is more difficult to identify. Particularly in industrialized countries the effects of interregional highway investment on the absolute levels of peripheral development are ambiguous and in most cases small (Frerich, 1974 and Dodgson, 1974).

● In general there is a lack of thorough empirical studies which evaluate the impact of improved accessibility between different types of regions (core regions, declining industrial regions, peripheral depressed regions, peripheral resource regions, etc.) on their rates of development.

Empirical findings on the *impact of financial incentives* are also to a certain extent ambiguous:

- Some studies (especially on Britain and Scotland) indicate the high importance of investment incentives and building grants for the creation of jobs in, and the movement of firms to, peripheral areas (e.g. Moore and Rhodes, 1975; Board of Trade, 1968);
- other studies (e.g. Wolf, 1974 for Hessen in West Germany) indicate that capital incentives are very weakly associated with investment decisions, especially with those for the expansion of existing plants.
- There is some agreement on the fact that investment incentives seem to have more impact on the establishment of capital-intensive branch plants and foreign firms than on the establishment or movement of complete firms (Fürst and Zimmermann, 1973; Wolf, 1974; Firn, 1975; McDermott, 1976; Dicken, 1976).

On the whole this may indicate that financial incentives mainly induce the establishment of branch plants and subsidiaries of core-region based enterprises but hardly the expansion of firms already existing in peripheral areas or the transfer of entire enterprises from core regions to peripheries.

Concerning the *impact of development controls in core regions*, the British experience seems to indicate that this instrument contributes to a considerable decentralization of industrial activities to peripheral areas.

B. Qualitative and Structural Aspects of Interregional and Regional Trends

In this section we shall analyze not how many but rather what kinds of plants and jobs have been created in peripheral areas either by policy support or by market forces.

The case studies have been selected with a view towards getting information on the following groups of questions:

- Which *sectors* have been promoted in or decentralised to peripheral areas? (sectoral growth characteristics, sectoral combination of production factors, wage levels, etc.) and
- which *level of technology* has been introduced to peripheral regions by the new plants? (highest, intermediate, low, "adequate" technology).
- What are the *control- and ownership relations* of the plants which were established in peripheral areas? (branch plants, subsidiaries with partial autonomy, autonomous firms, firms with total or partial extraregional or foreign ownership) and—associated with these questions—

- what are the *organizational characteristics* of these plants? (functions of production, trade, administration, decision-making, research etc.) and which kinds of jobs are associated with these characteristics? (blue or white collar, type of qualification, etc.).

Concerning the *sectoral characteristics and the level of technology* of new (mostly policy-supported) activities in peripheral areas the major conclusions from available studies are:

- The regional policies investigated tended to promote capital intensive and usually regional export-oriented "growth industries."* (Ohlsson et al., 1975, for Sweden; Penouil, 1969, for the Aquitaine Region in France; Sandmeyer, 1976, for the North-East of Brazil; Wolf, 1974, for Hessen in West Germany).
- For countries and regions with urgent unemployment problems these regional policies—because of the capital intensity of promoted firms—contribute little to the reduction of the unemployment problem (e.g. Sandmeyer, 1976, for Brazil).
- In problem regions of industrialized countries, policy-supported "growth sectors" and high productivity sectors have in many cases not been in a position to offset the market trend towards the establishment of low-wage industries in the peripheral areas (e.g. Pernitz and Kunze, 1970, and Bobek and Steinbach, 1975 for Austria; Lutz and Reyher, 1975, for Lower Bavaria in West Germany; Fleck, 1975, for West Germany).
- There exist too few empirical studies on the technology-impact of regional policies to permit general conclusions but there exist various examples of a rather undifferentiated promotion of "highest" and very capital intensive technology with a rather detrimental impact on regional employment (Sandmeyer, 1976, for the North East of Brazil).
- From the investigated case studies and examples of regional policies, no policy instruments oriented. specifically towards sectors with high intra-regional multipliers could be identified.

Concerning the *control, ownership and organizational characteristics of the newly established or expanded plants* in relation to their impact on regional development the following conclusions can be drawn:

- A large proportion of new activities in peripheral areas are branch plants or subsidiaries with extra-regional control and/or ownership

*These are usually industries with medium and long term production and/or employment growth.

(Bade, 1977, Fleck, 1975, Wolf, 1974, for West Germany; Board of Trade, 1968, Keeble, 1971 and 1972, for Great Britain; Firn, 1975, McDermott, 1976, and Lever, 1974, for Scotland).

● The findings on the performance and developmental effects of these branch plants or subsidiaries with extra-regional control and/or ownership are somewhat ambiguous:

Generally there seem to be differences in impact between (usually smaller) branch-plants, narrowly specialized in segregated routine functions of production in low wage sectors, on the one hand, and (usually larger) more diversified branch plants and subsidiaries with partial control functions on the other hand.

With respect to the narrowly-specialized branch plants the conclusions of a number of case studies are fairly unanimous:

● Branch plants seem more likely to be located in peripheral areas (in comparison with relocated firms) because they find it easier to bridge larger distances (Fürst and Zimmermann, 1973, Spanger and Treuner, 1975, and Fleck, 1975, for West Germany).

● Because of their large share of routine production processes and the lack of their own administrative and research activities, branch plants very often create relatively low-skill jobs and they are not able to stop outmigration of the younger and more qualified population (Kohler and Reyher, 1975, Wolf, 1974 for West Germany).

● Smaller branch plants and plants in certain sectors (leather, textiles and clothing, and electrical equipment) show more instability with respect to macroeconomic fluctuations because their headquarters tend to reduce employment at first in the peripheral branch plants (Clark, 1976, for Sweden; Fürst and Zimmermann, 1973, Gerlach and Liepmann, 1972, for West Germany).*

● Branch plants tend to have linkages over larger distances and therefore fewer regional purchases and multiplier effects (Spehl et al., 1975, for West Germany; Lever, 1972 and 1974, for West Central Scotland).**

● One of the most important findings of the studies seems to be that regional policy instruments (especially investment incentives) tend to support the establishment of branch plants and of subsidiaries with foreign ownership in peripheral areas (Wolf, 1974; Fürst and Zimmermann, 1973; Dicken, 1976; McDermott, 1976; Thoman, 1973).

*Concerning the stability prospects of branch plants Bade (1976) states that branch plants which are more integrated into the production process of the enterprise show more stability.

**Lever (1976) states in this connection, however, that while branch plants receive lower inputs from the local economy, they have a greater volume of regional exports compared to indigenous firms (p. 133).

• With respect to more diversified branch plants and subsidiaries with partial control functions, no clear findings emerge from available studies (Firn, 1975; McDermott, 1976; Pernitz and Kunze, 1970; O'Farrell, 1976; Thoman, 1973).

TOWARDS A THEORETICAL INTERPRETATION

Regional policies have essentially aimed at diffusing growth from highly developed core regions to less developed peripheral areas. In this section we shall try to interpret these policies in theoretical terms and show their implications for the operation of interregional systems.

We shall simplify regional systems by essentially discussing relations between highly developed "core regions" and less developed "peripheral areas" although there exist of course different intensities and types of these regions in a multi-regional setting.

A. The Theoretical Background

Interregional disparities and interactions are basically conditioned by regional differences in access to production factors and to markets. We shall concentrate first on differences in availability of production factors.

Core regions are characterized by a scarcity of natural resources and of labor, while peripheral areas usually have a scarcity of capital and technology. According to neoclassical economic theory, factor returns should be high in areas of scarcity and low in areas of abundance. Core regions should therefore have high returns for natural resources and labor while peripheral areas should have high returns for capital and technology. Under neoclassical assumptions (complete mobility and homogeneity of production factors, decreasing marginal returns, and so forth) factors are expected to move from areas of low return to those of high return. Natural resources and labor should therefore flow from peripheral areas to core regions, while capital and technology would be expected to flow in the opposite direction from core regions to peripheries. These flows would increase factor supply in areas of scarcity and reduce it in areas of abundance, whereby factor prices would be expected to equalize over space. As a consequence, income should also equalize over space (Richardson, 1969).

In reality, however, this is not the case. First, because not all production factors tend towards spatial equilibrium of supply and demand. Such a tendency is counteracted by different degrees of mobility and heterogeneity of factors and by increasing factor returns due to the unequal spatial distribution of external and scale economies. Second, there occur "leakages" of different types between regions (also outside the factor markets) which can lead to income disparities. Such leakages occur through interregional multiplier effects, through changes in import and/or export propensities and in the terms of trade, through organizational linkages, etc.

Regarding production factors, labor and capital in practice often do not tend towards equilibrium. Although labor in aggregate terms moves from (usually low wage) peripheral areas to (high wage) core regions, this movement should not be considered in aggregate terms but should be disaggregated, since migration is highly selective. Migrants from peripheral to core regions usually come from the more mobile and more productive population strata (i.e. the potential high-wage earners) of peripheral areas. This therefore tends to reduce the average of wage levels in peripheral areas still further rather than increasing average wage levels due to the reduction of aggregate labor supply, as neoclassical theory would have it. At the same time this selective outmigration reduces the production potential of peripheral areas still further.

Capital flows also do not tend towards a regional equilibrium of supply and demand. Empirical studies (Lasuén 1961, ECLA 1969, Griffin 1969) have shown that on balance capital flows from peripheral (high capital cost) areas to core regions (with relatively low capital cost). The major reason for this disequilibrating trend is the higher productivity of capital in core regions due to a comparative advantage in scale and external economies.

Regional policy instruments essentially have attempted to change these disequilibrating flows, but they have hardly made explicit attempts to control the leakages mentioned.

Since migration is outside of direct policy control in most market and mixed economies, policy instruments have concentrated on inverting flows of capital (along with technology, often incorporated in it) and on creating greater external economies in peripheral areas through public infrastructure investment (neatly summarized e.g. in Canada, Ministre, 1976).

In the following section the major instruments of regional policy in market and mixed economies will be briefly reviewed and related to some of the major findings of empirical evaluations of regional policy reviewed above. A synopsis of the policy instruments and related empirical findings is then presented on pp. 106–108.

B. Major Instruments of Regional Policy and Their Implications

(1) Capital and Technology Transfers to Peripheral Areas. These instruments are used in practically all countries analyzed. Essentially they are supposed to create, as far as factor availability and infrastructure are concerned, conditions in peripheral areas more like those of core regions. The strong emphasis of most regional development policies on capital incentives and on the introduction of high technology (often incorporated in capital) have stimulated the emergence of capital intensive industries in peripheral areas (Sandmeyer, 1976 for the northeast of Brazil; Penouil, 1969 for the Aquitaine region in France; Ohlsson, 1975, for Sweden; Holland, 1976 for Italy; Kerlikowsky, 1977 for Alabama in the USA) and have thereby *increased regional productivity and regional output*.

At the same time they have produced relatively *small employment effects*, and contributed comparatively little to solving the unemployment problems of peripheral areas (Sandmeyer, 1976; Kerlikowsky, 1977) in spite of the application of employment premiums in some countries.

(2) Promotion of "Modern" Industries in Peripheral Areas. Apart from the incentives offered for activities with high productivity, economic promotion was (often implicitly) oriented towards activities with high demand elasticity and with an "export base," i.e. catering to international and national rather than to regional demand (Lower Austria, 1971; Wolf, 1974, p. 168 for West Germany). This meant that economic activities in peripheral areas *increasingly* became *dependent* not only *on external production factors* (external capital and technology) but *also on external demand*.

Products with high demand elasticity imply "young" industries with a relatively high rate of innovation. Since the highly innovative phases in the product cycle usually last only for a limited time period there exists the danger of *relatively high structural instability*, especially if these new activities gain a predominant role in otherwise little-industrialized peripheral areas. In many cases this was aggravated by the fact that in such "young" industries (e.g. electronics, plastics) mainly *routine and less skilled sub-functions* were delegated to peripheral areas (see below). The heavy reliance on activities catering to national and international markets was in line with export base theory, which assumes that regional and national economic growth is mainly a function of the value of their exports. However, the emphasis of new plants on export base activities in many peripheral areas *increased the dependence on national and international cyclical fluctuations* (McDermott 1976, Novotny, 1977).

The emphasis of regional policy instruments on activities with high productivity and high demand elasticity, and on sectors catering to international or national demand (export base orientation), addressed itself to characteristics normally typical of core region activities. Very often, therefore, this encouraged the *transfer of expanding core-region activities* (or parts thereof—the socalled "extended work benches") which, due to increasing overall demand, met with bottlenecks in core regions (particularly shortages of labor and land). With the recent slow-down of national and international economic growth these bottlenecks were reduced (cf. Flore, 1976) and the new activities in peripheral areas represent an increased danger of cyclical and structural instability.

Due to the difficulties of overcoming distance from core regions, the major reaction to these instruments came from enterprises most able to overcome distance and locational deficiencies on account of their own organisational capacity and capital reserves: these were *to a great extent large-scale multiregional or multinational enterprises*, catering to large-scale (usually world) markets and able to shift resources and functions rather freely between areas and countries.

If the above-mentioned "extended work benches" in economically marginal peripheral areas belonged to multiregional or multinational firms their closure rates often were particularly high (cf. Bade, 1976; Fürst and Zimmermann, 1973; Clark, 1976) and thereby tended to increase still further the already existing cyclical and structural instability in peripheral areas.

Since multiregional or multinational firms were able to shift activities freely within their own highly specialized organizational structures, they usually shifted the low-skill, low-pay routine activities to peripheral areas, retaining more highly skilled non-routine jobs, including research and development functions, administrative functions etc. in core regions. This meant that the *newly created jobs were usually in the low-skill and low-wage categories*. (Westaway, 1974, for Great Britain; Wolf, 1974, Kohler and Reyher, 1975 for West Germany; Thoman, 1973, for Belgium). This may in fact have contributed towards a reinforcement of long-standing structural weaknesses of peripheral areas rather than to their relief.

Multinational or multiregional firms are better able to bridge the distance to peripheral areas. If these areas are favored by public incentives or subsidies, the firms will legitimately select the most accessible locations within them and thereby often *contribute to an increase of intraregional disparities*. The entrepreneurial objective of being competitive interregionally or internationally may in fact lead to increased intraregional disparities (Ray, 1976; Lasuén and Pastor, 1976).

When activities (or parts thereof) were relocated from core regions to peripheral areas there was a tendency, particularly on the part of multiplant firms, to retain previous input-output and service relations of their organisations wherever possible so that usually few *functional relations among these activities developed within peripheral areas.* This led to a *relatively high regional import propensity for inputs* and thereby *increased leakages from peripheral areas* (Lever, 1972 and 1974 and McDermott, 1976, for Scotland; Spehl et al., 1975, and Wolf, 1974, for West Germany). In fact it has been maintained that these leakages may often be greater than the transfers of capital or public investment undertaken (Lasuén and Pastor, 1976).

Due to the increasing reallocation of labor and capital to the most efficient activities and to effective (and increasingly external) demand, *scarce production factors* (skilled labor, capital) frequently were *withdrawn from privately-supplied basic needs sectors.* Regional basic needs became less relevant for investment decisions and since (particularly in poorer regions) they are usually backed by small purchasing power, became neglected both in quantitative terms and in their specific qualitative articulation. Producers increasingly had to concentrate on only a few locations or close down completely. With typically scarce population and low demand-density in great parts of peripheral areas the access to these basic needs and services deteriorated considerably, particularly in the case of the less mobile and/or economically less powerful population strata (the elderly, the poor, etc.), whose proportion of the total population was increasing due to the selective outmigration process. This meant that *intraregional disparities in access to basic needs facilities also increased* considerably. Access to basic needs services also deteriorated because the improvement of interregional accessibility (see below) increased competition from outside centers and *reduced the relative growth potential of regional service centres.* Marketing and service channels became increasingly oriented towards supraregional systems and often made investment in the less developed parts of peripheral areas uneconomic. This further increased the pressure for outmigration.

Furthermore, in most cases there were no explicit incentives for the utilisation of *regional natural resources,* so these often were *underutilized* (idle agricultural land, idle regional building materials, etc.).

The promotion of "modern" industries therefore usually led not only to *increasing reliance on external production factors and demand* but also to an *underemployment of regional resources and a neglect of regional basic needs.* It thereby contributed to an *increase in external dependence* and to a *reduction in regional self-reliance.*

(3) **Transfer of Public Investment to Peripheral Areas.** In most countries this is a major policy instrument intended to reduce spatial disparities. Its major thrust usually is to provide economic infrastructure for new economic activities. This is done mainly by investment in local infrastructure and in the interregional transport and communications network.

Local infrastructure investment will, apart from a demand multiplier, *create external economies* and thereby help to reduce the cost of production in peripheral areas. In cases where this is done by central agencies it will (as with multi-plant enterprises) favor the introduction of core-region based construction technology, building materials and (via core-region based construction firms) other extraregional inputs. This will tend to reduce potential regional employment effects and the mobilisation of other regional resources (building materials etc.), create *leakages*, and thereby *often considerably reduce the expected regional impact of such transfers* of public investment (Lasuén and Pastor, 1976). If administered by centrally steered agencies, it will also fail to help develop peripheral areas' abilities to mobilize and handle their own resources.

Finally, public investment in interregional transport and communications networks will increase accessibility between regions, a phenomenon that merits further discussion.

(4) **Extension of Transport and Communications Networks from Core-Regions to Peripheries.** Transport and communications investment is usually made *with priority between major urban centers and between core-regions and peripheries* in order to increase accessibility in these relations. Thus it follows existing traffic patterns and the thrust of major effective demand. Comparatively little investment is made in transport infrastructure between peripheral areas and for interactions within peripheral areas (Törnquist, 1973). Such investment implicitly follows the export-base conception that regional growth must be induced by extraregional demand and that increased specialization and accessibility within and between peripheral areas can contribute little to the development of peripheral areas because of their low density and low growth rate of demand.

The same applies to (mass) communications networks which essentially are extended from core-regions to peripheral areas. Communication flows emanate radially from core regions to peripheral areas; organizational and power centers that determine the kinds of information to be transmitted are also essentially core-region based.*

(5) Promotion of Functional Integration Between Core-Regions and Peripheries. The above policies are aimed at increasing inter-regional functional integration (input-output relations, factor flows, etc.) in order to reduce disparities between core-regions and peripheries. They are essentially based on the neoclassical assumption that with increased functional integration production factors and commodities will move to the locations of their highest return, and that factor and commodity prices will equalize over space and lead to a convergence of regional per capita income. It was shown above that this is not the case in reality.

The problem in question can also be posed in terms of comparative market access as a determinant of regional growth. The improvement of mutual accessibility between core regions and peripheries at first sight could be expected to give peripheral areas a comparative advantage through improved access to large core-region markets, whereas core regions would gain improved access only to the relatively small markets of peripheral areas and would consequently be expected to benefit less from integration. In reality however, the *already highly developed core regions gain much greater comparative advantage* from such functional integration because of their greatly superior capacity to utilize agglomeration and scale economies (Pedersen and Stöhr, 1971). Core regions are thereby able to increase their initial advantage cumulatively.

Major comparative advantages accrue to peripheral areas mainly if they possess considerable scarce and relatively immobile resources in sectors of rapidly increasing national and international demand (selected mineral resources, tourism, etc.) or if they offer comparatively greater external and scale economies than competing core-regions. The first is the case in a few highly developed countries only; the second is an objective of growth center strategies. An alternative strategy of increasing aggregate peripheral demand by improved intraregional accessibility within or between peripheral areas has rarely been attempted.

(6) Growth Center Policies. These essentially involve a combination of the characteristics of "modern" industries and the creation of agglomeration economies in an attempt to reduce the backwash

---

*This applies both to the national and to the international level. On the latter see Rhaghavan, 1976.

effects between peripheral and more developed regions and at the same time create spread effects to the growth centers' hinterlands. Empirical analyses indicate that this has been achieved only rarely. In the majority of cases it seems that where growth centers were able to increase their own dynamics it was due to increased backwash effects (withdrawal of labor and natural resources, deterioration of the hinterland's terms of trade). In consequence, therefore, even when growth center policies have increased the average growth rate of peripheral regions (and thereby reduced interregional disparities) *intra*regional disparities of living levels usually have increased. This means that *growth centers have essentially led to a shift of disparities from the interregional to the intraregional level*, but rarely seem to have led to an overall reduction of spatial disparities in living levels. In part this may be due to the lack of explicit incentives for the utilization of regional resources, particularly natural resources and labor, which are predominantly located in hinterlands. The second reason may be the lack of explicit sectoral specification.

(7) **Lack of an Explicit Sectoral Specification of Regional Development Policy.** Regional policy in most market and mixed economies has essentially been sectorially unspecified (Flore, 1976). With the application of regional incentives according to criteria of efficiency and growth it might be expected that those sectors which conform most to these criteria would be attracted to peripheral areas. The attraction of an efficient and fast growing activity, however, did not necessarily mean that the locality or region would actually benefit from faster growth. Activities with few local or regional linkages may in fact (e.g. Penouil, 1969) contribute much more to the growth of other localities or regions with which they maintain intensive functional interaction than to the growth of their own region. To become regionally effective, both regional policy and growth center policy need to be addressed more specifically to sectors which, beyond the criteria mentioned, also produce *intraregional income and employment multipliers*; functional relations between the "modern" export-base activities and intraregional sectors as well as linkages to regional resources and to regional demand seem important for this purpose. To comply with such rather complex characteristics a *more explicitly sectorally-oriented regional policy may be necessary.* Klaassen, Paelinck and Wagenaar (1976), for instance, propose the selection of activities for regional development according to three groups of criteria: regional income and employment multipliers, intra- and extraregional market potential, and locational profile. Similar suggestions are made by Strassert, 1976.

(8) **Extension of Core-Region Based Education and Training Facilities to Peripheries.** Educational policy in most countries tries to equalize educational and training opportunities in all parts of the national territory. In most countries, particularly those with a centralized educational policy, this means the introduction of *uniform (core-region based) educational standards and curricula*, even for peripheral areas. With standards and curricula oriented towards core-region needs, people from peripheral areas (and particularly the most highly trained among them) are often *forced to migrate to core-regions*, which *increases still further the spatially disequilibrating effects* already mentioned. On the other hand, the orientation of curricula and educational objectives to regional needs (without discriminating in levels of education) might be able to better serve both human needs and regional development by reducing the psychic and social costs of economically-induced migration.

(9) **Extension of Core-Region Based Public and Private Organizations to Peripheral Areas.** A major instrument for the development of peripheral areas in many countries has been the strengthening of national (core-region steered) administrative and planning systems for peripheral areas. This usually manifested itself in the establishment of new or the expansion of existing central government offices (or their dependencies) in peripheral areas; these offices were charged with designing and implementing plans for peripheral area development. These new or expanded core-region based organizations often helped to speed up material progress by facilitating the transfer of capital, technology and organizational skills to peripheral regions; however, they very often *supplanted existing autochthonous regional organizations and thus debilitated regional organizing capacity.* Only seldom have these centrally-guided institutions explicitly promoted the organizing capacity of autochthonous regional institutions, or voluntarily transferred powers to them. The forceful drive for the devolution of power on the part of peripheral communities in many countries (Great Britain, Spain, France, etc.) must be considered as a reaction to this fact. Similar arguments also apply to the extension into peripheral areas of core-region based private sector organizations such as branches of multiregional or multinational firms.

Apart from supplanting and debilitating the organizational capacity of local and regional institutions in peripheral areas, externally-based public or private organizations also *tend to apply uniformly to peripheral areas their central decision making criteria*, their high technology and their organizational principles. The impact on the underutilization of regional natural and human resources has already been discussed. Similar pressure is exerted on specifically regional cultural patterns, value systems, customs, and traditions, which are important ingredients of regional identity. They serve not only as "comforts" (Scitovsky, 1976) for non-material human satisfaction but also constitute an important prerequisite for sustained material progress.

Various unitary states (France, Great Britain, Sweden) have attempted to mitigate the high geographic concentration of administrative functions by *relocating public offices* from the capital to less developed areas. While this may have created a certain spatial redistribution of income in favor of peripheral areas, the effects on the redistribution of decision making were usually small because central decisionmaking structures were retained. Similarly *employment effects* were small because many posts were filled by employees who moved from core-regions together with the decentralized agencies (Sundquist, 1975).

In federal countries such as Austria, West Germany and the USA these problems seem to have been considerably smaller. Even weak regional policies in these countries seem to be accompanied by a convergence of regional development trends.

(10) Reinforcement of Core-Region Based Standards, Rules and Value Systems Over the Periphery. Along with the transfer of public investments, the extension of transport and communications networks, of education and training facilities, and of organizational structures from core-regions to peripheries, the extension to peripheral areas of core-region based standards, rules and value systems became reinforced. It is what Friedmann (1973, p. 70) has called "the extension over a given territory of a common basis for social life . . . a shared frame of socio-cultural expectations, including language, cultural values, political-legal-bureaucratic institutions, and a market economy."

As long as uniform national *standards and rules are set predominantly according to core-region value systems, peripheral areas will usually be at a comparative disadvantage in reaching them.*

The possibility of *maintaining a plurality of value systems* and life styles would give regions with different preconditions better chances to develop their respective potentials and reach a comparable degree of satisfaction within their respective value systems.

The following is a synopsis of the policy instruments that have been applied to peripheral areas and of the major empirical conditions which seem to be associated with them.

Synopsis

Major Policy Instruments for the Development of Peripheral Areas:

(1) capital incentives and technology transfer

(2) promotion of "modern" industries characterized by

—high productivity
—high demand elasticity of products
—export base orientation

Related Empirical Conditions in Peripheral Areas:

increased regional productivity and output, but small employment effect

increased reliance on external production factors and on external demand

increased underemployment of regional (natural and human) resources

predominance of branch plants of core-region based multiregional or multinational enterprises (possessing comparative advantage in bridging distance to peripheral areas); new "modern" industries, and particularly branch plants, in peripheral areas contribute to the following phenomena:

—new jobs mainly in low skill and low wage categories

—relatively high structural and cyclical instability

—few functional relations of new plants within peripheral areas contribute to small intraregional multiplier effects

—new activities create a relatively high regional import propensity, whereby part of their impact is lost through leakages to other regions

—comparatively high closure rate of new plants and jobs

—scarce production factors (skilled labor, capital) are withdrawn from regional basic needs sectors and intraregional disparities in access to basic needs facilities increase

Synopsis (continued)

(3) transfer of public investment — external economies reduce production costs in peripheral areas but leakages to other regions occur particularly in the case of centrally-steered public investments

reduction of peripheral areas' ability to mobilize and handle their own resources

(4) Extension of transport and communication networks from core-regions to peripheries — increase in accessibility mainly amongst core-regions and between core-regions and peripheral areas; little accessibility increase between and within peripheral areas

(5) promotion of core-periphery integration — comparative advantage of spatial integration accrues mainly to core regions (unless peripheries possess considerable scarce and immobile resources or offer other major external economies)

(6) growth center policies — often shift spatial disparities from one level (inter-regional) to another (usually intra-regional) but little reduction of overall spatial disparities in living levels

(7) lack of explicit sectoral specification of regional development policy — emphasis on efficiency and growth criteria but neglect of (sectorally differentiated) intra-regional income and employment multiplier effects

(8) extension of core-region based education and training facilities — uniform (core region based) curricula tend to neglect differentiated regional educational needs and increase pressure for selective out-migration from peripheral areas, thereby increasing disequilibrium effects

(continued overleaf)

Synopsis (continued)

Major Policy Instruments for the
Development of Peripheral Areas:

(9) extension of core-region based
public and private organizations
to peripheral areas

(10) reinforcement of core-region
based standards, rules and value
systems over peripheral areas

Related Empirical Conditions in Peripheral Areas:

core-region based institutions supplant autochthonous regional ones
and debilitate their organizing capacity

application of central decision-making criteria handicaps consideration
of differentiated regional needs and full utilization of peripheral resources

public offices relocated to peripheral areas have, particularly in unitary
states, relatively small positive employment and decision-making effects
for peripheral areas

due to their different starting conditions peripheral areas are at a
comparative disadvantage in reaching uniform core-region based
standards

possibility of peripheral areas to maintain a plurality of value systems
and life styles would improve their chances to develop their own
regional potentials to maximize satisfaction in terms of their respective
value systems.

C. Conclusions

Regional development trends and the effects of regional development policies as described above have been partly successful in their *quantitative aspects* (numbers of jobs created, amount of investment, level of regional unemployment, regional per capita income, gross or net outmigration etc.). Spatial disparities in living levels were reduced or at least stabilized in some countries, while in a number of others they have continued to increase or were merely shifted from one spatial level to another.

Qualitative and structural aspects of spatial disparities (skill structure and stability of new plants and jobs, wage levels and wage differentials, organizational linkages, control mechanisms and functional characteristics of new plants, degree of extraregional ownership, etc.), however, have essentially remained unsatisfactory and in some cases —partly as side-effects of traditional regional policy instruments— have even deteriorated.

In order to reduce spatial disparities of living levels, regional development policies have given major emphasis to the transfer of private and public resources from core regions to peripheries through capital incentives and public infrastructure investment. At the same time the promotion of new activities was based on efficiency criteria and on demand backed by effective purchasing power. New activities in peripheral areas therefore were to a great extent "modern" industries offering high productivity, high demand elasticity and export base demand. These policies increased production in peripheral areas (mainly for core-region or extraregional demand) but at the same time led to a reallocation of scarce production factors in peripheral areas from basic needs sectors (backed by insufficient purchasing power) to regional export products. This frequently led to a deterioration in the access to basic service facilities, particularly for the less mobile and less affluent population strata. At the same time this reallocation of factors led to an underutilization of factors that are relatively abundant in peripheral areas, especially natural resources.

Traditional regional development policies also led to the extension of core-region based private and public institutions (multiregional firms, large-scale public agencies), of transport and communications networks, and of core-region standards and value systems to peripheral areas. Consequently, peripheral areas, in addition to their increasing dependence on external production factors and external demand, also became increasingly dependent on external private and public decision-making. Increased external dependence and reduced self-reliance on regional resources therefore occured in all these respects. As both these factors have increasingly become objectives of development in their own right and at the same time are considered important prerequisites for sustained economic development, it is not surprising that both the degree of subjective and of objective satisfaction with the results of established regional development policies has been rather poor.

The increase in external dependence and the reduction in self-reliance of peripheral areas have led to a variety of "leakages" of the positive effects experienced in some quantitative indicators of economic development. Such leakages occur via organizational linkages of multiregional firms or public agencies and manifest themselves in the transfer of employment and income effects to other regions, through increases in the regional import propensity and a deterioration of the regional terms of trade, through the closure of employment or service facilities by extraregional decisions, etc. Similar disadvantages occur via the introduction of core-region based rules, standards and value systems which put peripheral areas at a disadvantage in reaching uniform national standards.

The moderate success of regional development policies so far seems to have been facilitated to a considerable extent by the relatively high rates of economic growth and expansion of demand in the past decades which, due to factor bottlenecks in the highly developed and often congested core regions, have—via the market mechanism—created "spill-overs" of development to peripheral areas. It appears that regional policy has in fact only accentuated and in some cases attempted to redirect the locational pattern of these spill-overs.

A positive net effect for peripheral areas may therefore be explained by a preponderance of these accentuated spill-over effects over the negative "leakage" effects mentioned above. If one assumes for the years to come a reduced rate of overall economic growth and of demand expansion, these spill-over effects are likely to decrease and thereby reduce still further the effectiveness of traditional regional policy instruments. On the other hand, the lack of these spill-over effects will also increase the magnitude of regional problems for the solution of which, due to the reduced rate of overall economic growth, less funds will be available. A grave negative spiral may therefore emerge.

Formal evaluations of regional policy (and particularly the more narrowly conceived impact studies) have mainly attempted to measure the relations between the magnitudes of specific policy instruments (magnitude of capital incentives, subsidies, public infrastructure investment, etc.) and the reduction of spatial disparities. From this approach it might follow that in order to reduce spatial disparities further, more resources should be devoted to some of the traditional policy instruments. Thus, one policy alternative, if the actual reduction in spatial disparities in living levels falls short of established goals, is to increase the magnitude of inputs going into existing policy instruments by making more funds available for direct incentives or for public transfers to less-developed areas. This may be economically and politically very difficult (if not impossible), particularly in the case of reduced rates of overall economic growth. Even if the latter were not the case, however, interregional leakages may increase at least at the same rate—and in part as a function of— increases in the magnitude of traditional policy inputs.

This would mean that traditional policy instruments have a built-in self-defeating mechanism. Our interpretations lend some support to this view, which also is in accordance with some of the major critiques which have been leveled against development and aid policies at the international level (Santa Cruz, 1976).

It may well be that the unsatisfactory results of regional development policies in some countries are not so much due to the insufficient resources allocated to regional development efforts as to an inadequate conceptual structure for regional development policies.

Alternative policies might have to be oriented more specifically towards changing the basic parameters underlying the "leakages" of developmental effects out of peripheral areas. Measures which already (usually intuitively and implicitly) are being taken in this direction in various countries were compiled in an earlier paper (Stöhr and Tödtling 1976), where they were subsumed under the heading of "measures of selective spatial closure." In practice, these measures have been used in isolated form and have therefore hardly been able to change the operation of spatial systems in a coherent way.

It would go beyond the scope of this paper to develop a coherent framework for an alternative regional development strategy. Such a strategy, however, would certainly need to give much more attention to counteracting the negative phenomena which have accompanied traditional regional development policies and a number of which are dealt with in this paper. In essence an alternative strategy would probably have to move in the direction of what in international development policy is vaguely called more "self-reliant" development (Erb and Kallab 1975).

At the regional or interregional level within countries an alternative policy would have to lay greater emphasis on:

- projects which mobilize and utilize regional (natural, human, etc.) resources and serve regional basic needs rather than projects based on satisfying external demand;

- utilizing and possibly transforming existing (or structuring new) regional institutions to promote peripheral development in line with self-defined objectives, instead of utilizing primarily extra-regional institutions to promote development by externally-defined standards;
- qualitative and structural aspects of regional development (diversity of employment opportunities, skill structure, wage level and stability of new jobs, regional income and employment multipliers, organizational and decision-making structures of new plants, etc.) rather than the present emphasis on mainly quantitative aspects (regional product, per capita income, number of jobs created etc.). Many of these quantitative advances are often considerably reduced and even nullified by disadvantages in qualitative and structural aspects and in less tangible areas such as changes in regional terms of trade, extraregional multipliers, increased dependence on extraregional decisions, etc.;
- accessibility increases within and between peripheral areas rather than on the improvement of accessibility mainly amongst core-regions and between core-regions and peripheries;
- including in the evaluation of regional policy instruments the repercussions at all important levels (not only the regional and national ones), in order to ascertain whether specific strategies and instruments actually reduce total spatial disparities in living levels or mainly shift them from one level to another;
- the accelerated devolution of decision-making powers from large-scale (private and public) functional units to territorial units at different scales; provisions facilitating the regional differentiation of value systems, cultural patterns, standards and organizational forms; and on the strengthening of organizational capacities for self-organization at the local and regional levels;
- equity in the satisfaction of (usually territorially provided) concrete basic needs, including employment and basic private and public services, rather than the present predominant emphasis on efficiency, growth and more abstract overall objectives such as increase in regional product, per capita income, number of jobs created, or the quantity of infrastructure and service facilities provided by large-scale (public and private) organizations, often with little consideration for the concrete needs of, and the active participation by, small-scale groups using and organizing them;
- selection of technologies which serve the above regional objectives instead of the present search for (or transfer of) the highest available technology chosen by growth and efficiency maximizing criteria. This might involve a certain degree of despecialization of

activities (Pedersen 1975a) and a reduction in large-scale interactions with a view to more energy-saving interaction patterns and radii.

Research in this direction needs to be continued and intensified.

BIBLIOGRAPHY*

Allardt, E. 1973. *About Dimensions of Welfare.* Research Report No. 1. Helsinki.

Allen, K. and MacLennan, M.C. 1970. *Regional Problems and Policies in Italy and France.* London.

Alonso, W. and Medrich, E. 1972. Spontaneous Growth Centres in Twentieth-century American Urbanization. In: Hansen, N.M. (Ed.) *Growth Centers in Regional Economic Development.* New York/London: The Free Press.

Appalraju, J. and Safier M., 1976. Growth Centre Strategies in Less Developed Countries. In Gilbert A., 1976.

Atkins, D.H.W. 1973. Employment Change in Branch and Parent Manufacturing Plants in the U.K.: 1966—71. *Trade and Industry* 12, 437—439.

Bade, F.J. 1977. Die Mobilität industrieller Betriebe. Discussion Papers/77—14. Berlin: Internationales Institut für Management und Verwaltung.

Becker, B.K. 1976. A Hypothesis Concerning the Origin of the Urban Phenomenon on a Resource Frontier in Brazil. Paper presented at the 3rd International Geographical Congress, Commission on Regional Aspects of Development, International Geographical Union, Dushanbe.

Berentsen, B. 1976. Regional Policy and Regional Inequalities in Austria: The Impact of Policy upon the Achievement of Planning Goals. Unpublished doctoral dissertation. The Ohio State University.

Board of Trade. 1968. The Movement of Manufacturing Industry in the United Kingdom, 1945—1965. HMSO, London.

Bobek, H. and Steinbach, J. 1975. *Die Regionalstruktur der Industrie Österreichs.* Wien: Verlag der Akademie der Wissenschaften.

Bölting, H.M. 1976. *Wirkungsanalyse der regionalen Wirtschaftspolitik.* Münster: Institut für Siedlungs- und Wohnungswesen.

Böventer, E.V. 1969. Regional Economic Problems in West Germany. In Robinson, 1969.

Brown, A.J. 1972. *The Framework of Regional Economics in the United Kingdom.* Cambridge: CUP.

Cameron, G.C. 1974. Regional Economic Policy in the United Kingdom. In Sant, 1974.

Cameron, G.C. and Clark, B.D. 1966. *Industrial Movement and the Regional Problem.* Edinburgh: Oliver and Boyd.

Canada, Ministre de l'Expansion économique régionale. 1976. Le contexte du Développement Régional. Document de travail présenté au Comité permanent de l'Expansion économique régionale.

Cao-Pinna, V. 1974. Regional Policy in Italy. In Hansen. 1974.

*See Editor's note, p. 85.

Clark, U.E.G. 1976. The Cyclical Sensitivity of Employment in Branch and Parent Plants. *Regional Studies*, Vol. 10, No. 3, pp. 293–298.

Courbis, R. 1975. Urban Analysis in the Regional National Model REGINA of the French Economy. *Environment and Planning A*, Vol. 7, No. 7, pp. 863–878.

Cumberland, J.H. 1973. *Regional Development Experiences and Prospects in the United States of America*, Paris/The Hague:Mouton.

Davin, L.E. 1969. The Structural Crisis of a Regional Economy. A Case Study: The Walloon Area. In Robinson. 1969.

Dawson, I. and Ulrich, M. 1975. MUPIM, Macro Urban Programming Impact Model. In *Proceedings of a Conference on National Settlement Systems and Strategies*, ed. by Swain H. and R. MacKinnon. Laxenburg: International Institute for Applied Systems Analysis. CP–19/4.

Dicken, P. 1976. The Multiplant Business Enterprise and Geographical Space: Some Issues in the Study of External Control and Regional Development. *Regional Studies*, Vol. 10, No. 4, pp. 401–412.

Dodgson, J.S. 1974. Motorway Investment and Sub-regional Growth: Case Study for the M62. *Regional Studies*, Vol. 8, pp. 75–90.

Erb G.F. and Kallab V. (Eds.). 1975. *Beyond Dependency: The Developing World Speaks Out*. New York, Washington/London: Praeger.

Economic Commission for Latin America. 1961. Economic Survey of Latin America. 1968. Part I. New York: United Nations.

Firn, J.R. 1975. External Control and Regional Development: The Case of Scotland. *Environment and Planning A*, vol. 7, pp. 493–414.

Fleck, W. 1975. Analyse und Prognose von Neuerrichtungen (Verlagerungen, Neu- und Zweigbetriebsgründungen in der Industrie). Berlin: International Institute of Management.

Flore, C. 1976. Regionale Wirtschaftspolitik unter veränderten Rahmenbedingungen. *Informationen zur Raumentwicklung*. 12/1976. pp. 775–792. Bonn-Bad Godesberg: Bundesforschungsanstalt für Landeskunde und Raumordnung.

Frerich, J. 1974. Die regionalen Wachstums- und Struktureffekte von Autobahnen in Industrieländern. *Verkehrswissenschaftliche Forschungen*, ed. F.Voigt, Band 28, Berlin: Duncker & Humblot.

Friedmann, J. 1966 a. *Regional Development Policy: A Case Study of Venezuela* Cambridge, Massachusetts and London: The M.I.T. Press.

Friedmann J. 1966 b. Poor Regions and Poor Nations. Perspectives of the Problem of Appalachia. *South-Economic Journal*, Vol. 32.

Friedmann, J. 1973. *Urbanization, Planning and National Development*. Beverly Hills/London: Sage Publications.

Fürst, D. and Zimmermann, K. 1973. Standortwahl industrieller Unternehmungen. Ergebnisse einer Unternehmensbefragung. Schriftenreihe *Gesellschaft für Regionale Strukturentwicklung*. Bonn.

Gauthier, J.L. 1968. Transportation and the Growth of the Sao Paulo Economy. In: *Transport and Development*, ed. by B.S. Hoyle. London and Basingstoke: MacMillan.

Gerlach, K. and Liepmann, P. 1972. Konjunkturelle Aspekte der Industrialisierung peripherer Regionen—dargestellt am Beispiel des Ostbayrischen Regierungsbezirks Oberpfalz. *Jahrbuch für Nationalökonomie und Statistik*, 187, S.1–21, Stuttgart.

Gilbert, A. 1975. A Note on the Incidence of Development in the Vicinity of a Growth Centre. *Regional Studies*, Vol. 9, 325–333.

Gilbert, A. (Ed.). 1976. *Development Planning and Spatial Structure*. London: John Wiley and Sons.

Gilbert, A.G. and Goodman, D.E. 1976. Regional Income Disparities and Economic Development: A Critique. In Gilbert, 1976.

Griffin, K. 1969. *Underdevelopment in Spanish America*. London: Allen & Unwin.

Hansen, N.M. (Ed.). 1974. *Public Policy and Regional Economic Development*. Cambridge, Mass.: Ballinger Publishing Company.

Hansen, N.M. 1975 a. *The Challenge of Urban Growth: The Basic Economics of City Size and Structure*. Toronto/London: Lexington.

Hansen, N.M. 1975 b. An Evaluation of Growth Centre Theory and Practice. *Environment and Planning*, Vol. 7, No. 7, pp. 821–232.

Helleiner, F.M. and Stöhr, W. 1974. *Spatial Aspects of the Development Process*. Proceedings of the Commission on Regional Aspects of Development of the International Geographical Union, Vol. II. Toronto: Allister Typesetting and Graphics.

Holland, S. 1976. *The Regional Problem*. London and Basingstoke: The MacMillan Press.

Hötger, H.E. 1974. Die Erfolge der regionalen Wirtschaftspolitik. *Informationen zur Raumentwicklung* 5/1974, pp. 187–192. Bonn Bad-Godesberg.

Katzmann, M.T. 1975. Regional Development Policy in Brazil: The Role of Growth Poles and Development Highways in Goias. *Economic Development and Cultural Change*, Vol. 24, No. 1, pp. 75–107.

Keeble, D.E. 1971. Employment Mobility in Britain. In *Spatial Policy Problems of the British Economy*, ed. by M. Chisholm and G. Manners. Cambridge: CUP.

Keeble, D.E. 1972. Industrial Movement and Regional Development in the United Kingdom. *Town Planners Review*. 43, 3–25.

Kerlikovsky, H. 1977. Nette Leute aus Germany: Die Degussa in Alabama. *Die Zeit*, No. 18, April 1977, p. 30.

Klaassen, L.H., Paelinck J. et Wagenaar, Sj. 1976. Recherches Recentes sur les Disparités Regionales. *Foundations of Empirical Economic Research*, 1976/ 14. Rotterdam: Netherlands Economic Institute.

Klaassen, L.H. and Venter A.C.P. 1974. SPAMO, een ruimtelyk model I. Nederlands Economisch Instituut. Rotterdam.

Kleinpenning, J.M.G. 1975. *The Integration and Colonisation of the Brazilian Portion of the Amazon Basin*. Nijmegen: Geografisch en Planologisch Instituut Katholieke Universiteit.

Kohler H. and Reyher L. 1975. Zu den Auswirkungen von Förderungsmassnahmen auf den Arbeitsmarkt des Regierungsbezirkes Niederbayern nach kreisfreien Städten, Landkreisen und Arbeitsamtsbezirken. *Beiträge zur Arbeitsmarkt- und Berufsforschung* 6. Nürnberg: Institut für Arbeitsmarkt- und Berufsforschung der Bundesanstalt für Arbeit.

Kuklinski, A.R. (Ed.). 1975. *Regional Development and Planning: International Perspectives.* Leyden: Sijthoff.

Kuklinski, A.R. 1977. *Social Issues in Regional Policy and Regional Planning.* The Hague/Paris: Mouton.

Lasuén, J.R. 1961. Regional Income Inequalities and Growth. *Papers and Proceedings of the Regional Science Association*, Vol. 14.

Lasuén, J.R. 1974. Spain's Regional Growth. In: Hansen, 1974.

Lasuén, J.R. and Pastor, A. 1976. International and Interregional Gaps, Madrid, mimeogr.

Lever, W.F. 1972. Industrial Movement, Spatial Association and Functional Linkages. *Regional Studies* 6, p. 371–384.

Lever, W.F. 1974. Manufacturing Linkages and the Search for Suppliers and Markets. In: *Spatial Perspectives on Industrial Organization and Decision-Making*, ed. by Hamilton, F.E.I. London: John Wiley & Sons.

Lever, W.F. 1976. Selectivity in British Regional Policies for Industry. In: *Regional Development and Planning*, ed. Compton, P.A. and M. Pécsi, Budapest: Akadémiou Kiadó.

Lower Austria. 1971. Raumordnungsprogramm zur Schaffung, Verbesserung oder Sicherung geeigneter Standorte für Betriebe des güterproduzierenden fernbedarfstätigen Gewerbes und der Industrie. LGB1. Nr. 255 v.30.11.197.

McDermott, P.J. 1976. Ownership, Organization and Regional Dependence in the Scottish Electronics Industry. *Regional Studies*, Vol. 10, pp. 319–335.

Mera, K. 1975. The Changing Pattern of Population Distribution in Japan and its Implications for Developing Countries. In: Nagoya Centre, 1975.

Moore, B. and Rhodes, J. 1973. *The Economic and Exchequer Implications of Regional Policy.* Minutes of Evidence taken before the Expenditure Committee (Trade and Industry Sub-Committee), House of Commons 42, XVI, HMSO, London.

Moore, B. and J. Rhodes. 1974a. The Effects of Regional Economic Policy in the United Kingdom. In Sant, 1974.

Moore, B. and J. Rhodes. 1974b. Regional Policy and the Scottish Economy. *Scottish Journal of Political Economy*, Vol. XXI, No. 3, pp. 215–235.

Moore, B. and J. Rhodes. 1975. Evaluating the Economic Effects of Regional Policy. Paper presented at the OECD Working Party No. 6 of the Industry Committee. Paris: Organization for Economic Co-operation and Development.

Morrill, R.L. 1974. Growth Centre- Hinterland Relations. In Helleiner and Stöhr, 1974.

Moseley, M.J. 1973a. The Impact of Growth Centres in Rural Regions—I. *Regional Studies*, 7, pp. 57–75.

Moseley, M.J. 1973b. The Impact of Growth Centres in Rural Regions—II. *Regional Studies*, 7, pp. 77–94.

Moseley, M.J. 1974. *Growth Centres in Spatial Planning.* Oxford: Pergamon Press.

Nagoya Centre. 1975. *Growth Strategy and Regional Development Planning in Asia.* Proceedings of the Seminar on Industrialization Strategies and the Growth Pole Approach to Regional Planning and Development: The Asian Experience. Nagoya, Japan.

Nichols, V. 1969. Growth Poles: An Evaluation of their Propulsive Effect. *Environment and Planning.* 1 (2), pp. 193–208.

Nordborg, K. 1967. Elit lokalisering och befolkningspotential. Svensk Geografisk Årbok 43, 93–100.

Novotny, E. 1976. Zur regionalen Differenzierung des Konjunkturverlaufes. *Berichte zur Raumforschung und Raumplanung,* Heft 3/4/76. Wien: Österreichische Gesellschaft für Raumforschung und Raumplanung, pp. 30–34.

Organisation for Economic Co-operation and Development (OECD). 1976. *Regional Problems and Policies in OECD Countries.* Paris.

Organisation for Economic Co-operation and Development (OECD), 1976. Regional Development Policies (Drafts of Parts II and III of the New Report), DDSTI/IND 6/76.21.

O'Farrell, P.N. 1976. An Analysis of Industrial Closures: Irish Experience 1960–1973. *Regional Studies,* Vol. 10, No. 4, pp. 433–338.

Ohlsson, K. et al. 1975. Assessing Swedish Regional Policy—Paper presented at the Working party No. 6 of the Industry Committee. Paris: Organisation for Economic Co-operation and Development.

Pedersen, P.O. 1975 a. Organization Structure and Regional Development. In: *Regional Development and Planning: International Perspectives,* ed. by Kuklinski, A.R. Leyden: Sijthoff.

Pedersen, P.O. 1975 b. *Urban-regional Development in South America.* Paris/ The Hague: Mouton.

Pedersen, P.O. and Stöhr, W. 1971. Economic Integration and the Spatial Development of South America. In: *Latin American Urban Policies and the Social Sciences,* ed. by J. Miller and R. Gakenheimer. Beverly Hills: Sage Publications.

Penouil, M. 1969. An Appraisal of Regional Development Policy in the Aquitaine Region, in Robinson, 1969.

Pernitz, K. and E. Kunze. 1970. Die Industriegründungen in Niederösterreich zwischen 1955 und 1968. *Kulturberichte* 5/1970, pp. 1–8.

Popescou, O. 1963. Probleme der wirtschaftlichen Entwicklung Lateinamerikas. *Jahrbuch f.d. Sozialwissenschaft,* Bd. 14.

Prud'homme, R. 1974. Regional Economic Policy in France, 1962–1972, in Hansen. 1974.

Raghavan, Ch. 1976. A New World Communication and Information Structure. *Development Dialogue* 1976:2, pp. 43–50.

Ray, M. (Ed.). 1976. *Canadian Urban Trends: National Perspective.* Vol. 1. Toronto: Copp Clark Publishing.

Richardson, H.W. 1969. *Regional Economics.* London.

Richardson, H.W. 1973. *Regional Growth Theory.* London: The MacMillan Press Ltd.

Richardson, H.W. 1975 *Regional Development Policy and Planning in Spain.* Lexington: Westmead.

Robinson, E.A.G. 1969. (Ed.). *Backward Areas in Advanced Countries.* Proceedings of a Conference held by the International Economic Association, London/Melbourne/Toronto: The MacMillan Press.

Rodgers, A. 1970. Migration and Industrial Development: The Southern Italian Experience. *Economic Geography* 46, pp. 111–135.

Rothschild K.W. and Lackinger O. 1971. *Betriebsgründungen und Arbeitsmarkt: Oberösterreichische Erfahrungen 1964–1969.* Veröffentlichungen des Österreichischen Institutes für Arbeitsmarktpolitik, Heft XI. Linz.

Ruehmann, P. 1968. *Die regionale Wirtschaftspolitik Belgiens.* Kieler Studien No. 93. Tübingen: Mohr.

Sandmeyer, U. 1976. *Wahl der industriellen Technologie in den Entwicklungsländern: Theoretische Grundlagen und Darstellung am Beispiel des Nordostens Brasiliens.* St. Gallen: Verlag Ruegger.

Sant, M. 1974. *Regional Policy and Planning for Europe.* Lexington: Westmead.

Sant, M. 1975. *Industrial Movement and Regional Development: The British Case.* Oxford: Pergamon Press.

Santa Cruz, H. 1976. Comments on the RIO projects. *Development Dialogue,* 1976/2, pp. 104–111. Uppsala.

Scitovsky, T. 1976. *The Joyless Economy, An Inquiry into Human Satisfaction.* New York: Oxford University Press.

Spehl, H., Töpfer, K. and Töpfer, P. 1975. Folgewirkungen von Industrieansiedlungen. Empirische Ermittlung und regionalpolitische Beurteilung der Einkommens- und Verflechtungswirkungen. Schriftenreihe *Gesellschaft für Regionale Strukturentwicklung* 3. Bonn.

Spanger, U. and Treuner, P. 1975. Standortwahl der Industriebetriebe in Nordrhein-Westfalen 1955–1971. Schriftenreihe *Landes und Stadtentwicklungsforschung* des Landes Nordrhein-Westfalen, 1.003.

Stöhr, W. and Tödtling, F. 1976. "Spatial Equity—Some Antitheses to Current Regional Planning Doctrine." Paper presented at the 13th European Regional Science Congress, Copenhagen, 1976. To be published in the *Papers of the Regional Science Association* (RSA), Vol. 38. 1977.

Strassert, G. 1976. Mehr Zielkonformität durch eine sektorale Differenzierung der regionalen Wirtschaftsförderung. *Informationen zur Raumentwicklung* 12/1976, pp. 793–800. Bonn-Bad Godesberg: Bundesforschungsanstalt für Landeskunde und Raumordnung.

Sundquist, J.L. 1975. *Dispersing Population: What America Can Learn from Europe.* Washington: Brookings Institution.

Thomas, R.G. 1973. *Foreign Investment and Regional Development: The Theory and Practice of Investment Incentives, with a Case Study of Belgium.* New York/Washington/London: Praeger.

Thoman, R.S. 1976. Appalachia after Ten Years. Paper presented to the Third Symposium, Commission on Regional Aspects of Development, International Geographical Union, Dushanbe.

Thoss, R. 1976. Identification and Measurement of the Effects of Regional Policy in the Federal Republic of Germany. Paper presented to the Working Party No. 6 of the Industry Committee. Paris: Organisation for Economic Cooperation and Development.

Törnquist, G.E. 1973. *Systems of Cities and Information Flows,* Lund Studies in Geography Series, B, Nr. 28, Lund.

Ullman, E.L. 1956. The Role of Transportation and the Bases for Interaction. In: *Man's Role in the Face of the Earth*, ed. by William L. Thomas, Jr., et al. Chicago: The University of Chicago Press.

Voigt, F. et al. 1969. Wirtschaftliche Entleerungsgebiete in Industrieländern. Forschungsberichte des Landes Nordrhein-Westfalen, No. 2061.

Waller, P. 1974. The Spread of a Growth Pole—A Case Study of Arequipa (Peru). In Helleiner and Stöhr. 1974.

Westaway, J. 1974. Contact Potential and the Occupational Structure of the British Urban System 1961—1966: An Empirical Study. *Regional Studies*, Vol. 8, No. 1, pp. 57—73.

Wilson, G. et al. 1966. *The Impact of Highway Investment on Development*. Washington: The Brookings Institution.

Wolf, F. 1974. *Effizienz und Erfolgskontrolle der regionalen Wirtschaftsförderung: Ergebnisse einer Untersuchung in Hessen*. Wiesbaden: Hessische Landesentwicklungs- und Treuhandgesellschaft.

Wolf, F. 1975. Wie effizient ist die regionale Wirtschaftsförderung. *Informationen zur Raumentwicklung*, 9/1975, pp. 431—438. Bonn-Bad Godesberg.

※ *Chapter 5*

On the Settlement System of the German Democratic Republic: Development Trends and Strategies

Heinz Lüdemann
Joachim Heinzmann

Since the foundation of the German Democratic Republic the state agencies have paid great attention to the comprehensive development of human settlements at the central, regional, and local levels. The main aim of the government policy in this field is the creation of the most favourable living conditions for the population: for their work, housing, education, and recreation. In the GDR the preconditions for achieving this aim have clearly existed, as can be seen from the results thus far obtained in the development of human settlements. This study presents some of the problems and results of this process.

REGIONAL DEVELOPMENT PROCESSES: THE ECONOMIC BASIS FOR CHANGES IN THE SETTLEMENT SYSTEMS

The development of human settlement systems is closely related to the dynamics of the productive forces and their regional distribution. Studying the development trends of settlement systems presupposes knowledge of the regularities of and the nature of the economic processes ruling them. To a high degree, long-term strategies for the formation of settlement systems—if they are to be realized in practice—depend on the extent to which they are in accordance with the regional policies for the economic base structure of a given country. A basic principle of the location of the productive forces in Socialist countries is the even distribution of production over the whole country. The realization of this principle is the presupposition for being

Table 5–1. **People Employed in Industry and Agriculture** *(percent).* *

	1895		1907		1925	
District	*Ind.*	*Agric.*	*Ind.*	*Agric.*	*Ind.*	*Agric.*
Rostock	32.5	67.5	32.9	67.1	34.3	65.7
Schwerin	19.7	70.3	31.8	68.2	29.5	70.5
Neubranden- burg	32.5	67.5	31.4	68.6	29.7	70.3
Halle	53.2	46.8	56.3	43.7	61.5	38.5
Leipzig	65.2	34.8	73.2	26.8	76.6	23.4
Karl-Marx- Stadt	80.8	19.2	86.9	13.1	86.3	13.7
GDR	48.5	41.5	64.2	35.8	65.5	34.5

Source: Ökonomische Geographie der DDR, Berlin 1969, p. 22–52,
Statistisches Jahrbuch der DDR, Berlin 1976, p. 58–59.
*For reasons of comparability, handicraft and building trade data have been included in industry.

able to offer the people in all parts of the country good conditions for work and living. This principle does not mean, as sometimes wrongly interpreted, an even distribution of all branches of industry over the whole country, i.e. a regional balance in the degree of industrialization. Rather, it involves the formation of regional centers in all parts of the country and the concentration of industries in those locations where the economic conditions are best for them. For example, the systematic development of industrial agglomerations and the utilization of their economic powers is part of this principle, just as the creation of predominantly agricultural production complexes in certain areas. The formation of a regionally differentiated but highly developed economic base in all parts of the country according to different historical, natural, and demographic conditions is a universal problem faced by most countries, though in varying degree according to specific conditions. Such a regionally differentiated structure of the economic base brings about regionally differing starting points and objectives for the dynamics of the human settlement systems. With regard to the GDR, some problems of the regional development of the economy and its relations to the settlement structure can be demonstrated by the example of structural shifts between the northern and southern parts of the country. Three representative districts of the north (Rostock, Schwerin, Neubrandenburg) and of the south (Halle, Leipzig, Karl-Marx-Stadt) serve as objects of comparison. On the territory now belonging to the GDR, there were very strong differences up to the end of World War II in

Table 5–1. continued

1939		1956		1966		1975	
Ind.	Agric.	Ind.	Agric.	Ind.	Agric.	Ind.	Agric.
45.4	54.6	48.4	51.6	57.4	42.6	69.3	30.7
32.5	67.5	34.1	65.9	42.5	57.5	59.7	40.3
33.4	66.6	24.7	75.3	31.4	68.6	51.2	48.8
69.4	30.6	73.8	26.2	78.7	21.3	83.7	16.1
80.4	19.6	78.8	21.2	80.9	19.1	85.1	14.9
86.0	14.0	85.7	14.3	88.3	11.7	91.2	8.8
69.9	30.1	68.6	31.4	74.3	25.7	71.2	18.8

the economic structure and level of development between the north and the south. Modern large-scale industry was situated almost exclusively in the southern part and in the area around Berlin, whereas the northern areas, with their one-sidedly agrarian structure, belonged to the economically underdeveloped regions. This fact is clearly seen by comparing the number of employees in industry and agriculture up to 1939 (see Table 5–1).

Taking into account the principle of the even distribution of industry over the whole country and the specific conditions of the territorial structure, the economic regional policy of the GDR in the past decades has been directed and will be directed in the future to the following aims:

- General strengthening of the economic base in the previously heavily-agricultural areas by new location and extension of industrial plants, with a simultaneous rapid development and modernization of large-scale agricultural production.
- Maximum utilization, reconstruction and modernization of the existing production potential of industrial agglomerations, with partial extension of industries and a simultaneous intensive development of agriculture.

This was and is no steady process. From time to time one side or the other has been stressed.

The results of this regional policy become apparent in the change of the economic structure of the northern districts that have developed from pure agrarian districts into agrarian-industrial districts (see Table 5–1). The growth rate of industry in the northern districts was higher than that of the heavily-industrialized southern districts (see Table 5−2). However, this has not resulted in basic changes in the regional proportions of industrial production in the GDR, nor are changes anticipated in the next few years. Moreover, in the southern districts industrial production is concentrated mainly in a few industrial agglomerations, so that there is a very differentiated territorial structure.

The experience of the GDR indicates that the economic level of a region cannot be judged on the basis of its industrial potential alone. Modern agriculture, for instance, by developing industrial methods of production, may strongly contribute to the strengthening of the economic base of certain regions. Consequently, the industrialization process also includes agriculture. Despite differing economic structures in individual districts of the GDR, the evenness of the regional distribution of productive forces becomes apparent by virtue of the facts that in all regions full employment is guaranteed, that there are no basic regional differences in the wage levels, and that in all parts of the country every citizen has the opportunity to make use of a wide range of work places.

The differences in the economic structure are reflected in the territorial differentiation of the settlement structure of the GDR and in its dynamics (Table 5−3).

For the highly industrialized and densely-settled south of the GDR, a high degree of urbanization and a dense network of towns and settlements are characteristic. In the more agriculturally structured regions, chiefly in the north, a lower degree of urbanization and a wide-meshed network of towns prevails. Another characteristic feature is a high concentration of population in towns (55 percent of the population lives in towns with more than 10,000 inhabitants) on

Table 5−2. **Northern Versus Southern Industry Growth Rate**

	Share of the Districts in the Industrial Gross Production of the GDR, 1975 (percent)	Index of Industrial Gross Production 1975 (1965 = 100)
Rostock	3.2	184
Schwerin	2.4	213
Neubrandenburg	1.7	232
Halle	14.3	180
Leipzig	8.5	173
Karl-Marx-Stadt	14.4	180
Dresden	12.1	176

Source: Statistisches Jahrbuch der DDR 1976, Berlin 1976, p. 71−99.

Table 5–3. Differences in Economic Structure as Reflected by Territorial Settlement.

District	Residential Population (1,000)	Population Density (inhabitants/sq. km.)	Settlement Density (Number of Settlements/ 1,000 sq. km.)	Degree of Urbanization (percentage of people living in towns > 10,000 inhabitants)
Rostock	868.7	123	254	58.7
Schwerin	590.3	68	144	44.4
Neubrandenburg	626.3	58	126	39.7
Halle	1,876.5	214	167	53.6
Leipzig	1,445.8	291	278	62.5
Karl-Marx-Stadt	1,976.9	329	215	53.6
Dresden	1,835.6	272	260	59.0
GDR	16,820.2	155	158	55.2

Source: Statistisches Jahrbuch der DDR 1976, Berlin 1976, p. 1 and 8.

the one hand, and at the same time a prevalence of many small settlements (the 7,634 municipalities of the GDR consist of 17,000 settlements and housing estates).

In spite of the relatively high stability of the settlement structure in the past two decades, some structural changes related to various planning measures have occurred. Despite a decrease in the population, the degree of urbanization (percentage of people living in towns with more than 10,000 inhabitants) increased between 1955 and 1975 from 49.3 percent to 55.2 percent (see Table 5—4). The rate of this development was considerably higher in the northern districts than in the southern districts, so that in general differences were reduced. These changes are the result of a purposeful planning of the regional distribution of production and housing construction.

With regard to their nature and their regional influence, the processes of industrialization and urbanization are closely interdependent. In the GDR, industrialization consists of intensive processes (rationalization and modernization of existing production complexes) and extensive processes (formation of new places of production). One reason why the working out of strategies for regional policy is very complicated is that these processes take place very inconsistently within themselves. Thus the industrialization process itself includes diverse trends that lead to varying effects on the settlement systems (see Figure 5—1).

The main orientation in the economic development of the GDR is towards intensification. With regard to the settlement systems, the following trends have to be expected from the intended regional distribution of industries:

Table 5—4. Changes in Degree of Urbanization in the GDR *(population in towns with more than 10,000 inhabitants) (percent).*

Districts	1955	1960	1970	1975	1975 / 1955
Rostock	48.2	49.9	55.7	58.7	+10.5
Schwerin	37.3	38.4	39.5	44.4	+ 7.1
Neubrandenburg	28.4	30.3	35.4	39.6	+11.2
Halle	48.7	49.7	52.4	53.6	+ 4.9
Leipzig	61.0	61.3	62.8	62.5	+ 1.5
Karl-Marx-Stadt	51.2	50.8	53.0	53.5	+ 2.3
GDR	49.3	50.2	53.6	55.2	+ 4.9

Source: Statistisches Jahrbuch der DDR 1976, Berlin 1976, p. 8—12.

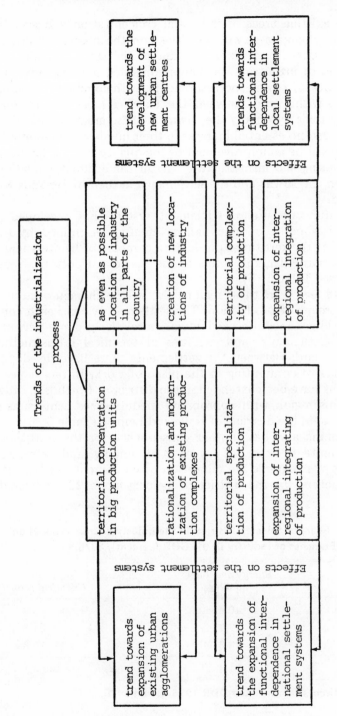

Figure 5—1. Effects of Industrialization Process on Settlement Systems

1. In the existing areas of industrial concentration and agglomeration primary emphasis will be placed on the maximum utilization, rationalization, and modernization of the stock of industrial machinery and of infrastructure. These congested areas already have a dense network of towns and settlements, with complex functional interrelations within and between the existing local and regional settlement systems. Normally the towns in these areas of concentration will undergo no essential increase in their number of inhabitants; rather, there will be an improvement of the quality of their facilities, especially housing and infrastructure. At the same time the relationships between the towns and the settlements in their hinterlands will be intensified.

2. A specific structure of settlement systems has developed in those regions whose economic base is chiefly determined by the development of the territorial production complex of lignite-energy-chemicals. In particular, this refers to the districts of Cottbus, Halle, and Leipzig (see Table 5—5).

In the next few years these regions also will be characterized by a rapid development of production. The settlement systems each comprise several larger medium-sized towns, a relatively dense network of workers' settlements, and facilities of technical infrastructure of a high standard. Between the settlements there have developed intensive fields of commuting to the place of work. In recent years selected towns have been extended in the district of Cottbus in order to provide this region with appropriate medium-sized centers, as is already the case in the districts of Halle and Leipzig (Table 5—6).

Lignite mining also has another consequence for the settlement structure. Lignite is extracted by open-pit mining, and extraction from the big pits requires the relocation of equipment, settlements, and infrastructure. In the district of Leipzig alone 22 settlements

Table 5—5.   Share of Selected Districts in the Industrial Gross Production of Selected Branches of Industry of the GDR (percent), 1975.

District	Energy and Fuel Industry	Chemical Industry
Cottbus	40.4	5.2
Halle	17.7	37.6
Leipzig	13.3	10.3
	71.4	53.1

Source: Statistisches Jahrbuch der DDR 1976, Berlin 1976, p. 71.

Table 5−6. Population Change in Selected Towns in the Districts of Cottbus, Halle, Leipzig *(in 1,000)*.

District	Town	1946	1950	1964	1971	1975
Cottbus	Cottbus	49.1	60.8	73.3	83.4	96.9
	Hoyerswerda	7.2	7.3	39.6	59.1	67.1
	Senftenberg	17.7	18.2	24.0	24.3	30.5
Halle	Bitterfeld/ Wolfen	44.2	44.5	54.8	56.8	55.3
Leipzig	Borna	18.4	17.8	19.9	22.1	22.1
	Altenburg	51.8	49.4	47.5	46.7	52.5

Source: Statistisches Jahrbuch der DDR 1976, Berlin 1976, p. 9−12.

have had to be transferred because of the opening up of new open-pit mines. The citizens of these hitherto mostly rural settlements were resettled mainly in small- or medium-sized towns of the region. Where resettlement is required by economic necessities, state authorities and mining enterprises together work out long-term programmes in order to avoid social stress on the citizens.

3. For some selected towns an increase in the number of inhabitants is planned. This growth will be the consequence of the systematic settling of workers and their families in towns where an extensive enlargement of industrial production is planned. This is why 140 large- and medium-sized towns and some small industrial towns have been included in the long-term central planning of the regional distribution of productive forces. Generally, planned growth of population of these towns is approximately 10 percent for the period from 1975 to 1990.

4. In the next few years far-reaching concentration and changes in industrialization processes will take place in agriculture. For example, this trend will include expansion of big specialized enterprises for plant and animal production, of agricultural services (agro-chemical centers, enterprises of agricultural engineering), and of the processing industry. This development will lead to concentration in the settlement network of rural areas, and there will be an increase in the importance of rural settlement centers. They will be given priority in the location of infrastructure and they will largely determine the development of local settlement systems.

To facilitate these objectively necessary trends of concentration in the settlement system, associations of communities (Gemeindeverbände) have been created. In many cases several municipalities have united on a cooperative basis. By a coordinated and concentrated utilization of their material and financial means, as well as by cooperation with the enterprises and cooperatives in their territory, a rapid improvement of the working and living conditions of their citizens is obtained. Together they decide which of the communities is to be the center of the association. All questions of the development of the association of communities are settled by common decisions of the elected representative of the people of the communities concerned. The associations are founded by the voluntary decision of the communes. By June 1976, 52 percent of all rural municipalities were members of such associations, which included about half of the rural population of the GDR.

MIGRATION AND SETTLEMENT SYSTEMS

Compared with other countries, migration plays a relatively small role in the dynamics of the settlement system in the GDR (Table 5–7). One reason is the fact that the population of the GDR has remained fairly stable for a longer time.

In this connection it can be stated that migration across subdistrict borders has been decreasing during the last two decades, and especially since the end of the sixties. There are several main reasons for this phenomenon.

1. Until well into the sixties a large number of industrial enterprises were established in formerly agrarian regions. In a number of cases this was connected with the creation of new towns in lesser-developed regions. Since then the intensification and rationalization of industry has been in the foreground. In certain cases this may also include the creation of new enterprises, but this usually takes place in already-industrialized areas, in which case existing towns are extended and modernized.

2. Especially since the end of the sixties, much progress has been achieved in the transition to industry-like production methods in agriculture. This is expressed, for instance, in the creation of large

Table 5–7. **Migration Across Subdistrict Borders According to Number of Registrations** *(per 1,000 people).*

Year	Rate	Year	Rate
1953	47.9	1969	15.6
1957	40.2	1973	15.7
1961	37.5	1974	16.7
1965	29.3		

Source: Statistisches Jahrbuch der DDR 1976, Berlin 1976, p. 398.

production units for animal husbandry, of agro-chemical centers, and of other central institutions.

As a result, the number of people employed in agriculture first went down rapidly, but in the last few years the decrease has been much slower. Thus, the trend towards concentration in the rural settlement network will strengthen, but it will take effect mainly in smaller spatial units and will concern migration across subdistrict borders only to a low degree.

3. Minimizing and in some fields even overcoming regional differences in the material and cultural living conditions of the people work against the trend towards migration and, to a certain degree, will be a factor of stabilization of the settlement system.

The predominance of migration within relatively small spatial units is illustrated by data from 1974, which are also representative for the years before (Table 5−8).

Migration within districts (65.4 percent of the total migration) reflects a tendency toward a gradual concentration of the population in the settlement network, caused by the requirements of industrial and agricultural production as well as the growing material and cultural needs of the population. It is complemented by a concentration of housing construction in the district and subdistrict towns as well as in local centers of rural areas. However, this process is occurring slowly; in 1974 the communes of the GDR with less than 2,000 inhabitants had a loss of 45,472 people due to migration, which corresponds to only 1.06 percent of the population living in this size-group of communes (Table 5−9).

In the GDR as a whole migration into other districts is also of low importance and does not have any fundamental effect on the development of the national settlement system.

For more than a decade the capital of Berlin and the districts of

Table 5−8.   Migration Across Municipality Borders According to Number of Registrations in 1974.

	Persons	Percentage of Migration
Total migration of which:	410,149	100
Within the subdistrict	128,265	31.3
Across subdistrict borders, but within the district	139,743	34.1
Into other districts	142,141	34.6

Source: Statistisches Jahrbuch der DDR 1976, Berlin 1976, p. 396−398.

Table 5—9.   Gains in Population by Migration in the Periods 1962—1965 and 1974.

District	Average Migration in the Period 1962–1965	Migrants per 1,000 Population	Average Migration in 1974	Migrants per 1,000 Population
Capital of Berlin	9,790	9.18	12,201	11.15
Cottbus	4,230	5.16	1,717	1.97
Frankfurt	3,521	5.37	1,260	1.83
Rostock	490	0.59	995	1.15

Source: Ökonomische Geographie der DDR, Berlin 1969, p. 96.   Statistisches Jahrbuch der DDR 1976, Berlin 1976, p. 396–397.

Cottbus, Frankfurt and Rostock have had the biggest gains in population due to in-migration.

The biggest increase in population due to migration has been in the capital of Berlin, a result of intensified reconstruction during the past decade. This gain was caused by inflows from all other districts of the GDR.

The districts of Cottbus and Frankfurt have also had an increase in population due to migration. The main cause was the creation— especially during the sixties—of a number of important industrial plants (e.g. coal and power, chemicals, electronics). With the beginning of production the rate of population increase in these districts went down considerably. Migrants into these districts came chiefly from the neighboring districts of Dresden and Neubrandenburg, as well as from the districts of Halle, Karl-Marx-Stadt and Rostock.

Because of the development of industry and of maritime and port traffic, the district of Rostock has had a small increase in population due to migration; the inflow has come primarily from the neighboring districts of Schwerin and Neubrandenburg.

In the past decade all other districts of the GDR had slight losses in population. The heaviest net outmigration occurred in the districts of Schwerin and Neubrandenburg, where the annual rates were, respectively, two and four persons per thousand population.

In summation, migration in the GDR has declined in importance. It occurs mainly in the gradual process of concentration in regional and local settlement systems. On a national scale it does not cause any fundamental changes, though it has contributed to a gradual increase in the population of Berlin and new industrial centers.

ON THE ROLE OF URBAN CENTERS IN THE NATIONAL SETTLEMENT SYSTEM

In the national settlement system of the GDR the capital of Berlin and 14 other district-towns are of greatest importance. They are the political and social centers of the country and the individual districts, but beyond that they are the most important centers of production, education, culture and science. Therefore, in the years to come a large amount of the funds intended for the development of the national settlement system will be allocated to them. In these centers priority will be given to the extension or improvement of the quality of technical and social infrastructure, including housing construction, the modernization of older residential districts, provision of services for the local population and visitors, and development of communication systems.

The further development of the settlement system in the GDR, especially under the specific prevailing conditions of urbanization, requires the rational organization of relationships between towns and their hinterlands.

1. This will allow an ever-increasing part of the population in smaller hinterland settlements to take advantage of the various services of the towns, and it will contribute considerably to the development of urban ways of working and living in smaller settlements, so that there will be a diminution of essential differences between town and country.
2. The rational organization of the relationships between towns and their hinterlands will mean greater possibilities for more people to use their leisure time for recreation and sports, cultural activities, and further education.
3. The potentials of the hinterlands can be put to better use through, for example, the establishment of recreation areas, fuller utilization of their labour potential, and the development of sites for the disposal of industrial and municipal waste without detrimental environmental effects.

The desirable size of a hinterland area is determined largely by the degree of accessibility to its urban center. In general, the maximum travel time should be 40 minutes in one direction for daily trips, and about 60 minutes for periodic or infrequent trips by public transport means. Though these figures are modified by personal transportation, they are not nullified by it.

Considering the 15 towns mentioned earlier from this point of view, it can be said that while their development is having an increasing effect on their hinterlands, they still influence the daily life of only part of the GDR population (see Table 5—10). In consequence, many other towns that are also centers of production, education and culture will be included in the development of the national settlement system of the GDR. The basis for their selection are data concerning accessibility to subdistrict towns, including the centers of a higher rank (see Table 5—11).

Over 80 percent of the GDR population lives in subdistrict towns or at a distance that allows them to go to these towns daily. Another 14.5 percent are within a reasonable distance with respect to important occasional trips. Only 4.2 percent of the GDR population needs

Table 5—10.   Accessibility to the District Towns of the GDR.

	(1,000 Population)	(Percent)
Capital and district towns including the 20-minute zone	4,268	25.1
20–40-minute zone	1,682	9.9
40–60-minute zone	1,684	9.9
Outside the 60-minute-zone	9,378	55.1
GDR	17,012	100.0

(Calculated by Institute of Geography and Geoecology).

more than 60 minutes to get to a subdistrict town by public transport. At the same time, there are differences between the northern and the southern districts; these arise because of differences in settlement network density, development of communications, and other factors.

On the basis of these data different variants of regional center systems were studied. The objective is to provide the distribution of centers over the entire national territory that will be of greatest benefit to hinterland residents, i.e. those persons living within the 40-minute zone. A considerable part of the GDR territory is already influenced by 115 of the 197 subdistrict towns and only very small areas lie outside of the influence spheres of 157 towns.

In conjunction with these investigations, detailed studies were made of 55 large- and medium-sized towns and their various interrelations with their respective hinterlands. Commuting, population and employment structure, supply and service functions, and stock of housing units according to number and quality were among the factors studied.

In the GDR city-hinterland-regions (Stadt-Umland-Regionen) are an important form of spatial organisation. Within these regions significant needs related to work, services, education and leisure can be satisfied in terms of ever-increasing quality and with a reasonable expenditure of time. From the aspect of the national settlement system these regions are elementary regional settlement systems.

The inner structure of these city-hinterland-regions is strongly influenced by regional differences as well as by the subcenters existing within them.

In a very generalized way, however, it is possible to distinguish three zones within the city-hinterland-regions.

Table 5–11.   Accessibility to the Subdistrict Towns in the GDR.

	GDR		Northern Districts		Southern Districts	
	in 1,000 Persons	Percent	in 1,000 Persons	Percent	in 1,000 Persons	Percent
Subdistrict towns including the 20-minute zone	11,263	66.2	1,154	56.0	5,051	68.1
20–40-minute zone	2,558	15.0	489	23.9	1,644	22.2
40–60-minute zone	2,469	14.5	196	9.5	507	6.8
Outside the 60-minute zone	722	4.2	222	10.8	213	2.9
	17,012	100.0	2,061	100.0	7,415	100.0

(Calculated by Institute of Geography and Geoecology).

ZONE I: the average radius from the center is 10 to 15 kilometers. All settlements within this zone are oriented clearly to the center of the city-hinterland-region.

ZONE II: the average radius from the center is 20 to 25 kilometers. The settlements within this zone are already strongly oriented to subcenters (usually smaller towns and other local centers). The relations with the main center of the city-hinterland-region are reduced, but there is daily commuting.

ZONE III: the average radius from the center is 20 to 30 kilometers. The most important relations exist between the main center and the subcenters. Periodic and occasional relations of the population of the hinterland to the main center predominate.

From these different investigations it was found that regional centers, usually certain subdistrict towns, play an important part in the decision-making process for the further development of the national settlement system. Planning of the development is done—in cooperation with local representatives of the people and their councils—for a considerable part on a central level (for 140 selected towns) but also on the district level.

The development of the 15 most important towns and a large number of other regional centers is the basic framework of the national settlement system of the GDR. At the same time, this process gives the development of other towns and municipalities a general orientation and important stimulation. On this basis, the local representatives of the people and their councils have full scope to develop the larger part of all other towns and communes in such a way that the working and living conditions of the people living in them will improve systematically.

OVERCOMING REGIONAL DIFFERENCES IN THE MATERIAL AND CULTURAL LIVING CONDITIONS OF THE PEOPLE

A fundamental problem of the development of national settlement systems is the gradual removal of regional differences, in some cases even of sharp contrasts in the material and cultural living conditions of the people. In a socialist society this is immediately connected with the socio-political task of overcoming differences between town and country.

In this connection the following facts should be taken into consideration:

1. An equalization of the living standard refers to *basic* problems of material living conditions, education, culture, public health, recreation, and related problems. Of course, it does not completely abolish differences conditioned by social, regional and individual particularities and interests.
2. An equalization of the living standard requires an efficient economic base in all parts of the country. Because of natural conditions, economic and technological requirements and demographic particularities, the regional structure of production will also be very differentiated in the future. Consequently, an equalization of the living standard can be realized not contrary to, but rather on the basis of, the territorial specialization and division of labor of production and certain branches of services.

By a systematic and purposeful development of the territorial structure of production and the national settlement system of the GDR (based on the principle of the unity of economic and social policy), a considerable diminution of former regional differences in material and cultural living conditions has been achieved in the past three decades. In certain spheres of human life they have been abolished completely: full employment, for instance, which has existed in the GDR for a long time, ensures an ever better basis of existence for the populations in all regions of the country. Nevertheless, the complete removal of all differences is a long-lasting process extending well into the future. These issues can be seen in the development of the northern and southern districts of the GDR where, as already mentioned, there are still distinct differences in the levels of industrialization and urbanization.

Before presenting relevant data it should be noted that because the material and cultural living conditions of people are extremely intricate phenomena, they cannot be simply characterized by a few indices. In addition, suitable primary data are not always available. Nevertheless, on the basis of the data available it can readily be seen that the great differences in population density and in levels of industrialization and urbanization between the northern and southern districts do not imply significant differences in material and cultural living conditions.

Retail-trade turnover per capita can, to a certain degree, be a basis for estimating the material living standards of the populations in different regions. But it should be pointed out that the facts are influenced by central functions of large cities (e.g. Leipzig and Dresden) and by special functions of individual regions (e.g. recreation and port functions in the district of Rostock). Nevertheless, this variable can give a rough orientation. The retail-trade turnover per capita of the population increased from 2,616 marks in 1960 to 4,870 marks in 1975, while retail prices in the GDR as a whole and in the regions remained constant. In terms of this variable, a very balanced development could be observed in the districts studied (see Table 5-12). The considerably higher development rate in the three formerly-backward northern districts in fact characterized even the earlier period not shown here.

Data on the stock of durable consumer goods, which is a good indicator of material and cultural living standards, provides similar results (see Table 5-13).

The level of education and of educational opportunities can be regarded as an important indicator of the cultural conditions in the different regions of a country. In the GDR, for instance, the percentage of employed persons who had completed a university or college education increased from 6.1 percent in 1961 to 13.5 percent in 1974. Although this percentage is much higher in significant centers of science, industry, and culture (e.g. in the cities of Berlin, Leipzig, Dresden, and Rostock), there are no fundamental regional differences outside these centers, even between the heavily industrialized and urbanized districts in the south and the formerly underdeveloped northern districts (see Table 5-14).

In the past three decades the groundwork has been laid to offer equal educational opportunities to the youth in all regions of the GDR. One of the prerequisites was the establishment of a complete network of polytechnical schools (10 or 12-year education-periods respectively) in all parts of the country. One indication of this development is the number of pupils per teacher employed full-time, which decreased from 24.9 in 1955 to 17.5 in 1974 (Table 5-15). A similar situation obtains with respect to the care of preschool age children, for which the parents have to pay only a small amount of money (Table 5-16). Again, the evidence indicates that in the past three decades good results have been achieved in the diminution and removal of regional differences in material and cultural living conditions. In the future intensive efforts will be made to continue and strengthen this process. Among others, the following problems may be noted here.

1. Solution of the housing problem, which may take until 1990. A housing construction programme provides for the new construc-

Table 5–12.   Retail-Trade Turnover per Capita of the Population.

	Northern Districts				Southern Districts		
	1960 (marks)	1975 (marks)	1960 = 100		1960 (marks)	1975 (marks)	1960 = 100
Rostock	2,735	5,251	192	Halle	2,492	4,526	182
Schwerin	2,349	4,606	196	Leipzig	2,784	4,956	178
Neubrandenburg	2,295	4,603	201	Karl-Marx-Stadt	2,665	4,805	180
				Dresden	2,666	4,855	182

Source: Statistisches Jahrbuch der DDR 1976, Berlin 1976, p. 1 and 250–251.

Table 5–13.   Selected Durable Consumer Goods per 100 Households of Workers and Employees in 1974.

	Northern Districts				Southern Districts		
	TV Sets	Refrigerators	Washing Machines		TV Sets	Refrigerators	Washing Machines
Rostock	91.3	84.7	74.2	Halle	89.2	85.7	81.9
Schwerin	92.1	84.5	75.2	Leipzig	88.8	88.1	77.6
Neubrandenburg	89.3	82.5	75.4	Karl-Marx-Stadt	88.4	85.7	80.5
				Dresden	85.6	86.1	75.4

Source: Statistisches Jahrbuch der DDR 1976, Berlin 1976, p. 313.

Table 5—14. Percentage of Employed Persons with University or College Education

| | Northern Districts | | | Southern Districts | |
	1964	1974		1964	1974
Rostock	8.4	15.0	Halle	6.9	12.7
Schwerin	6.8	11.6	Leipzig	7.6	15.4
Neubranden-burg	6.4	12.3	Karl-Marx-Stadt	5.6	10.9
			Dresden	7.1	11.8

(Calculated by the authors from diverse data in: Statistische Jahrbücher der Bezirke der DDR, 1961 and 1975/1976).

Table 5—15. Pupils per Teacher Employed Full-time at Schools of General Education.

| | Northern Districts | | | Southern Districts | |
	1960	1974		1960	1974
Rostock	22.5	17.8	Halle	26.1	17.6
Schwerin	21.1	16.4	Leipzig	25.1	18.1
Neubranden-burg	22.2	16.6	Karl-Marx-Stadt	24.4	16.8
			Dresden	24.0	17.7

(Calculated by the authors from diverse data in: Statistische Jahrbücher der Bezirke der DDR, 1961 and 1975/1976).

Table 5—16. Number of Children Cared for in Kindergartens per 1,000 Children in Preschool Ages (from 3 to 6 years), 1974 (GDR = 804).

Northern Districts		Southern Districts	
Rostock	780	Halle	815
Schwerin	788	Leipzig	782
Neubrandenburg	805	Karl-Marx-Stadt	756
		Dresden	784

(Calculated by the authors from diverse data in: Statistische Jahrbücher der Bezirke der DDR, 1961 and 1975/1976).

tion and modernization of 750,000 flats between 1976 and 1980. This will mean an immediate improvement of the housing conditions of about 2.1 million people within 5 years. In 1980 about 40 percent of the population will live in flats that were built or modernized after 1945. Main efforts will be concentrated on the bigger towns.

2. Measures for improving environmental conditions. These will be concentrated mainly on agglomerations and large cities. A reduction in the pollution of water and air as well as improvements in the disposal and utilization of municipal and industrial waste will be emphasized.

3. Quantitative and qualitative improvement of recreational opportunities for the populations in heavily industrialized and urbanized areas. For example, large recreation areas close to nature will be laid out in areas formerly used for lignite mining; such sites already can be found in the districts of Cottbus (e.g. Senftenberg Lake) and Leipzig.

4. With the further industrialization of agriculture there will also be a gradual concentration in the rural settlement network. However, this will not affect all villages. Emphasis will be given to the smallest villages situated relatively far from regional and local settlement centers, and especially to scattered settlements and single farms which do not provide favorable material and cultural living conditions.

REFERENCES

Grimm, F., R. Krönert; and H. Lüdemann (1975), Aspects of Urbanisation in the German Democratic Republic, in *National Settlement Strategies East and West*, IIASA Conference Proceedings, Laxenburg, Austria.

Krönert, R. (1976), *Zur Herausbildung und den Entwicklungsbedingungen von Gemeindeverbänden aus der Sicht der Stadt-Umland-Forschungen*, Institut für Geographie und Geoökologie der AdW der DDR, manuscript.

Lüdemann, H., and J. Heinzmann (1975), Zur Rolle der Stadt-Umland-Beziehungen bei der Entwicklung der Siedlungsstruktur, in *Wissenschaftliche Zeitschrift der Humboldt-Universität zu Berlin, mathematisch-naturwissenschaftliche Reihe, XXIV*, 1.

Lüdemann, H. (1972), The Process of Equalizing Levels of Regional Development in the German Democratic Republic, in *International Geography 1972, 1*, Montreal.

Lüdemann, H. (1975), The Interrelations Between the Process of Concentration and Territorial Development under Socialist Conditions in the German Democratic Republic, in *Regional Studies, Methods and Analyses*, Budapest.

Ostwald, W., and K. Scherf (1973), Probleme der planmäßigen, proportionalen Entwicklung der Siedlungsstruktur der DDR, in *Probleme der Entwicklung der Siedlungsstruktur.* Berichte und Mitteilungen, herausgegeben vom Wissenschaftlichen Rat für Fragen der Vervollkommnung der Planung und wirtschaftlichen Rechnungsführung, Nr. 4, Berlin.

Ostwald, W. (1976), Planmäßige, proportionale Gestaltung der Territorialstruktur der DDR als Beitrag zur Erhöhung der Effektivität der gesellschaftlichen Reproduktion, in *Wirtschaftswissenschaft*, Nr. 5, Berlin.

Ökonomische Geographie der DDR (1969), Herausgegeben von H. Kohl, G. Jacob, H.–J. Kramm, W. Roubitschek, G. Schmidt-Renner, Gothe/Leipzig.

Statistische Jahrbücher der Deutschen Demokratischen Republik, (1960 to 1975).

Statistische Jahrbücher der Bezirke der DDR, (1960 to 1975).

✳ *Chapter 6*

The Structure of Population and the Future Settlement System in Poland

Kazimierz Dziewoński

The present regional differentiation of the population structure in Poland, which results from past and present migrations, influences and will continue to influence deeply the whole settlement system and its transformations.

The following analysis attempts to give a general picture of past and future problems; the details are presented in a larger publication prepared by the Institute of Geography of the Polish Academy of Sciences (1976). Some of the supporting evidence and information concerning this outline may be found in numerous publications of the Central Statistical Office from the last ten years.

Poland belongs to the group of European countries which have a greater-than-average density of population, and are characterized by a larger-than-mean (although lately falling) rate of natural increase. The population forecasts recently published for Poland by the Central Statistical Office are very detailed and methodically subtle but clearly rather pessimistic. However, comparison with forecasts published for other countries shows them to be more optimistic. The explanation may lie in the fact that other countries take into account immigration from abroad, while the Polish forecast does not. Another reason may be the unduly pessimistic assumptions as far as the fall in the fertility and birth indices are concerned. The recent stabilization in fertility rates—which took demographers rather by surprise— is currently resulting in an upward revision of the forecasts. Whatever the explanation of these differences, one fact seems to remain certain —Poland, as all Europe, will face in the near future (not later than in the middle of the 21st century) a complete stabilization (or even a small decline) in its population. This number may be assumed to be somewhere in the vicinity of 40 million, or at the most 45 million, inhabitants. However, closer analysis indicates that it is not the number of the whole population which really matters; far more important is the number of the working or productive part, and its reproduction. This obviously introduces structural problems as well as the issue of proper proportions between people in the preproductive, productive and postproductive age-classes.

It is readily observed that while the number of people in the preproductive ages is decisive for the later size of the productive-age population, the number of people in the postproductive group is a simple function of longevity, or the average length of life. At present it is already comparatively high, and although it will still grow in the coming years the rate of growth is clearly diminishing. Except for some unforeseeable breakthrough in medicine, the average age will be stabilized somewhere around 75 years of age. The very large percentages of older people may turn out to be a rather mixed blessing for the social and economic life of a nation, but the proper size of population in the preproductive ages is crucial not only for the growth but for the very existence of the nation. Hence any rational population policies have to take care that the number of births not fall below a specific level, which is possible to define as one ensuring the proper reproduction of the productive (or working) population. All these rather abstract statements may be reduced to and expressed in a more practical, operative way by stating that the most important element for a community in its demographic aspects and prospects is the family and its prevailing types and models.

From that point of view the spatial differentiation of population in Poland is very large and the existing disparities are indeed very significant, both for the present and the future. This differentiation depends on the past history of individual regions and recent migratory movements. The consequences of historical regional differences for their economic, cultural, and political development are rather difficult to define clearly; moreover, they have lost most of their importance because of the high present integration of Polish society, which is the result of the great economic, social and cultural upheavals of the war and postwar years. On the other hand, the great migrations of the past form the main basis of present regional differences in demographic structure.

Generally speaking, one has to deal here with the three most important migratory phenomena and processes: first, the economic and partly political emigration to foreign countries at the end of the 19th and the beginning of the 20th centuries (caused on the one hand by the population explosion after the abolition of serfdom and the agrarian reforms of the 19th century, and on the other by the economic and social stagnation and underdevelopment in what used to be Polish lands, the result of their political division at the time between three occupying powers); second, the transfers of population in the 20th century, caused by the changes in the size and boundaries of the national territory, especially at the end of the Second World War; and third, modern industrialization and urbanization, the full, intense growth of which has taken place only since the last war, in connection with the development of the socialist planned economy.

The first of these three migratory movements and processes, although it ended practically with the First World War, has left significant disparities among various regions of Poland, with large tracts of densely populated agricultural land in the southern, eastern and some central parts of the country, and areas of much smaller densities in the remaining parts. The densities in the former areas were so large that they were considered in the interwar years to be grossly overpopulated and characterized by "hidden unemployment," i.e. overemployment in agriculture. As a result, these areas served in the postwar period as the main sources of new population in the resettlement of the western and northern parts of the country, recovered after the war; in the last thirty years they have supplied the largest number of migrants to the urban and industrial agglomerations, yet the fragmentation of peasant holdings and the dispersal of agricultural settlements were and are still significantly high.

The second process of the postwar resettlement has diminished the earlier differences in the distribution of the population but it has very greatly increased the age-structure variances because of the dominance of younger people among migrants. The northern and western regions have areas of very high rates of natural increase, which will tend to recur (although on a slowly diminishing scale) with every generation (i.e., every 25–30 years).

The third process, the migrations to industrialized or urbanized zones (both old and traditional or new), reached its peak intensity in the fifties; in spite of a certain slowing down it is still continuing strongly. It leads to heavy concentrations of population around the largest industrial and urban centers. The research carried out for almost twenty years by A. Jelonek indicates some significant changes in the importance and influence of these migratory waves on the actual population distribution and on structural differences of the population by regions. His studies show that the regional differences created by the first two migratory movements are losing their importance and are slowly fading away. They have been replaced by the spreading of industrial civilization and urban culture. But this is neither a simple phenomenon nor is its structure straightforward. Even migration patterns themselves do not present a consistent picture.

One explanation, a traditional interpretation, is that the population tends to concentrate in industrial and urban areas (the larger the city, the bigger the concentration) and that the process of polarization into urban and rural ways of life is going on at a steadily increasing rate. A closer analysis, however, shows that this is a very schematic and evidently an oversimplified point of view. First, the line of division between rural and urban seems to have changed. It runs now rather between urban agglomerations and larger cities on one side, and the remaining areas with their characteristic local rural-urban settlement complexes on the other.

But even this corrected view is oversimplified. Urban agglomerations, with their specific population structures, are growing but their growth is based on an influx of population from the outside. But areas that are increasing in size and relative importance have to be contrasted with other areas that are losing population and relative importance. However, the latter do not fully correspond to the agricultural and rural territories. The outflows are not the same everywhere. To understand this phenomenon it is necessary to study the mechanism of migrations.

Research carried out in the Institute of Geography of the Polish Academy of Sciences gives some insight into this question. A. Zurek, in her monograph on migrations to cities and towns in the voivodship of Kielce, shows that there exist three different types of rural-urban migration: local, regional and interregional.

Two main motives lie behind these migrations: the search for work and the search for better living conditions. A third one which is sometimes mentioned, i.e. the reunion of families, may be treated as secondary when one considers that people live in families and all migrations of individuals are in reality migration of families, even when the migration of some members of the family is delayed in time. To the search for work (supply) corresponds the search for workers (demand). The first is expressed spatially by the distribution of productive population, the second by the labor market. It is obvious that the urban agglomeration and larger industrial regions represent highly concentrated labor markets—hence their attraction and importance; while the rural, mainly agricultural areas represent very dispersed labor markets—hence their small power of attraction. The second motive, i.e. the search for better living conditions, is much more difficult to identify. However, recent sociological studies indicate that such aims (as far as the living conditions are concerned) are very similar among various groups, types of settlement, and regions and that only in cities with over 100,000 inhabitants are the available services generally considered to be relatively satisfactory. In addition, in their choice of services people are starting to be more selective. For instance, generally speaking parents consider the services available for their children to be of greater importance than those available for themselves. This of course means that urban agglomerations and larger cities have at present an additional power of attraction. Whether, with rising living standards, some other areas with more agreeable natural environments will become major points of attraction for migrants is still an open question, though this seems likely in the light of recent evidence.

However, there exists at present a very effective constraint on a stronger influx of immigrants to the large cities, namely, the lack of available housing. Workers in these cities often have to wait for years before obtaining a satisfactory place to live. As a result rural-urban migrations take a distinctly different form depending on whether they are directed to smaller towns or to larger cities.

It may be said that the influx into smaller towns is similar to the traditional model, i.e., the surplus of younger and more active groups of the population in search of nonagricultural employment moves into these towns. In labor-shed terms, the drainage areas of such towns are comparatively large but the number of migrants is not very high. The spatial pattern of drainage areas develops according to patterns of central place theory, with some hierarchical elements (drainage areas of towns of higher order superimposed on places of lower order).

In the case of larger cities there are two patterns. First, central areas have a high influx from comparatively small areas (the immigrants had already been working in and commuting to the central area, but after receiving a suitable dwelling they moved there permanently). Second, there is a surrounding ring of rural areas and adjacent smaller towns into which migrants moved from a more distant outer ring (or drainage area), mainly in order to commute to the central area.

It is characteristic of the present situation that with very few exceptions the influx to the outer ring is greater (although dispersed over a much larger surface) than the influx to the central area. Thus, there are two or even three-stage migrations, often within the lifespan of one generation. The question whether this type of rural-urban migration is stabilized and permanent or whether when the deficit of housing is liquidated it will first diminish and then disappear remains open. An additional stage of migration, characteristic of large urban agglomerations, may take the form of a movement from the central area to the inner suburban ring in search of better living and environmental conditions. This stage may also be connected with the construction of satellite (and, at the worst, dormitory) towns and cities.

The first or traditional type of rural-urban migration is essentially local and only rarely regional in scale; the second most prevalent in terms of the number of migrants involves larger cities (urban agglomerations) and regional drainage areas. Another type of rural-urban migration, which is interregional in scale, concerns only the largest agglomerations, whose deficit of manpower is so large that they have to draw migrants from the most distant regions (with the phenomenon of intervening opportunity strongly influencing the spatial patterns). This type of migration has been observed so far only in the case of the Upper Silesian Mining and Industrial Region. Some traces have also been evident in the case of Warsaw, the political and cultural capital of the whole country, as well as in some of the new mining and industrial districts. However, from the point of view of interregional migration, the most important movements are, and increasingly will be, urban-to-urban, including those between urban agglomerations and those from smaller towns to larger cities. The first reflect adjustments in the distribution of skilled personnel; the second are caused by better possibilities for employment in larger cities and by better conditions of living there, especially where services of a higher order are concerned. The future of migration from smaller towns to larger cities is not very clear. There are two opposite tendencies. On the one hand, with growing standards of living the services now available only in the largest cities may also be present in the smaller ones; at the same time, the growing concentration of population may easily lead to deterioration of the quality of the environment and of living conditions. On the other hand, with technological progress and given the essentially polycentric structure of the network of urban agglomerations in Poland, their attractiveness may not diminish but may grow even stronger over time.

In discussing interregional migration problems in present-day Poland another type of migration also has to be taken into account. The Poles possess, generally speaking, a very strong sense and even love of the locality and region where they were born and have grown up. Thus, the phenomenon of return migration occurs frequently whenever new possibilities for nonagricultural employment are created or when the conditions of living improve significantly in the regions from which the migrants originally came. Return migration may also occur at retirement age.

In assessing the spatial patterns of migration it is necessary to take into account the differentiation which exists in spatial patterns of labor markets for men and women. Such differentiation is a direct result of the dominance of men or women in various professions and employment groups. In particular, men form a strong majority among miners, in heavy industries and in building and construction industries; women are employed mainly in light industries and in services. Moreover, there is a general prevalence of women in the field of education, especially in humanities. The spatial consequence of this division is that there is a larger than average percentage of women in the central areas of cities (sometimes up to 130 women per 100 men), with a close positive correlation between the size of the city and the percentage of women. On the other hand, in areas with a greater influx of industrial workers, (in particular in new mining and industrial districts), as well as in the suburban areas of rapidly-growing agglomerations, the number of men is higher than that of women.

Such differences in the distribution of male and female populations have consequences for the development of family life and rates of natural increase. In eastern regions with very low-quality rural housing the rates of natural increase are significantly (even 50 percent) higher in cities than in the surrounding communes.

The greater influx of women to urban agglomerations has its correlate in their outflow from rural (especially backward) areas and is marked by a negative influence on families and on natural increase. The fall of the birthrate in some rural areas is very rapid and in fact there are already some areas where the indices do not show a marked difference from those of large cities or urban agglomerations.

Therefore with the steady growth of urban agglomerations specific social support for young families seems to be necessary, even if the simple reproduction of population is to be achieved. Incidentally, this may involve changes in housing policies and even efforts to diminish the rates and the tempo of migration from rural to urban areas, steering people away from the largest concentrations.

Thus the next issue which obviously must be considered and scrutinized in this context is the settlement system and its problems. It will be recalled that in present-day Poland there are three main forms of settlement, three specific settlement subsystems; first, urban agglomerations; second, regional and subregional centers (some of which will certainly grow into urban agglomerations); and third, local rural-urban complexes. These were recently made the basis for the administrative-territorial division of the whole country into the smallest units, grouping all agricultural settlements around the largest one (usually a small town), in which all basic services, and especially those of a higher level, are to be concentrated. The hypothetical existence of such subsystems has been confirmed by research findings to date.

Research into structures of local settlement complexes indicates the existence of large regional variations. No model can serve all cases; in fact, the prevalent opinion holds that settlement policies should vary regionally. At issue is the optimal degree of concentration of services and of dwellings. These depend on the natural environment (and needs for its conservation), on the value of the settlement pattern as it has developed historically, on the fixed assets represented by the existing buildings and transport lines, and on other factors.

The regional centers and smaller and younger urban agglomerations are developing at much higher rates than the largest agglomerations. This phenomenon is typical not only of Poland but also of other more developed countries. It is taken into account in the national plan of physical development up to 1990, which calls for a strengthening of the polycentric, moderately-concentrated structure of settlement at the regional level.

The number of developed, developing and potentially developing agglomerations is such that the whole country may be considered in the future as a set of urban regions, each of which has an agglomeration in its center. Some larger agglomerations may grow to cover whole urban regions, in which cases the respective regions and the agglomerations will become identical. There may even be cases where agglomerations overflow regional boundaries. But for a long time to come in the majority of regions there will be some differentiation between the area of the agglomeration and that of the region. It may be interpreted in terms of migration rings. The central area with a suburban ring will form the agglomeration proper; the outer ring and the migratory drainage zone will form the remaining part of the region. From the social point of view it is very important that every settlement or community in this outer zone should have easy access to the higher-level services located in the agglomeration, mostly in its central area. Another possible new pattern would involve a discontinuous and dispersed structure of agglomeration, with elements of all three zones (central, suburban and remaining) being fragmented and intermingled. Such a pattern is highly probable (perhaps it already exists) but it will involve the need for very careful and stringent planning.

These three basic forms of settlement are each heavily involved in problems of migration and natural increase. The local settlement complexes having the highest rates of natural increase generate flows of migrants. Higher wages, urban culture and better living conditions have been the economic and social factors inducing such flows, but such a characterization has to be qualified. The increased migration of younger people, in particular of women, has led in recent years to a significant fall in rates of natural increase. Additional factors which may impede further migration are the socialization of agriculture (transforming farmers into wage earners with limited hours of work), the improvement in living conditions and services in rural areas, and the spread of the urban way of life there through easily accessible mass media. So in the future only those areas where emigration has not distorted the age structure will be able to supply migrants to other urban areas larger and more distant than local service centers. Such areas are located mainly in the northern part of the country. The regional growth centers, if they are to grow, will have to absorb to a greater extent and at a faster rate population surpluses from rural areas and smaller towns within their own regions. For the next twenty or thirty years perhaps there are still sufficient reserves for such migrations. The positive factor is that they are still able to ensure the simple reproduction of their present populations.

The large urban agglomerations are in the worst position. Even maintaining their populations at the present levels involves immigration. Their growth has been completely dependent on the influx from other areas. The magnitude of their needs will make interregional migration necessary. The northern part of the country is in the best position, because migrants move shorter distances and do not encounter serious intervening opportunities. The urban environment of these regions is healthier and amenities are higher in quality. The surrounding regions possess at present the highest natural increase and birth rate indices and all available information suggests that the relative proportions between these regions and other parts of the country as far as birth rates are concerned will remain unchanged. For the first time the number of urban immigrants in relation to the total population is higher in these areas than in the southern and central regions. This means there already has been a complete change in relation to past directions of population movement.

Given the state of our present knowledge it may be concluded that to preserve and to ensure even a moderate population growth rate in urban agglomerations, without at the same time endangering the population equilibrium of the whole nation and of settlement subsystems, significant changes in family models and in the natural increase of population in those agglomerations are necessary. This requires specific policies concerning population, housing and services. In addition, it should be stressed very strongly that such national policies should be regionally adjusted and diversified.

REFERENCE

Institute of Geography of the Polish Academy of Sciences (1976), "Rozmieszczenie i migracje ludności a system osadniczy Polski Ludowej (Distribution of Population, Migration and the Settlement System of People's Poland), *Prace Geograficzne, 117*, Warszawa and Wrocław.

Chapter 7

Population Concentration and Regional Income Disparities: A Comparative Analysis of Japan and Korea

Koichi Mera

INTRODUCTION

In most countries, national policy-makers are seriously concerned with the increasing concentration of economic activities and population in primate cities. Although the economic damages which are thought to result from such concentration may not be real [1], they create socio-political problems which are essentially related to the distribution of opportunities. Consequently, an increasing number of countries have started to adopt "decentralization policies;" this study is addressed to the question of population concentration as related to such policies.

In a paper dealing with the Japanese experience concerning population concentration in the largest metropolitan areas, I noted an extremely rapid shift of population into the largest metropolitan areas during the period of rapid economic growth and a declining rate of concentration after about 1970 [2]. After examining alternative factors which might have contributed to population concentration, the paper concludes:

The foregoing analysis has revealed that the recent emergence of a new pattern of population shifts, which can be characterized by a lesser degree of incremental population concentration in large metropolitan areas and a lesser number of depopulating prefectures, does not necessarily imply changes in the preferences of the population. Rather, it can be explained by continuing changes in economic variables. Specifically, the slowing down of the economic growth rate and the declining income disparity among prefectures are considered to be largely responsible for the recent change. It is to be emphasized that these two factors outweighed the continuing upward trend of population concentration which can be considered to be a result of general improvement in transport and communication over time. Intensified concern over the environment and a possible change in values in life might have contributed to some extent to the change, but the evidence is too uncertain to conclude this [3].

In the variables mentioned above, income disparity among regions is, as was noted earlier by Williamson, related to economic growth [4]. In the case of Japan, the converging trend of income disparity began in 1961 and has continued since then in parallel with a generally high rate of economic growth. Convergence started before the implementation of government policies for decentralization of major economic activities.

Therefore, it can be inferred, as Williamson found earlier, that as the economy develops from a low level, income disparity among regions intensifies for some time, but when a certain stage of development is reached income disparity begins to decline with economic development. Thus, economic growth and regional income disparity tend to intensify population concentration during the initial phase of development, but during the second phase the trend for greater population concentration will be substantially reduced or even reversed as regional income disparity diminishes. Therefore, the problem of population concentration is "a temporary problem for developing countries" [5]. In this view a higher and sustained rate of economic growth appears to be a means for overcoming the problem of population concentration in developing countries.

Although it would be a temporary problem, it still might take several decades before the problem of population concentration is ameliorated to a satisfactory level (this appears to have been the case with Japan). If so, the economic growth approach to the problem of population concentration, as suggested by me, would be too roundabout to consider seriously.

Recently, I have had an opportunity to examine spatial population distribution issues in the Republic of Korea. What is striking in this case is the fact that similar developments have been taking place but at much faster rates and earlier in relation to "the level of development." The Korean case implies that the economic growth approach may be successful in coping with the problem of population concentration within a time span of about ten years and that this may be true for a number of developing countries.

The Japanese and Korean cases are of interest because each country has gone through both the ascending and descending stages of regional income disparity. In this chapter I shall attempt to identify the causes of differences in the two cases and attempt to draw policy implications.

THE JAPANESE EXPERIENCE

The growth rate of population has varied widely among the 47 prefectures. Since World War II the general situation has been one of increasing concentration into the two largest metropolitan areas, the Capital Region and the Kinki Urban Region, which have Tokyo and Osaka as their respective centers [6]. Within these urban regions, the population growth rates of prefectures were generally higher than the national average rate of growth and often exceeded 6 percent per year (Figure 7—1). The growth rate was generally higher in the Capital Region; the Tokyo prefecture recorded the highest rate among the four prefectures in the region in almost every year from 1952 to 1959, but since then the surrounding prefectures of Kanagawa, Saitama and Chiba have grown more rapidly. As a result of generally high growth rates in the Capital Region, its share of the national population increased from 15.69 percent in 1950 to 23.26 percent in 1970. The Kinki Region also increased its population share from 8.62 percent in 1950 to 11.85 percent in 1970.

In contrast, most prefectures in the Northeast and Western Regions have had declining shares of the national population in every year since 1950. The share of the six northeastern prefectures as a group went from 10.84 percent in 1950 to 8.71 percent in 1970 and the seven Kyushu prefectures went from 14.55 percent to 11.63 percent during the same period [7].

This pattern of shifts in population distribution also can be seen in the number of depopulating prefectures. According to population registration records maintained by the Ministry of Local Autonomy, the number of "rapidly depopulating prefectures" (RDP), which are defined to be those prefectures having a growth rate of population more than 1 percentage point below the national mean, exceeded 20 in six years out of nine from 1952 to 1960, and ranged from 20 to 28 between 1961 and 1970. However, since then, the number has been declining (there was only one in 1975), indicating a marked departure from the past trend (see Table 7—1).

The pronounced change in the shifts of population distribution can also be seen in the degree of change in population concentration in the largest metropolitan regions. This variable can be measured by the proportion of the annual incremental population which has been absorbed within them. Two alternative measures will be used for the purpose of analysis:

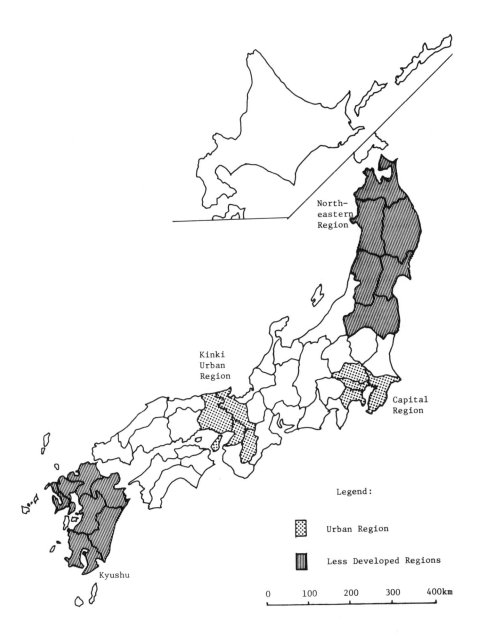

Figure 7–1. Urban Regions and Less Developed Regions in Japan

Table 7–1. Selected Development Indices: Japan, 1954–1975.

Year	PCC[1]	PCCK[1]	GR[2]	ID1[3]	ID2[3]	T	TD	RDP[4]
1954	27.0	42.5	2.8	93.9	0.18	0	0	6
55	26.9	45.4	10.8			1	0	4
1956	33.0	53.6	6.2	99.1	0.20	2	0	15
57	44.3	67.2	7.8	93.3	0.20	3	0	21
58	37.0	59.3	6.0	91.2	0.19	4	0	20
59	43.9	71.4	11.2	93.7	0.19	5	0	24
60	62.2	94.6	12.5	94.1	0.19	6	0	21
1961	75.9	120.0	13.5	99.5	0.20	7	0	22
62	86.4	132.5	6.4	97.8	0.20	8	0	24
63	64.4	99.8	12.5	92.8	0.20	9	0	22
64	62.1	91.6	10.6	90.8	0.19	10	0	24
65	61.7	90.7	5.7	84.9	0.17	11	0	28
1966	72.3	103.1	11.1	83.2	0.16	12	0	21
67	74.2	117.9	13.1	80.0	0.16	13	0	21
68	87.9	127.5	12.7	78.5	0.15	14	0	23
69	82.8	117.1	11.0	78.3	0.15	15	0	20
70	67.3	95.5	10.4	77.9	0.16	16	1	21
1971	49.7	72.5	7.3	73.3	0.15	17	1	18
72	44.7	64.5	9.8	71.1	0.15	18	1	13
73	39.1	56.4	6.1	66.8	0.13	19	1	7
74	35.4	50.7	-0.6	65.8	0.13	20	1	3
75	37.1	51.8	1.6			21	1	1

Sources: 1. Computed from Japan Ministry of Local Autonomy, *Population and Household Statistics, 1976* (Tokyo: Ministry of Finance Printing Office, 1976).

2. Japan Economic Planning Agency, *Annual Report on National Income Statistics, 1975* (Tokyo: Ministry of Finance Printing Office, 1975) for 1954 to 1973 and Japan Economic Research Center, *Quarterly Economic Projections* for 1974 and 1975.

3. Mera, *op. cit.*, p. 11 for 1955 to 1972 and Japan Economic Planning Agency, "Outline of Prefectural Incomes, 1974," mimeographed, 1976, for 1973 and 1974.

4. Mera, *op. cit.*, p. 5 for 1954 to 1974 and Ministry of Local Autonomy, *Population and Household Statistics, 1976*, Tokyo, Ministry of Finance Printing Office, 1976, for 1975.

PCC — Percentage of incremental population absorbed in the
Capital Region, and

PCCK — Percentage of incremental population absorbed in the
Capital and Kinki Urban Regions together.

The values of these indices during the past 22 years are presented in Table 7−1.

As discussed, the rate of population concentration is postulated to be a function of the following factors:

1. the change in value orientation from economic affluence toward environmental amenities;
2. the rate of economic growth;
3. the degree of income disparity among prefectures, and
4. the time trend.

The change in value orientation is not directly measurable, but it is believed to have set in around 1970 [8]. Therefore, it will be represented by a time dummy variable (TD) which takes the value of one since 1970 and zero before.

The growth rate of the economy (GR) is considered to be a factor causing population concentration; a considerable literature confirms a positive association between population concentration and economic growth [9]. Interregional income disparities have been used already to explain migration flows within Japan [10].

Two alternative indices of income disparity will be used for analytic purposes:

Range of Income Disparity (ID1)
- the difference between the highest and the lowest indices of prefectural per capita personal income when the national average is set at 100, and

Coefficient of Variation (ID2)
- the unweighted coefficient of variation of all prefectural per capita incomes

The values of these variables are presented in Table 7−1 and graphically shown in Figure 7−2. The table also shows the time variable (T), which represents the general trend. This trend may be interpreted to represent general improvements in interregional transportation and communication over time.

As can be seen from Figure 7−2, the rate of population concentration stayed at a high level from 1960 to 1970 and peaked in 1962

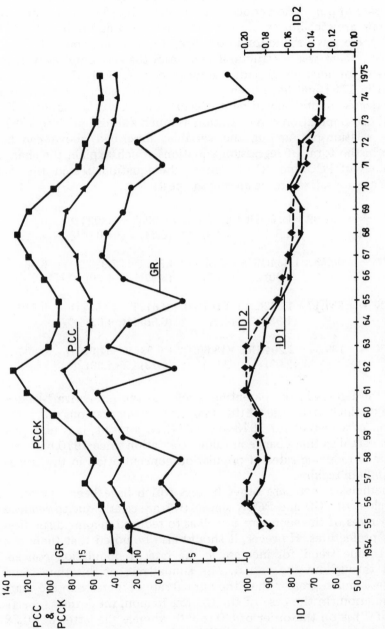

Figure 7–2. Selected Development Indices: Japan, 1954–1975

Source: Table 7–1.

and 1968. A high rate of economic growth started in 1959 and was more or less maintained until 1972. Consequently, it can be said that a high rate of population concentration was induced by a high rate of economic growth, but as the economy kept growing for an extended period there was a reduction in the rate of population concentration. However, there was a structural change in the economy, as seen in the trend of income disparity among regions. Both ID1 and ID2 peaked in 1961 and have been generally declining since then. With a lower degree of income disparity, economic growth apparently did not induce population concentration as much as it did prior to 1961.

The relationship among the variables described above can be shown in the form of regression equations which explain the changing values of PCC and PCCK. Among the equations tested, the following are considered to be among the best:

$$R$$

1) PCC $= -182.99 + 1.190\text{GR} + 2.041\text{ID1} + 6.026\text{T} - 30.92\text{TD}$ 0.915
   $\quad\quad\quad\ \ (1.83)\quad\quad (3.89)\quad\quad (6.64)\quad (-4.02)$

2) PCC $= -90.55 + 1.434\text{GR} + 535.6\text{ID2} + 4.955\text{T} - 37.97\text{TD}$ 0.881
   $\quad\quad\quad\ (1.90)\quad\quad (2.63)\quad\quad (5.37)\quad (-4.36)$

3) PCCK $= -281.17 + 1.832\text{GR} + 3.181\text{ID1} + 8.619\text{T} - 43.95\text{TD}$ 0.919
   $\quad\quad\quad\quad (1.98)\quad\quad (4.27)\quad\quad (6.68)\quad (-4.02)$

4) PCCK $= -139.84 + 2.204\text{GR} + 848.60\text{ID2} + 6.996\text{T} - 54.92\text{TD}$ 0.883
   $\quad\quad\quad\quad (2.02)\quad\quad (2.88)\quad\quad (5.23)\quad (-4.36)$

where the figures in the parentheses refer to the respective t-values.

One distinct advantage of this analysis over my previous one is the addition of variables for 1973 and 1974. As a result, it is now possible to establish that change in value orientation since 1970 has been a factor in reducing rates of population concentration in the largest metropolitan regions.

Nonetheless, there are other factors which have been operative. Low values of PCC and PCCK since 1971 are clearly due to reduced growth rates of the economy as well as to reduced income disparities among prefectures. However, it should also be noted that there is a distinct time trend for increase in the rate of population concentration throughout the period. The annual rate of this time trend increase is much greater than the annual rate of increase in the share of population. In the case of the Capital Region, the former (coefficient of T) is on the order of 5.0 to 6.0, whereas the latter was 0.38 on the average from 1950 to 1970, since its population share increased by 7.6 percent during the 20-year period.

Comparing the situation in 1974 with that of 1961 in terms of Equation 1, each factor contributed to the change in PCC as shown below:

Factor	Contribution to Change in PCC [11]
GR	−17
ID1	−69
T	78
TD	−31
Net Change	−39

Thus, it can be concluded that the reduction in regional income disparities has been the most important factor in reducing the rate of population concentration in the Capital Region in the past. A similar statement can also be made for the rate of population concentration in the Capital and Kinki Urban Regions combined.

THE KOREAN EXPERIENCE

The Korean experience can also be expressed by similar variables, which are shown in Table 7−2 and Figure 7−4. Due to the use of census data, the rate of population concentration can only be derived for intercensus periods. Three indices for the rate of population concentration are used:

PCS — Percentage of incremental population absorbed in the Special City of Seoul,

PCC — Percentage of incremental population absorbed in the Capital Region comprising Seoul and Gyeonggi Province, and

PCCB — Percentage of incremental population absorbed in the Capital Region and the Special City of Busan together.

The rate of population concentration stayed at a low level until about 1966, but it went up sharply during the four-year period after 1966. During this period, the rate of population absorption in Seoul was particularly high. Since 1970, the rate of population concentration in these two metropolitan areas has declined. In particular, the rate of absorption in Seoul has dropped sharply. It is to be noted that this whole pattern of rise and fall is quite similar to the one observed in the Japanese economy during the past twenty years. But,

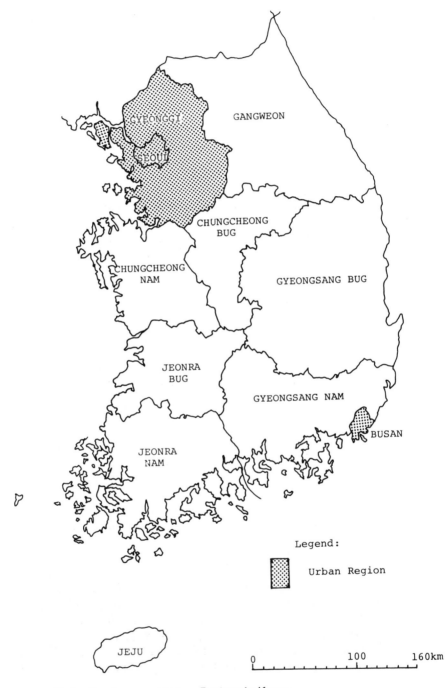

Figure 7-3. Provinces and Urban Regions in Korea

Table 7–2. Selected Development Indices: Korea, 1955–1975.

Year	PCS[1]	PCC[1]	PCCB[1]	GR[2]	ID1[3]	ID2[3]	MG[4]
1955				5.4			
56				0.4			
57				7.7			
58				5.2			
59				3.9			
60	25.1	36.2	40.9	1.9			
1961				4.8			
62				3.1			
63				8.8	92	0.266	
64				8.6	72	0.194	
65				6.1	94	0.291	
1966	32.4	40.9	47.2	12.4	110	0.337	
67				7.8	127	0.371	3.2
68				12.6	107	0.335	3.4
69				15.0	85	0.292	2.8
70	76.7	87.6	107.5	7.9	84	0.291	4.1
1971				9.2	62	0.224	4.3
72				7.0	65	0.213	3.4
73				16.5	66	0.241	4.4
74				8.6	57	0.218	4.8
75	41.7	62.7	80.4				

Sources: 1. Computed from Korea Economic Planning Board, *Korea Statistical Yearbook 1975 and Preliminary Release of 1975 Population Census.*

2. Bank of Korea, *National Income in Korea, 1975,* Seoul, 1975.

3. Computed from Korea Ministry of Home Affairs, *Annual Report of Gross Regional Products, 1972 and 1974,* and *1974 Estimates of Regional Incomes* (in Korean) and Robert R. Nathan Associates, Inc., *Seoul Metropolitan Region First Cycle Report, 1975,* p. 47.

4. Korea Economic Planning Board, *Yearbook of Migration Statistics, 1974.*

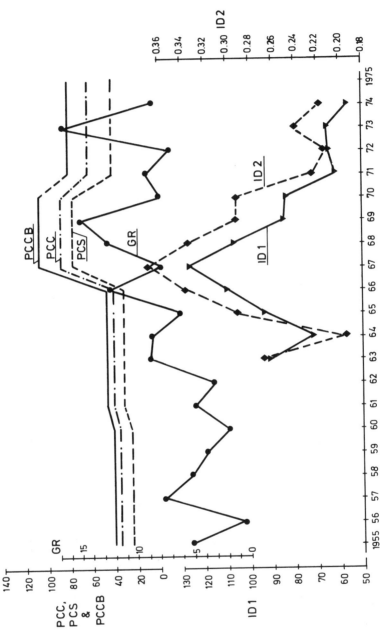

Figure 7–4.   Selected Development Indices: Korea, 1955–1975

Source: Table 7–2.

in Korea the process evolved in a much shorter span of time. As far as the last five to six years is concerned, the pattern is quite similar.

The growth rate of the economy, however, is not so similar. The growth rate went up in 1961 and stayed at a generally high level, and it is still going up rather than down. Therefore, in this case the change in the growth rate of the economy cannot explain the declining rate of population concentration.

This puzzle can be largely resolved by examining the trend in income disparities among regions. In terms of the range of disparity (ID1) or the coefficient of variation (ID2), regional income disparities were high from 1965 to 1970, reaching a peak in 1967. The high rate of population concentration in the largest metropolitan areas during the period must have been induced by a high rate of economic growth coupled with large income disparities among regions.

However, income disparities have been declining rapidly since 1967, which must have substantially removed perceived economic benefits derivable from migration to the largest metropolitan areas. It is noteworthy that the declining rate of PCC or PCCB is taking place in the face of increasing mobility of population since 1967, which is represented in Table 7–2 by

MG — Percent of interprovincial migrants in relation
to the total population.

Although no regression analysis can be undertaken due to insufficient population data, the relationships found in the Korean case are similar to those found in the Japanese case: economic growth and regional income disparities both initially increase the rate of population concentration. More recent declines in the rate of population concentration can be attributed to reduced income disparities among provinces. This process is taking place despite the increasing mobility of population among provinces.

INTERPRETATION OF THE TWO OBSERVED PATTERNS

The major findings can be summarized as follows: (1) the rate of population concentration has now passed its peak and is declining, and (2) the declining rate of population concentration is, wholly or in large part, attributable to declining income disparities among regions. Since the first finding is considered to be a result of declining regional income disparities during recent years, attention will now be turned to the trends observed in the two countries in this regard.

In Williamson's frequently-cited paper on regional income disparities and economic development, he states that:

> Increasing regional inequality is generated during the early development stages, while mature growth has produced regional convergence or a reduction in differentials [12].

According to this interpretation, the Japanese economy reached "maturity" around 1961 and the Korean economy around 1967, a difference of some 6 years. However, the level of development achieved by each country at its year of "maturity" cannot be said to be similar by almost any standard. As shown in Table 7−3, Japan in 1961 was far more developed than Korea in 1967 in terms of any of the indices shown. Similarity is found only in population density, which is not a development index by itself.

From the above comparison, it can be said that although the general rule of Williamson may hold true, the turning point in regional income disparities takes place within a wide range along the axis of development stages. This fact has an important policy implication. Williamson's rule may well be taken in a deterministic sense, in that the relationship between income disparities and economic development may be taken to mean that a nation should give up trying to reduce income disparities among regions until a certain, perhaps fairly advanced, stage of development is attained. But, the Korean case demonstrates that this stage could occur at a fairly early phase of development. If the experience of Korea is used as the basis and per capita income is taken as the index of development, 85 out of 125 countries listed in the World Bank Atlas already had passed this stage in 1973 [13]. In addition, 8 out of the remaining 40 countries which were below the per capita income level of $240 can reach this level by an increase in per capita income of 50 percent or less.

Granting that a wide range exists for the turning point, the next question is: what accounts for the early turn demonstrated by Korea? Geographic factors such as the small size of the country or physical features might be considered as possible factors. Although smallness might be a reason for having a lower degree of disparities, as expressed by our indices, it would not account for an early reduction in disparities. However, physical features might be a factor. The southeast and southern coasts are endowed with better natural conditions for ports for ocean-going vessels. In addition, these coastal locations are closer to the two major trading partners, the U.S. and

Table 7–3. Development Indices at "Maturity."

	Per Capita GNP in 1973 Dollars	Percent of Labor Force in Primary Sector	Per Capita Electric Power Generated (KWH)	Motor Vehicles Registered Per 1000 Persons	Population Density (Persons/km²)
Japan, 1961	1,300	29.8	1,384	24.4	250
Korea, 1967	240	55.2	166	2.1	299

Sources: For Japan, Office of the Prime Minister, *Japan Statistical Yearbook, 1975* (Tokyo: Ministry of Finance Printing Office, 1975), Economic Planning Agency, *Annual Report on National Income Statistics* (Tokyo: Ministry of Finance Printing Office, 1975).

For Korea, Economic Planning Board Bureau of Statistics, *Korea Statistical Yearbook, 1975* (Seoul: EPB, 1975).

Japan. These considerations might have helped the less-developed southern regions as the economy developed significantly through growth in exports, but they would not have been sufficient to alter the trend.

As far as explicit locational policies of the Government are concerned, none appears to have been instrumental. A National Land Construction Plan was prepared in 1967, but it merely paved the way for a more detailed national land-use plan which was completed in 1971. Dispersion of industrial development into less-developed regions became an explicit policy of the Government, but the relevant legislation was enacted only in 1970. A New Community Movement was started in 1970 and a tax aimed at discouraging residence in the largest metropolitan areas was instituted in 1973, but these deconcentration policies could not be credited for the declining income disparities since this process started in 1968.

One exception, however, is the pricing policy for farmers. Due to Government policies for farm products and inputs, the terms of trade for farmers started to improve in 1968 and the improvement was substantial from 1970 to 1973. The impact of the pricing policies can be seen in Tables 7-4 and 7-5, which show per capita income indices by province in current and constant prices, respectively. Although no estimate of per capita income is available for the Special City of Seoul from 1966 to 1969, data for the urbanized province of Busan are available. The terms of trade for the lowest-income province improved relative to Busan about 2 percent between 1967 and 1968, 6 percent between 1968 and 1969, and 9 percent between 1969 and 1970. The terms of trade for farmers from 1968 to 1975 are shown in Table 7-6. These figures indicate that the declining income disparities which started to appear in 1968 were largely due to pricing policies of the Government.

Nonetheless, the terms of trade for farmers cannot be improved indefinitely. In fact, they reached a peak in 1973 and since then they have been gradually eroding. However, income disparities have not necessarily widened again. Thus, Korea might have shifted the turning point in income disparities by several years by improving the terms of trade for farmers.

By the time the terms of trade reached a practical limit, other factors appear to have become operative in preventing regional income disparities from widening again. One would be the set of locational policies already described; another would be the maintenance of high growth of the economy for an extended period of time, which certainly has reduced the labor surplus within the economy. For example, within the agricultural sector, the percentage of workers who

Table 7–4. Index Values of per Capita Gross Regional Product by Province, Based on Current Prices, 1963–1974[a]

Province/City	1963	1964	1965	1966	1967	1968	1969	1970	1971	1972	1973	1974
Seoul	220	185	221	246	303	263	218	218	180	183	188	176
Busan	174	134	196	201	247	251	223	211	182	169	188	182
Gyeonggi	131	117	110	119	150	137	134	135	126	122	139	141
Gangweon	115	101	108	109	142	127	111	114	103	101	100	103
Chungcheong Bug	114	111	115	117	137	138	125	124	117	116	118	120
Chungcheong Nam	119	106	106	109	134	135	114	113	109	108	108	111
Jeonra Bug	123	115	108	108	117	114	110	113	109	112	101	106
Jeonra Nam	104	102	100	100	100	100	100	100	100	100	100	100
Gyeongsang Bug	120	106	118	111	130	123	117	109	106	104	107	111
Gyeongsang Nam	100	100	117	109	132	134	131	130	138	132	140	154
Jeju	108	113	146	125	133	149	124	116	113	112	122	121
Range of Disparity[b]	120	85	121	146	203	163	123	118	82	83	88	82
Coefficient of Variation[c]	0.266	0.194	0.291	0.337	0.371	0.335	0.292	0.291	0.224	0.213	0.241	0.218

Note: [a] The lowest province = 100.
        [b] The highest index minus the lowest index.
        [c] Standard deviation divided by the mean.

Source: Computed by the author from Ministry of Home Affairs, *Annual Report of Gross Regional Products, 1972 and 1974*, and *1974 Estimates of Provincial Incomes* and Bank of Korea, *National Income of Korea, 1975.*

Table 7–5. Index Values of per Capita Gross Regional Product by Province, Based on Constant Prices, 1963–1974[a]

Province/City	In Constant 1965 Prices								In Constant 1970 Prices				
	1963	1964	1965	1966	1967	1968	1969	1970	1970	1971	1972	1973	1974
Seoul	254	213	220	235	241	250	238	246	218	212	206	210	202
Busan	191	145	195	140	146	138	141	148	211	213	192	206	206
Gyeonggi	136	125	110	140	146	138	141	148	135	142	133	150	148
Gangweon	123	111	107	129	134	125	115	122	114	115	107	102	109
Chungcheong Bug	113	111	114	145	143	141	131	137	124	103	118	121	122
Chungcheong Nam	118	109	106	132	134	133	120	125	113	122	112	113	118
Jeonra Bug	124	118	108	130	112	111	112	114	109	100	111	101	105
Jeonra Nam	101	100	100	121	100	100	100	100	100	108	100	100	100
Gyeongsang Bug	123	109	117	137	132	124	122	123	109	100	108	110	116
Gyeongsang Nam	100	100	117	100	132	138	134	140	130	151	139	148	162
Jeju	109	105	145	150	142	162	137	123	116	120	116	124	132
Range of Disparity[b]	154	113	120						118	113	106	110	106
Coefficient of Variation[c]	0.329	0.253	0.292						0.291	0.296	0.222	0.283	0.257

Note: [a]The index is based on the lowest province = 100.
[b]The highest index minus the lowest index.
[c]Standard deviation divided by the mean.

Source: Same as in Table 7–4.

Table 7–6. Terms of Trade for Farmers, 1968–1975

Year	Index
1968	94.3
69	97.7
70	100.0
71	106.1
72	113.3
73	114.7
74	112.0
75[a]	111.6

[a] Average for the first eleven months.
Source: Economic Planning Board, *Monthly Statistics of Korea*, January 1976, pp. 77–78.

worked 26 or less hours per week declined from 25.1 percent in 1968 to 11.5 percent in 1974, and within the combined sectors outside of agriculture, it went down from 5.0 percent to 1.7 percent during the same period [14]. This reduction in surplus labor must have led to a narrowing of income disparities among regions. As far as the recent locational policies are concerned, their effects are known to have been rather marginal as of 1974.

Therefore, the substantial reduction in the rates of population concentration in Korea observed in recent years can be said to be mainly attributable to (1) the pricing policies for farmers, and (2) the maintenance of high growth of the economy. The first factor was predominant in the years immediately following 1967, but recent reductions are mainly due to the second factor. The high rate of economic growth works to reduce the rate of population concentration through reducing interregional income disparities.

CONCLUSIONS

Comparison of the development experiences of Japan and Korea reveals that Williamson's rule concerning regional income disparities and level of economic development leaves a wide margin of flexibility with respect to per capita income. Korea reversed the widening trend of income disparities at a substantially earlier stage than did Japan, initially by improving the terms of trade for farmers through pricing policies. When this approach was about to reach its limit, the high rate of economic growth, which had already been experienced for more than 10 years, started to have an effect by reducing income disparities among regions. This reduction apparently contributed materially to the recent slowing in the rate of population concentration in the primate urban regions. In the case of Japan, a process essentially identical with the latter just described also reduced income disparities and, subsequently, the rate of population concentration. But the process took a much longer period of time.

From the observation of these two cases, it appears quite probable that the maintenance of high growth of the economy is an effective way of reducing the rate of population concentration as well as reducing income disparities among regions once the economy reaches a certain stage. The Korean case also demonstrates the possibility of shifting the turning point in income disparities backward by several years through the use of pricing policies in favor of farmers. In this way Korea was successful in reversing the widening trend of regional income disparities when per capita GNP was only $240. The Korean experience is particularly encouraging for currently-developing countries, because of the success in reversing worsening trends at a fairly early stage of development.

NOTES TO CHAPTER 7

1. Refer to Alonso, William, "The Economics of Urban Size," *Regional Science Association Papers* 26 (1971), pp. 67–83 and Mera, Koichi, "On the Urban Agglomeration and Economic Efficiency," *Economic Development and Cultural Change* 21 (January, 1973), pp. 309–324.

2. Mera, Koichi, "The Changing Pattern of Population Distribution in Japan and its Implications for Developing Countries," to appear in *Habitat*; University of Tsukuba Institute of Socio-Economic Planning, Discussion Paper Number 4, November, 1975.

3. Mera, op. cit., p. 26.

4. Williamson, J.G., "Regional Inequality and the Process of National Development: A Description of the Patterns," *Economic Development and Cultural Change* 13 (July, 1965), Part 2.

5. Mera, op. cit., p. 28.

6. The Capital Region is defined here to comprise the prefectures of Tokyo, Saitama, Chiba and Kanagawa, and the Kinki Urban Region to comprise the prefectures of Osaka, Kyoto, Hyogo and Nara.

7. The Northeastern Region comprises the prefectures of Aomori, Iwate, Miyagi, Akita, Yamagata and Fukushima, and the Kyushu Region comprises the prefectures of Fukuoka, Saga, Nagasaki, Kumamoto, Oita, Miyazaki and Kagoshima.

8. The environment became a major political issue in 1970 and a task force was established within the Cabinet for establishing policies for pollution control and abatement. The Environmental Protection Agency was established in 1971.

9. Particularly, William Alonso, "The Economics of Urban Size," *Regional Science Association Papers* 26 (1971), pp. 67–83; Koichi Mera, "On the Urban Agglomeration and Economic Efficiency," *Economic Development and Cultural Change* 21) January 1973), pp. 309–324; and L.A. Sveikauskas, "The Productivity of Cities," *Quarterly Journal of Economics* 89 (August 1975), pp. 393–413.

10. Minoru Tachi, "Regional Income Disparity and Internal Migration of Population in Japan," *Economic Development and Cultural Change* 12 (January 1964), pp. 184–204; M. Shinohara, "Industrial Growth, Growth Regional Structure and Differentials in Japan," *Hitotsubashi Journal of Economics* (February 1967), pp. 1–37.

11. The contribution is defined to be the difference of the value of each variable in 1970 and its value in 1950, multiplied by the respective coefficients shown in Equation 1.

12. Williamson, *op. cit.*

13. Countries having a population of less than one million are excluded. The source is published by IBRD, 1975.

14. Economic Planning Board, Bureau of Statistics, *Korea Statistical Yearbook, 1975*, Seoul, 1975, p. 72.

Chapter 8

The Dynamics of Human Settlement Systems in Less Developed Countries: The Priorities for Urban Policy Formulation

Alan G. Gilbert

During the past decade our ideas about the nature of underdevelopment have changed profoundly. In the same period many new elements have entered our thinking about national settlement systems. Unfortunately, rather than leading to synthesis the two trends have diverged in terms of policy recommendation for the Third World. Many urban strategies have been intended for use in the developed nations and therefore fit uneasily with the kinds of problems facing urban areas and governments in most Third World countries. The problem is not that these strategies do not fit at all, it is rather that they are appropriate only to part of a more complex reality. And in tackling the problems afflicting one part of a whole, policy recommendations are in danger of accentuating the problems facing the poorer groups within Third World societies. It is the basic theme of this chapter that the urban problems of less developed countries often require different kinds of treatment than those of most developed countries. Appropriate policies can only be worked out if more regional economists, planners and geographers interested in urban problems pay specific attention to the situations of different poor countries. Currently, it is too often assumed that urban policies which have proved of value in developed countries will be equally useful in the poorer parts of the world. This study challenges that assumption and suggests that it rests on a misunderstanding of the problems facing most less developed countries.

THE PROCESS OF DEPENDENT
DEVELOPMENT

The 1950s were a period of optimism about the problems of the less developed world. As more and more countries in Africa and Asia became independent and were faced by the challenge of defeating poverty, development economists were not slow to suggest ways of achieving rapid economic growth. At the time relatively little interest was expressed in defining the nature of economic development and economic growth was commonly used in a laudative rather than in a perjorative sense. Interest seemed to focus less upon the nature of barriers to development than upon the ways in which such barriers might be overcome. Pessimistic views such as that of Boeke (1953) on the incompatibility of imported and indigenous cultures in a dual economy were in a minority compared to the predictions of a bright future. Foremost in his optimism was Rostow (1960), who at one point in his *Stages of Economic Growth* suggested that "the tricks of growth are not all that difficult" (p. 166). Today, few observers are so hopeful and few are willing to embrace the virtues of growth without severe qualification.

If I am correct in depicting the fifties as the age of optimism, then the seventies must surely be the age of pessimism. The United Nations Development Decades have passed almost without trace. Rapid rates of economic growth have been experienced in numerous Third World countries without solving the problems of the poor majority. And as a result of recent rises in petroleum prices, the dilemma of the poorest countries is apparent for all to see. Today, pessimism is rampant in the Third World development literature. Many elements which used to be seen as progress are now seen as further signs of underdevelopment. There has been a rise in the popularity of neo-Marxist interpretations such as those of Gunder Frank (1967a, 1967b). Attitudes to modern technology and company organization have changed dramatically. In the fifties, Higgins (1954) could argue that the introduction of modern techniques into poor societies would bring about development and higher material standards of life. While he believed that institutional and cultural barriers slowed down the process of development "they (were) not immutable . . . cultures can change with astonishing rapidity, and apparently with little pain, if the right formula is found." Today the benefits of modern technology are viewed more sceptically. Indeed an influential school of thought argues that it is the very intrusion of a foreign modern sector into indigenous cultures which originally stimulated the condition of underdevelopment.

Cardoso and Faletto (1969), Furtado (1970, 1972–73), Sunkel (1969) and other writers of the so-called "dependency" school have offered interesting insights into the present dilemma of Third World countries. The intrusion of capitalist modes of production into indigenous economies from the sixteenth century began the process of "dependent development." Under colonial rule most of today's Third World countries were turned into primary goods producers and into markets for the manufactured products of Great Britain and later the other developed countries. Before and after political independence this process created elites within these colonies whose economic interests were closely tied to the existing trade and dependency patterns. Attempts after the Second World War to reduce economic dependence by stimulating industrial development failed to resolve this problem. Rather than limit the power of the dependent elites, industrialization and import substitution frequently increased it and created other elites who benefited from it. In addition, forms of economic dependence were deepened. Instead of leading to the substitution of imports, industrial development created new demands for imported machinery and intermediate products. Rather than generating large scale employment opportunities, capital intensive technology produced goods but few jobs. Rather than reducing dependence upon foreign finance and technology dependent development encouraged higher levels of foreign debt as nations invested in new factories and urban infrastructure. The principal internal consequences of the process were far reaching. On the one hand, an enlarged "formal" sector emerged which offered material standards equivalent to those available in developed countries. On the other, a still larger "informal" sector was created where the population was partially integrated into modern life but left without the opportunity of achieving similar levels of living. In effect, dependent development perpetuated rather than removed the condition of dualism.

The general symptoms of dependent development are widely diagnosed in the literature. Even conservative institutions such as the World Bank now accept that an imbalance has been introduced into most Third World countries which demands new remedies (IBRD, 1975a; 1975b). Among the principal internal features of this process the following may be included.

First, the formal sector is dominated by large scale, high technology and capital intensive processes. The technology is imitative or is imported from the manufacturing plants of Detroit, Tokyo and Frankfurt. Limited numbers of workers earn above-subsistence salaries and are protected by social security benefits and trade union organization. Finance and commerce are increasingly dominated by conglomerates and by techniques of business imported from the developed world. Related to this sector but in some ways marginal to it are the activities of the informal sector. Productivity is generally low, the technology simple and organizational structures frequently personal. Those dependent on this sector suffer from low incomes and from high levels of underemployment. There is increasing evidence that operations in the formal sector harm those in the informal. Finance from the formal sector frequently takes over informal enterprises, products from the modern sector replace artisan goods, and legislation designed to protect workers in the modern sector reduces the demand for more workers. The formal sector is expanding but too slowly. It gradually employs more workers from the informal sector but cannot absorb the increases in the labor force occasioned by high rates of population increase. Increases in the *relative* size of the formal sector are associated with increases in the *absolute* size of the informal sector.

Secondly, the formal sector is dominated by foreign and transnational enterprises. Not only is the technology imported but the products manufactured in Buenos Aires or Khartoum are the same as those produced in the cities of the developed world. The problem that arises is that most of these products have been designed for high income populations. In the developed countries the majority have access to some if not all of these products. In the less-developed countries it is a minority who purchase most manufactured goods. It is clearly not in the interests of a transnational company to modify products on which a great deal of research and development has taken place. Once the product has been developed maximum profits can be achieved by encouraging subsidiary companies to produce it. The outcome in the poorer countries is that changes in product models occur frequently despite the fact that most potential consumers are excluded from the market. The formal sector is thereby dominated by expensive products with limited life spans, a tendency which accentuates differentials within the urban areas.

Thirdly, the bulk of the population is excluded from the formal sector and is unlikely to be absorbed in the future. It is unlikely that the poorest 80 percent of the population in most African countries will benefit from modern health care, own a car, or achieve secondary levels of education during the next fifty years. Because of the absolute growth rates of these populations and the limited ability of the formal sector to absorb labor the outlook appears bleak in most countries. The implications are serious insofar as the formal sector is revealing the advantages of modern life to increasing numbers of people without providing them with the means to satisfy their newly-awakened demands. Personal and regional inequalities in income, which it is often assumed will diminish as development occurs, will be perpetuated because high levels of material living can benefit only the few. Rather than disappearing the absolute numbers of poor will remain more or less constant. Economic development, therefore, is making more people richer than ever before but is unable to raise the standards of the majority.

Clearly the situations of different less developed countries vary. A glance at levels of per capita income in Asia, Africa and Latin America demonstrates the huge range of conditions included in that inadequate term, the Third World. But the difference in many respects is only one of degree. In Brazil or Argentina some 50 or 60 percent of the population may be absorbed by the formal sector by the year 2000; in Ethiopia or India the percentage is unlikely to rise above 15 or 20 percent. In many poor countries, the informal sector will persist and grow in size. Despite continuing per capita income growth rates of 5 percent or more there are few signs that economic development will eliminate widespread poverty.

THE URBAN CONSEQUENCES

The process of economic development has favored the concentration of human and financial resources in the urban areas. Industrialization has been encouraged by most Third World governments and has in turn stimulated urban growth. Infrastructure has been built to facilitate modern commercial and industrial development. This process of modernization has been financed in part by foreign loans. Private and public enterprises have borrowed money to build industrial plants; governments have entered into financial agreements to improve roads, increase electricity output and to provide better sewerage facilities. The opportunities for profit in the urban sector have encouraged private groups to invest in secondary and tertiary activities rather than in agriculture. The very process of urban development has created opportunities for land and building speculation. Many governments have oriented their investment programs towards the urban areas and in some cases agricultural marketing boards have shifted resources to the urban sector. In addition, policies such as subsidizing transport, maintaining low prices for agricultural products, and protecting home industry have favored urban activities at the expense of the rural sector.

Economic development in the urban areas has increased national wealth and created greater employment opportunities. One result has been the migration of large numbers of workers and their families from the rural areas and the small towns. In general the opportunities in the cities have attracted the better educated, more highly skilled and younger groups from the poorer regions of the Third World (Simmons, 1976). This concentration of more highly qualified groups is a possible further limit on the development potential of the rural areas though it has certainly stimulated economic expansion in the cities.

The process of economic development has led not only to urban growth but has encouraged metropolitan expansion. The scale of industrial operations, the quality of urban infrastructure, the concentration of higher income groups and the presence of the national bureaucracy are only some of the factors which have encouraged industrial activity to locate in the largest cities (Alonso, 1971b; Gilbert, 1974). Urban primacy and metropolitan dominance have increased in most places. Several enormous cities have emerged and within twenty years metropolitan complexes of 20 or 30 million people will exist in Latin America (Fox, 1975). Many governments have tried to slow this trend but few have had real success. The most likely modification is that resources will continue to concentrate in the main city regions but within those regions a process of deconcentration will take place. This is already occurring in the larger metropolitan areas of Latin America such as São Paulo, Buenos Aires and Mexico City (Rofman, 1974; Gilbert, 1974).

Economic development has had a distinctive effect on the cities themselves. Governments and international organizations are becoming increasingly concerned about the problem of unemployment (IBRD, 1975a; Friedmann and Sullivan, 1974). The shortage of high productivity jobs creates a mass of workers who are only partially employed or who are engaged in petty services and other low income activities (McGee, 1976). Although these workers are usually better off than their rural counterparts, they are faced by numerous difficulties in the urban areas. Insecurity of income and inadequate protection from the worst excesses of the free market make life difficult for a large section of the urban community. The physical consequences of this concentration of low income families is the emergence of spontaneous housing solutions (Dwyer, 1975; Abrams, 1964). Low income housing varies widely across the Third World but certain generalizations are possible. At the poorest levels are the street dwellers who represent a tiny fraction of the population in Latin American cities and a much higher proportion in cities like Calcutta. This group is unable to take advantage of even the worst accommodation. The slightly less poor tend to rent rooms in tenements in the decaying central areas or in the older established squatter settlements. The hope among this group is that they may eventually acquire their own property. Such an opportunity is normally available only in do-it-yourself forms, either in squatter settlements or in pirate urbanizations (that is on land which has been purchased but which lacks planning permission). Despite the problems facing these settlers spontaneous housing of this form normally offers the only real chance for urban consolidation (Turner, 1967). Given the right conditions, particularly security of tenure and a period of regular employment, these settlements gradually develop into ordinary low income communities. Services are gradually installed, either illegally or by canvassing the urban authorities, and conditions gradually improve. In most parts of the Third World such informal responses are the only means by which families can improve their housing conditions. Few governments are sufficiently prosperous that they can supply conventional housing for the poor. As a consequence most Third World cities are dominated increasingly by informal housing areas.

Parallel to the expansion of informal housing and employment solutions is the growth of the "modern" city. Car ownership rates have risen rapidly, urban motorways and underground railways have become increasingly common and large areas of attractive upper middle-class housing have developed. It is this juxtaposition of prosperity and poverty that is one of the basic features of Third World cities. The immediate threat of social revolution can be ruled out in most places, but one of the dilemmas of urban growth is that satisfying the needs of the formal sector often accentuates the difficulties of the urban poor.

Nowhere is this conflict better seen than in the social distribution of urban economies and diseconomies. At an aggregate level it is probable that urban economies outweigh urban diseconomies in most large cities. The evidence available in developed countries certainly suggests that per capita incomes and levels of productivity in large cities more than balance increased costs of living and producing in those cities (Hansen, 1975; Alonso, 1971; Mills, 1975; Richardson, 1973; Mera, 1973). It is also true that many of the problems which arise in large cities are the consequence of poor organization rather than of size *per se.* However, even if these arguments are correct the situation is only beneficial to the poorer groups insofar as they participate in the benefits and do not suffer disproportionately from the costs of urban growth. Unfortunately, I do not believe that this is the case nor do I believe that urban planners are always able to rectify the situation (Gilbert, 1976a).

Most urban groups suffer from diseconomies but, unlike the prosperous, the poor cannot avoid the worst consequences nor do they share in the urban economies. In the case of traffic congestion, for example, most groups suffer the consequences but whereas the poor tend to be crowded together on buses, the rich travel in their own cars. Most groups suffer from air pollution and high population densities, but while the higher income groups can afford to live in more salubrious and less polluted areas, the poor have little real choice over their location. Similarly the distribution of urban econo- mies is highly concentrated and the informal sector receive only minor advantages from agglomeration. Most of the advantages accrue to the formal sector and since employment opportunities in this sec- tor are limited, large groups are excluded from the benefits of urban expansion. There is no doubt that urban growth creates external economies but in most Third World cities the poor are largely ex- cluded from the benefits. In its most extreme form, therefore, the formal sector's expansion generates benefits for higher income groups but by stimulating rising land values, greater traffic volumes, air pollution, etc. creates problems which the poor cannot avoid. Quantification of this argument is clearly difficult but similar argu- ments have been offered in the context of cities in developed coun- tries (Harvey, 1973; Pahl, 1970). What is especially worrying in the Third World context is that planning seems unable to remedy the situation.

THE PLANNING RESPONSE

That the planners and administrators of Third World cities face an uphill struggle need not be emphasized. The fact that those cities form integral parts of less-developed economies means that resources are limited. Even though large urban complexes tend to absorb more than their population share of national resources the funds are always inadequate for the task. Many of the problems are worsened by the rates of population growth and the low levels of skill and education among Third World populations. In addition, the actions of urban authorities are normally constrained by the political environment of which they form a part. This environment is frequently conservative and does not permit policies which would restrict the private sector. Thus many elements of city growth which are contrary to the wider public interest cannot be controlled; good examples are the undesir- able effects of land speculation and increasing private car ownership. The dilemma of the urban authority in a less-developed country is that it is situated at the interface of conflicts between national, regional and local, formal and informal, and private and public interests. Many urban authorities are pawns in a much larger chess game over which they have no control. In such circumstances planners have little opportunity to implement effective programs. More common, however, is the situation where urban authorities can modify current conditions providing that they act swiftly, take advantage of fortuitous political situations and select appropriate strategies. What concerns me in this chapter is the relative shortage of appropriate strategies in the urban and regional planning literature. One reason is that wrong assumptions are often made about the nature of planning in less-developed countries, about the forms of urbanization and indeed about the process of development. Among such assumptions the following may be included.

Firstly, it is assumed that Third World cities will eventually resemble those in the developed countries today. The same assumption is also made about national urban systems and regional patterns of development, income and economic activity. Secondly, a related assumption is that many of the solutions to the difficulties of Third World cities can be found in the experience of the developed nations. While there is some truth in this belief there are also grave dangers. The solutions available from the developed world tend to be capital-intensive, high-technology approaches which require high levels of administrative ability. They are consequently often inappropriate to the needs of the poor cities. Moreover, their adoption often precludes the acceptance of simpler, lower technology strategies which may be more economical in terms of foreign exchange and may benefit greater numbers of people. Thirdly, urban and regional planners are optimists. They assume, as they must to maintain their sanity, that the quality and the effectiveness of planning improves over time. Experience, gradual improvements in the quality of planners and administrators, allied to a belief that politicians and military dictators cannot be as mindless as in the past, ensures that planning practice makes perfect. Empirical evidence provides only partial support for that optimism.

It is my contention that these assumptions are too often erroneous. As a result many of the strategies available to planners in the Third World are inappropriate. What is needed is a greater awareness on the part of "academic planners" of the reality of the Third World urban situation. While different cities require different solutions there is a need throughout the Third World to replace complex, imported high-technology strategies with simpler, local, low-technology approaches. If the typology of formal and informal sectors is accepted, a shift is required away from strategies which treat only the modern sector, to approaches which face up to the difficulties of the informal sector. If the informal sector will not eventually disappear then it must be organized and assisted; it is no longer adequate to assume that by encouraging the development of the modern sector the informal sector will fade away.

Clearly, there has been a movement in this direction in recent years. Approaches to housing the poor have been modified and site and service schemes have entered the conventional wisdom of planning. Nevertheless it is still true that urban policies tend to be oriented towards the formal sector. One example is the approach used in urban decentralization programs. Throughout Latin America and even in Africa and Asia the favored tools for decentralization have been growth-center strategies based upon industrialization (Stöhr, 1975; Gilbert, 1974). The fact that industrial employment occupies a small fraction of the population in many of these countries has not prevented planners relying wholly on this approach. Nor has the fact that growth has normally failed to spread from such growth centers led to their rejection (Robinson and Salih, 1971; Gilbert, 1975). Within Third World cities another example of the emphasis upon the modern sector can be seen in the approach to zoning and to traffic congestion. Most Latin American cities have been zoned along the lines of their North American counterparts. The more prosperous areas conform to these regulations and are preserved from the incursions of informal housing, but the poorer areas have not benefitted from planning at all. In fact where clandestine housing has developed which ignores the planning decrees it is often ineligible for public services. Similarly, approaches to traffic control have favored high technology solutions. Caracas and Rio have constructed expensive motorway systems rather than acting to control the flow of traffic. Mexico City, Lima, Rio, Caracas and San Juan have all opted for high technology underground railways rather than simpler solutions. Traffic engineers even more than urban planners are easily enticed by sophisticated solutions.

There is an important political element in the espousal of "big" projects. Few politicians are reluctant to use urban or decentralization programs for electoral purposes. The construction of concrete memorials for future generations to revere and contemporary electorates to applaud is all too common in Third World countries. The Perons, the Nkrumahs, the Sukarnos, etc. will continue to be attracted by popular schemes. What planners ought to provide is a means for channelling these gestures into more broadly based and less conspicuous programs. In order to do this the financing institutions such as the IBRD, IDB and the Export-Import Bank need to be convinced that planning for the informal sector is just as vital as that for the modern sector. Lenders, academic planners, politicians and urban administrators must be reminded constantly that planning and urban projects should be designed with all sectors of the population in mind. If the informal sector and poverty are likely to remain with us then they must be accommodated in the plans of the future.

A second, related problem is the belief among many planners that there is a fund of relevant urban strategies available in the developed nations. As I have argued elsewhere (Gilbert, 1976b) such a belief rests upon two assumptions; that urban policies have been effective in the developed countries and that they can be easily modified for use in the Third World. Neither assumption is water-tight. The new town policies in the United Kingdom or the Mezzogiorno program in Italy have contributed to the resolution of urban and regional problems in those countries. By no stretch of the imagination, however, can they be claimed to have resolved the problems which made such programs necessary. Indeed, very recently the British Secretary for the Environment questioned the wisdom of decentralizing industry and office employment at a time when the central city areas were suffering from high levels of unemployment.

Similarly, the assumption that urban programs can be transferred is subject to a series of difficulties. There are numerous barriers to transfer in the sense that the situations in less developed countries are often very different from those in the "donor" country. The level of resources available to implement projects obviously differs but in addition internal differences in language, religion, economic development and levels of education are often very dramatic within poor nations. Similarly there are major administrative and political barriers to successful planning in many Third World nations; the relationships between planners and politicians is often very different from the idealized situation presumed to operate in Western Europe or the United States. Finally, there is frequently an unwillingness or an inability to modify transferred techniques before use. Far too often reasonable approaches have been ruined by a failure to accommodate local reality.

Willingness to transfer techniques across cultures has been encouraged by the modern tradition of the social sciences. Generalization, cross-cultural comparisons and quantitative analyses are a vital ingredient in most social science approaches. Notwithstanding the advantages, there are dangers inherent in its influence on urban programs. One example is provided by the literature on innovation diffusion. The ideas of Lasuén (1969; 1973), Gould (1970), Pred (1966), Soja (1968), Pedersen (1970) and Berry (1969; 1972) had a major impact upon national settlement and economic decentralization programs in many Third World nations. The concept of hierarchical and spatial diffusion was integral to the widespread acceptance of growth-center strategies. Unfortunately, as Pred (1976) and Hansen (1976a) have reiterated, not all forms of diffusion spread in these ways. Still more vital is the fact that diffusion has been seen to be a desirable process whatever the innovation concerned. Little work until recently really questioned whether all forms of diffusion were desirable (Brookfield, 1973). The burden of work was upon demonstrating why the process of diffusion did not occur more rapidly, simulating diffusion processes, or recommending means by which it might be accelerated. The assumptions behind this approach are that diffusion is a neutral concept (which in certain respects it undoubtedly is); that the unfortunate effects of diffusion are frequently a necessary precursor to future benefits; and that inequalities brought by innovation diffusion will eventually be removed by natural forces. Unfortunately, reality seems to suggest that these assumptions are invalid. For example, the frequently-espoused view that regional income inequality rises to a peak and then declines as economic development proceeds has recently been disputed on the basis of new evidence (Williamson, 1965; Gilbert and Goodman, 1976). Convergence in regional incomes is not inevitable, especially once it is questioned whether all countries in the world will one day become developed. If current forms of dependent development are seen as a means of accentuating inequality or at best as a barrier to eventual widespread development, then this assumption is invalid. Many other similar examples might have been included.

Finally, much of the literature on urban planning in the Third World is predicated on the belief that the quality of urban administration will improve. Such an assumption must be used with care. In some respects it is clearly true; the quality of urban plans, the preparation of urban projects and the sophistication of arguments used in the literature on planning in the Third World have improved greatly. As planners, urban economists, transport engineers, etc. receive better training there is bound to be an advance. But growing sophistication of this kind is very different from the implementation of those plans and projects. The introduction of sensible plans often requires firm commitment by politicians and administrators but there is no evidence to suggest that the level of such commitment is bound to rise. Indeed implementation and growing sophistication frequently proceed in opposite directions. A recent sad example of this was the failure of the 1973 Colombian Census. Despite more sophisticated sampling techniques, better trained technicians and new computer facilities, the results were unreliable and have been shelved. If a process as comparatively simple as producing a census deteriorates over time why not urban and regional planning? Even if my pessimism is only partly right the lesson is clear—advice on urban planning should be as simple and as unsophisticated as possible. The quicker plans can be understood, the less sophisticated their technology, and the lower their cost, the more likely they are to be implemented.

CONCLUSION

So far my main argument has been that urbanization reflects the kind of economic and social development that is occurring in the Third World. The prerequisites for effective urban and regional planning, therefore, are a clear understanding of the nature of that development and an accurate assessment of the potential of different Third World countries to actually develop. Too often these prerequisites have been ignored and planners have been too optimistic about what could or could not be achieved. Such optimism has led to a continuing search for panaceas to underdevelopment. The key difficulty with such an approach is that beyond the discovery of oil very few panaceas are available. Consequently, the achievement of higher levels of material living is likely to be reached only after a long and a difficult struggle. Nor is there any single route that can guarantee a solution. Despite the important similarities which I have emphasized in this chapter, the internal characteristics and indeed the development potential of less developed countries differ widely. These differences are demonstrated in Table 8–1, which represents an attempt to classify the development and urban growth potential of different Third World countries. Whether or not one agrees with the details the fundamental point of this table is clear. Whatever the similarities between Brazil, Haiti, Upper Volta, Nigeria, India and Thailand, the differences among them are vast.

This very diversity demands that urban and regional development strategies be flexible. It is implausible to discuss the virtues and problems related to centralization or to agropolitan development without taking full account of differences in natural resources, development experience, class structure, distribution of income and political ideology. It is arguable that many offerings from spatial planners in the past have erred in this direction. Did not the appeal of the "growth center" lie in part in its universal applicability? Not only was it neutral politically and was therefore accepted in both communist and capitalist nations, but it was seen to be equally appropri-

Table 8—1. A Typology of Economic Development and Urban Growth Potential.

Type I. Those countries in which the process of urbanization is well underway. The population is already more than half urban, incomes relatively high and there is little pressure of population on arable land and natural resources. The end of the urbanization process will occur before the turn of the century when most of the population will be in urban areas and rural areas will begin to experience absolute declines. Category includes most of Latin America.

Type II. In these countries the urbanization experience is more recent. Over half the population is still in rural areas. Population pressures exist on the land and incomes are at relatively low levels. If population pressures can be eased and resource constraints overcome, this group of countries by the turn of the century should obtain levels of urbanization similar to those found in the Type I countries today. Category includes the semiindustrialized countries of Asia and North Africa such as Egypt, Korea, Malaysia and the Philippines.

Type III. This group of countries is predominantly rural but urbanizing rapidly. Even so, by the year 2000 they will still be predominantly rural with high rates of growth of the rural population. The outcome of the race between population growth and resources (and the resulting growth of per capita income) is uncertain. Category includes most of Africa south of the Sahara.

Type IV. These countries are dominated by severe pressures on the land in largely rural, subsistence-level-income societies. If the projected population growth rates are sustainable they will still be characterized in the year 2000 by large and growing rural populations living in absolute poverty. Category includes most of the large countries of Asia.

Source: IBRD (1975b), 5–11.

ate to developed and less-developed countries. Perhaps it was just this universality that was one of the reasons for recent disappointment with its effects (Hansen, 1972; Moseley, 1974)?

Clearly a balance between nomothetic and idiographic approaches is necessary. But at present the tendency is for the former to dominate our thinking and planning policies. When such an approach is associated with the search for panaceas to underdevelopment then the poor of the Third World are in danger of neglect more than salvation. It was for this reason indeed that I entered the debate about optimum city size (Gilbert, 1976). It seemed that despite the logic of the argument that it was not size *per se* which was the cause of urban problems but the nature of the society and its organization, the intellectual balance was being tipped towards a policy norm. Since such a norm would be appropriate in some societies but not in others a warning was necessary.

No urban or regional policy can ignore local political, social and economic realities. Unfortunately, due to the similar forms of training received by planners throughout the world and the impact of modern forms of communication, less-developed countries use strategies which were devised to solve specific difficulties in much richer societies. The consequence too often is that the new planning methods are applied to the formal sector of the poor economies and the informal sector is either neglected or even harmed by the new policies. Clearly the transfer of planning wisdom can be a two-edged sword.

Spatial planners need to devote more attention to the processes of underdevelopment and their local variations. We have begun to shift in that direction but there is still a long way to go. It still feels a little improper to be pessimistic in planning circles about the future of the Third World. Too many urban planners in poor countries want elegant and up-to-date solutions for their problems. If we are not careful more and more urban centers will be dominated by motorway systems, modern shopping centers and towering skyscrapers even where the majority of the population can never share in the benefits of a mass consumption society. The appeal of the sophisticated is universal but most less developed countries will imitate such sophistication at the expense of accentuating the differentials between the formal and the informal sectors. It is the duty of writers in developed countries who devise normative spatial strategies to draw attention to the dangers of their application in inappropriate circumstances. This is especially important when those strategies are large scale, expensive and sophisticated. If my contention that many Third World countries will fail to achieve high material standards of living is correct, then these countries require strategies which are small, cheap and simple. Small may not always be beautiful but in poor countries large can be very ugly indeed.

REFERENCES

Abrams, C. *Man's Struggle for Shelter in an Urbanizing World.* Cambridge, Mass., The M.I.T. Press, 1964.

Alonso, W. "Urban and Regional Imbalances in Economic Development," *Economic Development and Cultural Change, 17* (1969), 1—14.

Alonso, W. "The Economics of Urban Size," *Papers and Proceedings of the Regional Science Association, 26* (1971a), 67—83.

Alonso, W. "The Location of Industry in Developing Countries," in *Industrial Location and Regional Development,* edited by UNIDO. New York: United Nations, 1971b, 3—36.

Berry, B.J.L. "Relationships between Regional Economic Development and the Urban System: the Case of Chile," *Tijdschrift voor Economische en Sociale Geografie, 60* (1969), 283—307.

Berry, B.J.L. "Hierarchical Diffusion: the Basis of Developmental Filtering and Spread in a System of Growth Centres," in *Growth Centres in Regional Economic Development*, edited by N.M. Hansen. New York, The Free Press.

Boeke, J.H. *Economics and Economic Policy of Dual Societies*, New York, Institute of Pacific Relations, 1953.

Brookfield, H.C. "On One Geography and A Third World," *Transactions of the Institute of British Geographers, 58* (1973), 1–20.

Cardoso, F.H. and Faletto, E. *Dependencia y desarrollo en América Latina: ensayo de interpretación sociológica*. México D.F., Siglo Veintiuno Editores S.A., 1969.

Dwyer, D.J. *People and Housing in Third World Cities*. London, Longman, 1975.

Fox, R.W. *Urban Population Growth in Latin America*. Washington, D.C. Inter-American Development Bank, 1975.

Frank, A.G. *Capitalism and Underdevelopment in Latin America*. New York, Monthly Review Press, 1967a.

Frank, A.G. "Sociology of Development and Underdevelopment of Sociology," *Catalyst, 3* (1967b), 20–73.

Friedmann, J. *Urbanization, Planning and National Development*. Beverly Hills, Sage, 1973.

Friedmann, J. and M. Douglass, "Agropolitan Development: Towards a New Strategy for Regional Planning in Asia," in *Growth Pole Strategy and Regional Development Planning in Asia*. Nagoya, United Nations Centre for Regional Development, 1976.

Friedmann, J. and F. Sullivan. "Labour Absorbtion in the Urban Economy: the Case of the Developing Countries," *Economic Development and Cultural Change, 22* (1974), 385–413.

Friedmann, J. and R. Wulff. *The Urban Transition: Comparative Studies of Newly Industrializing Societies*. London, Edward Arnold, 1976.

Furtado, C. *The Economic Development of Latin America: A Survey from Colonial Times to the Cuban Revolution*. London, Cambridge University Press, 1970.

Furtado, C. "The Post–1964 Brazilian 'Model' of Development," *Studies in Comparative International Development, 8* (1972–1973), 115–127.

Gilbert, A.G. *Latin American Development: A Geographical Perspective*. Harmondsworth, Pelican.

Gilbert, A.G. "A Note on the Incidence of Development in the Vicinity of a Growth Centre," *Regional Studies, 9* (1975), 325–333.

Gilbert, A.G. (ed.) *Development Planning and Spatial Structure*. London, John Wiley, 1976a.

Gilbert, A.G. "The Arguments for Very Large Cities Reconsidered," *Urban Studies, 13* (1976b), 27–34.

Gilbert, A.G. and Goodman, D.E. "Regional Income Disparities and Economic Development: A Critique," in *Development Planning and Spatial Structure*, London, John Wiley, 1976, 113–142.

Gould, P.R. "Tanzania 1920–1963: the Spatial Impress of the Modernization Process," *World Politics, 22* (1970), 149–170.

Hansen, N.M. (ed.) *Growth Centres in Regional Economic Development.* New York, The Free Press, 1972.

Hansen, N.M. *The Challenge of Urban Growth.* Lexington, Massachusetts, Lexington Books, 1975.

Hansen, N.M. *Growth Strategies and Human Settlement Systems in Developing Countries.* Laxenburg, IIASA, 1976a.

Hansen, N.M. *Systems Approaches to Human Settlements.* Laxenburg, IIASA, 1976b.

Harvey, D. *Social Justice and the City.* London, Edward Arnold, 1973.

Higgins, B. "Economic Development of Underdeveloped Areas: Past and Present," *Ekonomi dan Keuangan Indonesia,* 1954.

IBRD. *The Urban Informal Sector.* Washington, D.C., Bank Staff Working Paper No. 211, 1975a.

IBRD. *The Task Ahead for the Cities of the Developing Countries.* Washington, D.C., Bank Staff Working Paper No. 209, 1975b.

Lasuen, J.R. "On Growth Poles," *Urban Studies, 6* (1969), 137–161.

Lasuen, J.R. "Urbanization and Development: The Temporal Interaction between Geographical and Sectoral Clusters," *Urban Studies, 10* (1973), 188.

McGee, T.G. "The Persistence of the Proto-proletariat: Occupational Structures and Planning of the Future of Third World Cities," *Progress in Geography, 9* (1976), 1–38.

Mera, K. "On the Urban Agglomeration and Economic Efficiency," *Economic Development and Cultural Change, 21* (1973), 309–324.

Mills, E.S. "Do Market Economies Distort City Sizes?" in *Issues in the Management of Urban Systems,* edited by H. Swain and R.D. Mackinnon, Laxenburg, IIASA, 1975.

Moseley, M. *Growth Centres in Spatial Planning.* Oxford, Pergamon Press, 1974.

Pahl, R.E. *Whose City?* London, Longman, 1970.

Pedersen, P.O. "Innovation Diffusion within and between National Urban Systems," *Geographical Analysis, 2* (1970), 203–254.

Pred, A.R. *The Spatial Dynamics of U.S. Urban-Industrial Growth 1800–1914: Interpretive and Theoretical Essays.* Cambridge, Massachusetts, M.I.T. Press, 1966.

Pred, A.R. "The Interurban Transmission of Growth in Advanced Economies: Empirical Findings versus Regional Planning Assumptions," Paper presented at the International Institute for Applied Systems Analysis, Laxenburg, 1976.

Richardson, H.W. *The Economics of Urban Size.* Westmead, Saxon House, 1973.

Robinson, G. and Salih, K.B. "The Spread of Development Around Kuala Lumpur: A Methodology for an Exploratory Test of Some Assumptions of the Growth Pole Model," *Regional Studies, 5* (1971), 303–314.

Rofman, A.B. *Dependencia, Estructura de Poder y Formación Regional en América Latina.* Buenos Aires, Siglo XXI, 1974.

Rostow, W.W. *The Stages of Economic Growth: A Non-Communist Manifesto.* London, Cambridge University Press, 1960.

Simmons, A.B. "Opportunity Space, Migration and Economic Development:

A Critical Assessment of Research on Migrant-Characteristics and Their Impact on Rural and Urban Communities," in *Development Planning and Spatial Structure*, edited by A.G. Gilbert, London, John Wiley, 1976, 47–76.

Soja, E.W. *The Geography of Modernization in Kenya.* Syracuse, Syracuse University Press, 1968.

Stöhr, W.B. *Regional Development Experiences and Prospects in Latin America.* The Hague, Mouton, 1975.

Sunkel, O. "National Development Policy and External Dependence in Latin America," *Journal of Development Studies, 6* (1969), 23–48.

Turner, J.F.C. "Barriers and Channels for Housing Development in Modernizing Countries," *Journal of American Institute of Planners, 33* (1967), 167–181.

Williamson, J.G. "Regional Inequality and the Process of National Development: a Description of the Patterns," *Economic Development and Cultural Change, 13* (1965), 3–43.

Part II

Systems Approaches
to Human Settlements

✳ *Chapter 9*

A Theory of Movements

William Alonso *

INTRODUCTION

In the past few decades a great many models of movement
have been developed in the social sciences, including input-
output models of the economy, models of urban traffic, of
migration, of social mobility, of the changes in status of employees
in organizations, and many more. The theory here seeks a more general theory of movement systems to offer a common logical and
mathematical framework, of which various particular models are
special cases.

Keep in mind what it is the theory does and what it does not do.
It does not speak to the empirical correctness of particular models,
and it does not offer, in itself, recommended alternatives. It does, I
hope, offer a more general framework for thinking about these diverse models, a common notation, and thus a way of comparing one
model to another in their logic and suppositions, many of which are
usually implicit and unrecognized. Thus, divergent empirical findings
and theoretical conclusions among models may stem not from the
perversity of nature, but rather from the fact that diverse investi-
gators draw various portraits of nature which differ at their inception
in the implicit logic of particular models. This more general framework may help to trace unrecognized implications of the forms of

*This work is being carried out under grant #SOC7681736 from the National
Science Foundation. This is an expanded version of my paper "A Theory of
Movements: (I) Introduction," Working Paper No. 266, Institute of Urban and
Regional Development, University of California, Berkeley, June 1976.

particular models and thus sometimes help to open new ideas or to discard old ones.

The theory is quite brief in its formal expression, but it is highly involuted, in that many variables are implicit functions of each other. This makes certain questions difficult to analyze except in the simplest cases. Further, the general theory is highly circular. Certain suppositions and relations may be used as a point of departure in the construction of certain models, while other relations are derived or implied from these first ones. In other models, on the other hand, first and derived relations may be quite the other way around. But the circularity and tautological nature of the theory is its strength: wherever particular models hop onto the circle, if logical consistency is applied, it will carry them all the way around. The exposition of the theory which follows. therefore, is only one way making this circle.

In the second part of the chapter I will use the theory to contrast various models of migration in common currency.

THE THEORY IN BRIEF [1]

Movements Originating from *i*

There is a number n of classes of origins and destinations. These classes may be regions, populations, occupations, and so forth according to the particular model. Movements out of class i depend on certain characteristics of this class and its population.

We may write this as

$$M_{ij} = v_i D_i^{\alpha_i} \qquad (9-1)$$

where M_{ij} = movement from class i to class j;

M_{ix} = $\Sigma_j M_{ij}$, total movements from i;

v_i = a function of characteristics of class i and/or its population;

D_i = the draw or pull of the system at i, a function of the relation of class i to the rest of the system, per unit of v_i;

α_i = rate (elasticity) or movement response from i to its relation to other classes in the system (D_i).

Several observations are in order;

(a) What v_i may be varies widely from model to model. In some it is an extensive measure, such as population; in others, it is an intensive measure such as an unemployment rate; in others it is a value derived from complex relations of attributes of the class (such as climate in a region) and of its elements (such as age, sex, education of its population); finally, in others, such as input-output models, v_i may simply be zero or unity as a dimensionless variable indicating the existence of this class as a possible origin.

(b) Some models consider only moves *out* of the class, while others allow for "moves" within the class; i.e. staying as a form of moving. The practical difference is that in the former M_{ii} is set equal to zero. This difference among models does not matter for our purposes at this time, as it only involves whether a transitional variable t_{ii} (to be introduced below) is set equal to zero or some other constant value. In a later paper I will analyze the rather straightforward consequences of these different types of models.

(c) D_i, the relation of i to the system, remains formally undefined for the moment; it will be derived below. Its intuitive interpretation, however, is the pull which the rest of the system (including or not $i = j$) exerts for movements from i. D_i are the attractions of the system, the opportunities available per unit of v_i. It may be thought of as a demand or a draw, hence the notation D.

(d) Whereas v_i, however, constructed, is the result of the characteristics of class i, D_i is a function of the entire system, a scalar systemic variable evaluated at i. By analogy, D_i is the local value of a magnetic field. I will show later that, although this variable is seldom explicitly set forth, it is always imbedded in the various models by logical necessity.

(e) The responsiveness of moves from i to the attractions or draw D_i is measured by the elasticity α_i. In some models, the number of moves originating in i are unaffected by the attractions D_i. In such models $\alpha_i = 0$, and departures M_{ix} are a function only of local attributes v_i; however, as I have said, the variable D_i will of necessity exist in other relations of the system. In other models, the number of moves is fully proportional to D_i, and in these $\alpha_i = 1$. Although I have not encountered in the literature any models where α_i is greater than unity or smaller than zero, these are logically possible. An instance of α_i being negative might occur when increasing draws upon elements of a class result in greater class cohesiveness to combat such temptations, as might be the case for an ethnic nationality embedded in an integrationist nation-state. An instance where α_i is greater than unity is "gold rush" situations. On the other hand, while α_i values intermediate between zero and unity do not appear explicitly in the literature they make a great deal of sense: the response of moves to attractions may exist but be less than fully proportional. Therefore I shall pay considerable attention to such intermediate values.

Movements Arriving at *j*

The moves arriving at a particular class *j* may be similarly set as

$$M_{xj} = w_j C_j^{\beta_j} \tag{9-2}$$

where M_{ij} = movement from class *i* to class *j*;

M_{xj} = $\Sigma_i M_{ij}$, total arrivals at *j*;

w_j = a function of the characteristics of class *j* and/or its population;

C_j = competition, crowding, congestion or potential pool of moves into *j* per unit of w_j; a function of the relation of *j* to rest of the system, per unit of w_j;

β_j = rate of expansion (elasticity) or arrivals to competition at *j*.

Again, some remarks are in order:

(a) What w_j may be varies widely among models, from extensive, to intensive, to mixed, to existence. Intuitively, w_j may be thought of as the attractiveness or pull of *j*. In some models w_j is equal to v_j, but more commonly they are different functions of different variables.

(b) Some models allow $i = j$ in M_{ij}, and some do not. This does not affect our general discussion.

(c) C_j is the relation of *j* to the rest of the system, and remains formally undefined for the moment. Its intuitive interpretation in the case of migration models, for instance, is a weighted measure of the supply or pool of migrants available to *j* per unit of w_j. It may be thought of as a measure of crowding, competition, or congestion, hence the notation C.

(d) As with v_i and D_i, w_j is a function of characteristics evaluated totally within class j, whereas C_j is a systemic variable, a function of the whole system evaluated at j.

(e) In some models the number of moves into j is determined exclusively by w_j. In such models the potential pool of movers does not matter and $\beta_j = 0$. In other models, it is fully proportional, and $\beta_j = 1$. For the same reasons as for α_i I shall concentrate on the range $0 \leq \beta_j \leq 1$ in later papers.

Movements from i to j

If we think of the total arrivals and departures to and from each class as the marginals of an $n \times n$ matrix, it becomes clear that there is no unique way of filling the cells for class to class movements. The sum of rows and columns consistent with these marginals provides $2n$ equations, while there are n^2 unknowns. Therefore the particular form of the M_{ij} relation cannot be derived from Equations (9–1) and (9–2), and some further suppositions are needed.

A possible set of further suppositions is that the share of departures from i going to j will be (a) proportional to the attractiveness of $j(w_j)$; (b) proportional to the probability of a potential arrival's entry into j, to enjoy its attractiveness ($C_j^{\beta_j-1}$); (c) proportional to any special relation that may obtain between i and j, such as ease of movement or special affinity (t_{ij}); and (d) inversely proportional to the total opportunities or alternative attractions available to a departure from i (D_i^{-1}).

In formal terms, this amounts to:

$$\frac{M_{ij}}{M_{ix}} = w_j C_j^{\beta_j-1} \, t_{ij} D_i^{-1} \qquad (9-3)$$

where $\dfrac{M_{ij}}{M_{ix}}$ = share of i's departures going to j;

w_j = a value representing the attractiveness of j determined by the characteristics of this class or its population;

$C_j^{\beta_j-1} = C_j^{\beta_j}/C_j =$ entry rate or probability of a potential arrival's entry into j; this is the ratio of actual to potential arrivals at j; by Equation (9–1), $C_j^{\beta_j}$ are the actual arrivals per unit of w_j, and C_j is the pool of movers available to j per unit of w_j;

t_{ij} = a special relation obtaining between class i and class j, such as ease of movement in a traffic or migration model, a transitional probability in a Markov model, or a technical coefficient in an input-output model;

D_i = total draw, attractions or opportunities offered by the system to a departure from i.

By combining Equations (9−1) and (9−3), and rearranging terms, we obtain the equation for the number of moves from i to j:

$$M_{ij} = v_i D_i^{\alpha_i - 1} w_j C_j^{\beta_j - 1} t_{ij}. \qquad (9-4)$$

C_j: Competition, Congestion, Potential Pool of Moves

I will now derive and interpret the systemic variable C_j. By summing equation (9−4) over i, we obtain

$$M_{xj} = \Sigma_i M_{ij} = w_j C_j^{\beta_j - 1} (\Sigma_i v_i D_i^{\alpha_i - 1} t_{ij}). \qquad (9-5)$$

Combining Equations (9−2) and (9−5), we have

$$M_{xj} = w_j C_j^{\beta_j} = w_j C_j^{\beta_j - 1} (\Sigma_i v_i D_i^{\alpha_i - 1} t_{ij}),$$

which simplifies to

$$C_j = \Sigma_i v_i D_i^{\alpha_i - 1} t_{ij}. \qquad (9-6)$$

We have thus arrived at an operational definition of C_j, derived from Equations (9−1), (9−2), and (9−3).

Its interpretation may be visualized more easily if we rewrite equation (9−6) by using Equation (9−1) as

$$C_j = \Sigma_i (M_{ix}/D_i) t_{ij}.$$

C_j, the pool of potential arrivals per unit of w_j, is equal to the sum over all possible origins of the total departures from each origin

(M_{ix}), relative to the total opportunities or draws open in the system to each mover from each origin (D_i), and weighted in each case by the affinity or ease of transition between each origin and destination j (t_{ij}). In other words, potential arrivals C_j per unit of attraction at j are simply the system's departures per opportunity, weighted from j's perspective.

D_i: Demand, Draw, or Opportunities

We can derive D_i similarly by summing Equation (9–4) over all destinations j,

$$\Sigma_j M_{ij} = v_i D_i^{\alpha_i - 1} \Sigma_j (w_j C_j^{\beta_j - 1} t_{ij}).$$

Combining it with Equation (9–1) $M_{ix} = v_i D_i^{\alpha_i}$, we obtain

$$M_{ix} = v_i D_i^{\alpha_i} = v_i D_i^{\alpha_i - 1} \Sigma (w_j C_j^{\beta_j - 1} t_{ij})$$

which reduces to

$$D_i = \Sigma_j w_j C_j^{\beta_j - 1} t_{ij}. \tag{9-7}$$

The total opportunities, draws, or attractions from the perspective of a unit of v_i are all of the attractions w_j, weighted by the entry rate $(C_j^{\beta_j}/ C_j)$ of actual to potential arrivals per unit of w_j and by the ease of movements from i to each j (t_{ij}).

In addition, we could write

$$D_i = \Sigma_j (M_{xj}/C_j) t_{ij}$$

This may be interpreted as stating that the system's opportunities available to a mover from i consist of the actual entries (M_{xj}) at each destination j, negatively weighted by the degree of competition (C_j) per unit of w_j (e.g., jobs), weighted by the ease of access (t_{ij}). In other words, opportunities per prospective mover from i are the system's successful entries per try, weighted by ease of access, from i's perspective.

Total Moves

It can be readily seen that total moves in the system are

$$\Sigma_i \Sigma_j M_{ij} = \Sigma_i v_i D_i^{\alpha_i} = \Sigma_j w_j C_j^{\beta_j}$$

This simply says that in the matrix of moves the sum of all the cells is equal to the sum of the row marginals and to the sum of the column marginals. Or most simply, that total departures equal total arrivals in a closed system.

The Full Set of Relations
and Alternative Derivations

Equations (9—1), (9—2), (9—4), (9—6), and (9—7) describe the fundamental relations of this theory of movements. This full set of relations is redundant, as we have seen by deriving Equations (9—6) and (9—7) from the primary relations (9—1), (9—2), and (9—4). We could equally have picked another set of relations as primary and derived the remainder.

For instance, I may start by postulating that the moves from i to j depend on the local characteristics at i (v_i) and at j (w_j), and to their degree of connectedness (t_{ij}). I also postulate that the moves from i to j are proportional in some degree to the alternative demands on moves from i, where D_i are these demands and Ψ_i is the degree of response or elasticity, resulting in $D_i^{\Psi_i}$. Similarly I postulate that the moves will be proportional to the competition or congestion at j, C_j, modified by some elasticity or rate of adjustment η_j of j's capacity to this congestion, resulting in $C_j^{\eta_j}$. From these postulations I obtain the equivalent of Equation (9—4):

$$M_{ij} = v_i D_i^{\Psi_i} w_j C_j^{\eta_j} t_{ij} .$$

A prospective mover from i views the universe of his opportunities (D_i) as the attractions or characteristics of each destination (w_j), weighted by their accessibility, (t_{ij}), by their congestion and by their elasticity of adjustment $(C_j^{\eta_j})$. This results in an equation equivalent to (9—7):

$$D_i = \Sigma_j w_j C_j^{\eta_j} t_{ij} .$$

Similarly from a destination j, the level of congestion (C_j) may be viewed by the aggregate of the characteristics of the sources of moves (v_i), weighted by their accessibility (t_{ij}) and by their response to opportunities $(D_i^{\Psi_i})$. This provides an equation equivalent to (9—6):

$$C_j = \Sigma_i v_i D_i^{\Psi_i} t_{ij} .$$

Now we may derive the equivalents of Equations (9–1) and (9–2) for M_{ix} and M_{xj}. Summing the equation for M_{ij} over j we obtain

$$\Sigma_j M_{ij} = M_{ix} = v_i D_i^{\Psi_i} (\Sigma_j w_j C_j^{\eta_j} t_{ij}) .$$

And since the expression within the parenthesis is the definition of D_i, we can say

$$M_{ix} = v_i D_i^{\Psi_i + 1}$$

Similarly, by summing over the i's we obtain

$$\Sigma_i M_{ij} = M_{xj} = w_j C_j^{\eta_j} (\Sigma_i v_i D_i^{\Psi_i} t_{ij})$$

and since the expression within the parenthesis is C_j, we have that

$$M_{xj} = w_j C_j^{\eta_j + 1} .$$

Thus we have all five relations again, having derived the equivalent of Equations (9–1) and (9–2) from the equivalent of Equations (9–4), (9–6), and (9–7). The only difference is that here we have exponents Ψ_i and η_j instead of α_i and β_j. These translate readily as

$$\Psi_i = \alpha_i - 1$$

$$\eta_j = \beta_j - 1 .$$

However, the difference is more than one of notation and it is instructive to examine it in greater detail. In this last derivation Ψ_i was called the rate of response or elasticity of an origin from the point of view of a prospective destination; η_j was characterized as the rate of response or elasticity of a destination from the point of view of a particular origin. In fact, these rates of response are the result of two distinct effects. Thus, an increase in available opportunities will elicit more moves from a source if α_i is greater than zero. At the same time, this increase in alternative opportunities will reduce the share

$$\frac{M_{ij}}{M_{ix}} = w_j C_j^{\beta_j - 1} t_{ij} D_i^{-1} = w_j C_j^{\beta_j - 1} t_{ij} / \Sigma_j w_j C_j^{\beta_j - 1} t_{ij}$$

that goes to a particular destination unless the elasticity of outward moves is equal to or greater than unity (i.e., $\alpha_i \geq 1$). Thus the total effect ($D_i^{\Psi_i}$) in place to place flows (M_{ij}) is derived from both the effects on total flows ($D_i^{\alpha_i}$) and the effect on a particular flow (D_i^{-1}). The equivalent analysis shows that $C_j^{\eta_i}$ is the composite of local expansion ($C_j^{\beta_j}$) and reduced shares from invariant sources (C_j^{-1}). For this reason the use of α_i and β_j is preferable to that of Ψ_i and η_j.

There are obviously many ways of arriving at this redundant set of consistent relations. From the point of view of elegance, a parsimonious set would depend on which are the initial and which are the derived relations. Similarly, in applied problems, the count of unknowns and equations will depend on the data and the questions at hand. Various models and applied theories enter this logical circle.

SOME MIGRATION MODELS IN THE GENERAL FORM

Most migration models seem to get along just fine without concerning themselves with such abstruse matters as the systemic variables D and C, or their elasticities or rates of response α and β. But this is only because these models are only partially stated, and in fact some form of D, C, α, and β are the logical if unexplored consequences of the models [2]. In some ways, D, C, α, and β remind one of economic rent. Wherever it is suppressed in one form, it pops up in another. Models which ignore them while focusing on point to point movements (M_{ij}) filling the cells of the matrix, will have them pop up in the marginals (M_{ix} and M_{xj}). Conversely, models which ignore them while concerning themselves with total departures or arrivals (M_{ix} or M_{xj}) implicitly carry them in the point to point cells. All models, like Moliere's *bon homme*, speak this prose whether or not they know it.

Let us examine some of these models.

Markov Models of Migration

A great deal of valuable work has been done on probabilistic models of migration, either in the form of Markov chains or more recently in logit models.

Examining the simplest of these, we find a set of populations P_i, which in a given period of time distributes itself among destinations according to a probability ρ_{ij}, where $\Sigma_j \rho_{ij} = 1$. Normally, ρ_{ij} is calculated from the observed behavior in a prior period by simply dividing the number of those who arrived at any given destination (including the origin) from a given origin by the population of the origin.

In my notation, then, v_i is simply P_i, and $M_{ij} = \rho_{ij} P_i$. The "special relation" t_{ij} is ρ_{ij}. Total "departures" (including staying) are $M_{ix} = P_i$. Total "arrivals" (including staying) are $M_{xj} = \Sigma_i \rho_{ij} P_i$. This is all straightforward, and there is no need for the systemic variables. But let us consider them.

One may begin by asking what are the form and characteristics w_j of any destination j. Obviously, these are very minimal. Indeed the only characteristic of j as a destination is its existence, which is to say $w_j = 1$. Presumably there is also an infinite and ghostly set of "destinations" which have the other value of the binary choice between existence and nonexistence, but these need not concern us, since they will receive no migrants.

Next we may easily deduce the values of α and β. Since the number of "departures" is fixed at P_i, it is invariant or inelastic with respect to opportunities available to migrants from i, and therefore $\alpha = 0$. Total departures may be seen as $M_{ix} = P_i = v_i = v_i D_i^0$. Conversely, destination j is totally passive, accepting all migrants under an open admissions policy. Therefore, successful arrivals are fully elastic to the supply of migrants, and $\beta = 1$. Then $M_{xj} = w_j C_j^1$, and, since $w_j = 1$, $M_{xj} = C_j$.

All that remains is to specify D and C. $D_i = \Sigma w_j C_j^{\beta-1} t_{ij} = \Sigma_j 1 C_j^0 \rho_{ij} = \Sigma_j \rho_{ij} = 1$, which is to say the model views opportunities as invariant for the prediction of behavior. Similarly, we can start with the theoretical definition of $C_j = \Sigma_i v_i D_i^{\alpha-1} t_{ij} = \Sigma P_i D_i^{-1} \rho_{ij} = \Sigma_i P_i 1^{-1} \rho_{ij} = \Sigma_i P_i \rho_{ij}$. Thus, when we concluded above that, since $w = 1$ and $\beta = 1$, $M_{xj} = C_j$, we can now say that $M_{xj} = \Sigma_i P_i \rho_{ij}$. This takes us back to the simple and direct formulation at the beginning.

What purpose is there, then, in complicating life in this case? Perhaps none, but some points may have become clearer: (a) destinations have no attributes other than existence ($w = 1$); (b) the elasticity of entrants to the supply of potential immigrants is unity ($\beta = 1$); (c) the behavior of prospective migrants is unaffected by opportunities at home or abroad ($\alpha = 0$); and (d) whether many or few are competing for arrival at a destination does not affect the

Table 9–1. General Model of Interregional Gross Migration and Special Cases

	Flow from i to j M_{ij}	Departures $\sum_j M_{ij} = M_{ix}$	Arrivals $\sum_i M_{ij} = M_{xj}$
General model	$v_i\,w_j\,t_{ij}\,D_i^{\alpha-1}\,C_j^{\beta-1}$	$v_i D_i^{\alpha}$	$w_j C_j^{\beta}$
Push model (e.g., Markov)	$v_i\,w_j\,t_{ij}\,D_i^{-1}\,C_j^{0}$	$v_i D_i^{0}$	$w_j C_j^{1}$
Pull model (e.g., economic base)	$v_i\,w_j\,t_{ij}\,D_j^{0}\,C_j^{-1}$	$v_i D_i^{1}$	$w_j C_j^{0}$
Elastic gravity model	$v_i\,w_j\,t_{ij}\,D_i^{0}\,C_j^{0}$	$v_i D_i^{1}$	$w_j C_j^{1}$
Inelastic gravity model (e.g., "entropy" traffic)	$v_i\,w_j\,t_{ij}\,D_i^{-1}\,C_j^{-1}$	$v_i D_i^{0}$	$w_j C_j^{0}$

Note: The point of departure of the various special case models is indicated by a frame around the expression.

probability ($C^{\beta-1}$ = 1) of successful entrance of any migrant. These may be excellent simplifying assumptions to study or simulate certain situations, but alternative ones may be more useful in other cases. The Markov migration models are pure "push" models, in which the push and its directions are invariant.

Other Models

Other models differ in their assumptions. Table 9–1 summarizes their general characteristics. Without going into detail, the Markov model just discussed is one of simplest of the "push" models; others instances of push models including logit models and studies that relate local rates of outmigration to such variables as local economic distress or age composition.

Pull models are quite common, particularly in the literature of urban and regional economics. Typically, some form of economic analysis (sometimes very simple, sometimes very complex) arrives at some projection of the economy and the number of jobs in region j. This is w_j. It is assumed that exactly *that* number of workers will materialize [3], whether there is a vast reservoir of potential mi-

Table 9–1. continued

Opportunity D_i	Competition C_j	Elasticities α	β
$\sum\limits_j w_j t_{ij} C_j^{\beta-1}$	$\sum\limits_i v_i t_{ij} D_i^{\alpha-1}$	$0 \le \alpha \le 1$	$0 \le \beta \le 1$
$\sum\limits_i w_j t_{ij} C_j^0$	$\sum\limits_i v_i t_{ij} D_i^{-1}$	0	1
$\sum\limits_j w_j t_{ij} C_j^{-1}$	$\sum\limits_i v_i t_{ij} D_i^0$	1	0
$\sum\limits_j w_j t_{ij} C_j^0$	$\sum\limits_i v_i t_{ij} D_i^0$	1	1
$\sum\limits_j w_j t_{ij} C_j^{-1}$	$\sum\limits_j v_i t_{ij} D_i^{-1}$	0	0

grants or a great number of competing opportunities elsewhere. This amounts to setting $\beta = 0$.

These models seldom go into tracing the sources and flows of migrants. But, to suggest the implicit logic, one might construct a model where each region of origin is characterized by a value v_i which is a function of its population, skill levels, and other social and economic characteristics, and a relation to each region t_{ij}, which might take account of prior migration (contacts, information) economic distance, sectoral complementarity, etc. At the other extreme, one author has suggested a very simple model, where the proportion of migrants arriving from each region of origin is proportional to the share of past migrants coming from that region. This is, in effect, the equivalent of a technical input coefficient a_{ij} into labor at the destination.

The general point, however, is that pull models appear not to include consideration of C because, by not referring to it explicitly, they are in fact assigning to it the exponent $\beta = 0$. Since they do not concern themselves with the implications at the origins, they miss the fact that they imply that $\alpha = 1$, and that D must appear explicitly in M_{ix}. And since they do not consider the network of implied point to point movements, they fail to realize that in these M_{ij}'s of necessity

C must appear, with an exponent of -1. On the other hand, it must be noted, D need not be stated in the M_{ij} equations of these models because its exponent will be $\alpha - 1 = 0$.

All models of movement in the social sciences that have come to my attention fit into one or another of the four special cases in Table 9–1. The gravity model, such as that used by Ira Lowry, has exponents $\alpha = \beta = 1$. That is to say, it implies that departures are fully elastic to opportunities, and that opportunities will expand with unit elasticity to the flow of arrivals. This can be easily seen by drawing the necessary conclusions from its basic equation: $M_{ij} = v_i w_j t_{ij}$ [4]. We can see that total arrivals are $M_{xj} = w_j \Sigma_i v_i t_{ij}$, and total departures $M_{ix} = v_i \Sigma_j w_j t_{ij}$. From this it follows that $D_i = \Sigma_j w_j t_{ij}$ and $C_j = \Sigma_i v_i t_{ij}$, and that they have unit exponents in total arrivals and departures, and consequently null exponents in the point to point equation and in their internal definitions.

The final case is that of the by now classic, if comparatively recent, doubly-constrained model of traffic by Alan Wilson, where neither D nor C appear in the total departures or destinations because $\alpha = \beta = 0$, and therefore these variables are "silent" in the marginals. But, of course, they then must appear explicitly (if not easily interpreted) in the point to point flows, as discussed in an earlier note [5].

Thus, existing models of movement settle themselves in the corners of the rectangle in Figure 9–1. The "push" model $(0,1)$ may be long-windedly termed an "inelastic leave-elastic arrive" model, while the "pull" model is in reality an "elastic leave-inelastic arrive" model. The gravity model is an "elastic leave-elastic arrive" model, and Wilson's doubly constrained model is an "inelastic leave-inelastic arrive" model, and hence might properly be called an inelastic gravity model.

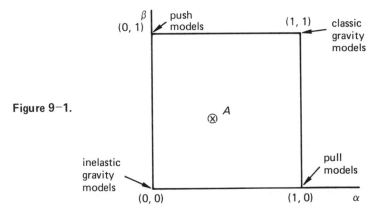

Figure 9–1.

In reality, as has been mentioned, most real-life movements might be expected to be intermediate between full and null elasticity, and the values of α and β may be expected to correspond to some interior point within the rectangle in Figure 9—1, such as A. Just what their intermediate elasticities might be is a matter of empirical determination, and they might differ from case to case and over time. For instance, during a labor shortage one might expect a small α and a large β, and the opposite during a depression.

Whether models which set α and β at zero or unity are good enough approximations must remain a matter of judgment at this time, and surely it must vary from case to case. But it seems to me important that we realize the implicit logic of our various models, the differences among them, and the structure of their variables. Further, although elasticities other than zero or unity present some thorny problems of mathematical analysis and statistical estimation, they carry with them the inescapable need to state D and C in each and every equation, by taking away the option of rendering them silent by an implicit zero exponent in the particular equation being examined.

NOTES TO CHAPTER 9

1. Earlier versions of this theory were presented in two of my papers: "National Interregional Demographic Accounts: A Prototype," Monograph #17, Berkeley: Institute of Urban and Regional Development, University of California, February 1973; "Policy-Oriented Interregional Demographic Accounting and a Generalization of Population Flow Models," WP–247, Berkeley: Institute of Urban and Regional Development, University of California, March 1975. The notation used there was somewhat different, and the analysis less advanced. I am currently writing a series of papers exploring the ramifications of the theory.

2. An exception is Alan Wilson's "family" of spatial interaction models (see A.G. Wilson [1970] *Entropy in Urban and Regional Modelling*, Pion, London) which incorporate systemic variables comparable to D and C (A^{-1} and B^{-1} in his notation). His consideration of "unconstrained," "production-constrained," "attraction-constrained," and "production-attraction-constrained" models correspond implicitly to α and β values of (1,1), (0,1), and (0,0) respectively. He also derives these from entropy maximization on flows subject to diverse constraints on total cost, departures and arrivals.

3. I omit discussion of the conversion from labor force to population figures, which is normally trivially handled.

4. In the paleolithic form of the gravity model, of course, $v_i = P_i$, $w_j = P_j$, $t_{ij} = d_{ij}^{-2}$; but by now v, w, and t have assumed all manner of baroque variations without, however, modifying the underlying logical structure.

5. It is worth noting that any singly-constrained or unconstrained model may be reformulated *ex post* as a doubly-constrained one.

Chapter 10

MULTIREGION: A Socioeconomic Computer Model for Labor Market Forecasting

*Richard J. Olsen**

INTRODUCTION

For at least a decade there has been a growing recognition of the need for a national/regional impact accounting system to help evaluate the interregional tradeoffs and displacements caused by national and regional policies and projects (Leven, *et al.*, 1970; Garnick *et al.*, 1971; and Alonso, 1973). This study describes a research project that has been oriented to this need. In particular, it focuses on some of the dimensions of MULTI-REGION—a computer model of regional and interregional socioeconomic development which interprets the economy of each BEA (functional) economic area (Figure 10-1) as a labor market, measures all activity in terms of people as members of the population or as employees, and simultaneously forecasts the demands and supplies of labor in all 173 areas at five-year intervals.

The following topics will be briefly considered: (1) the elements of a region's economy when viewed as a labor market; (2) the general computational sequence built into MULTIREGION; (3) the labor market equilibrating forces found in empirical analyses of regional population and employment; (4) the process of employment and population reconciliation embedded in MULTIREGION; (5) access

*This chapter is based on research performed at Oak Ridge National Laboratory with support from the National Science Foundation RANN Program and the Energy Research and Development Administration. Charles River Associates, Inc., has provided assistance for the preparation and presentation of this study. The views expressed are solely those of the author and in no way reflect the official or unofficial positions of NSF, ERDA, or CRA.

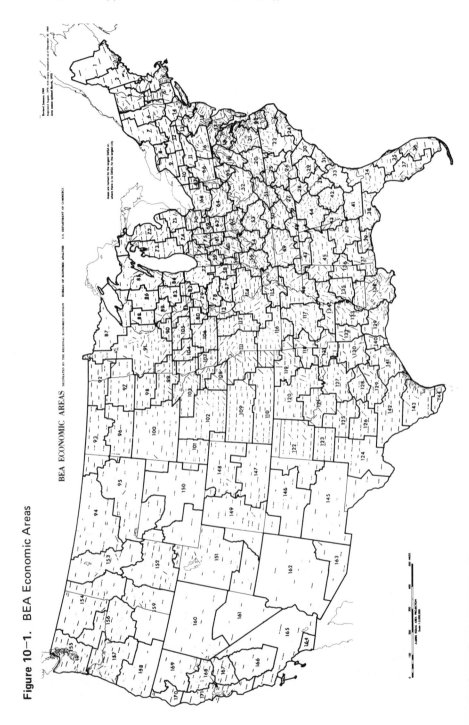

Figure 10–1.   BEA Economic Areas

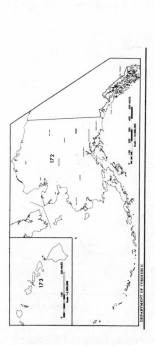

1 Bangor, Maine
2 Portland-South Portland, Maine
3 Burlington, Vt.
4 Boston, Mass.
5 Hartford, Conn.
6 Albany-Schenectady-Troy, N.Y.
7 Syracuse, N.Y.
8 Rochester, N.Y.
9 Buffalo, N.Y.
10 Erie, Pa.
11 Williamsport, Pa.
12 Binghamton, N.Y.–Pa.
13 Wilkes Barre-Hazleton, Pa.
14 New York, N.Y.
15 Philadelphia, Pa.–N.J.
16 Harrisburg, Pa.
17 Baltimore, Md.
18 Washington, D.C.–Md.–Va.
19 Staunton, Va.
20 Roanoke, Va.
21 Richmond, Va.
22 Norfolk-Portsmouth, Va.
23 Raleigh, N.C.
24 Wilmington, N.C.
25 Greensboro-Winston Salem-High Point, N.C.
26 Charlotte, N.C.
27 Asheville, N.C.
28 Greenville, S.C.
29 Columbia, S.C.
30 Florence, S.C.

31 Charleston, S.C.
32 Augusta, Ga.
33 Savannah, Ga.
34 Jacksonville, Fla.
35 Orlando, Fla.
36 Miami, Fal.
37 Tampa-St. Petersburg, Fla.
38 Tallahassee, Fla.
39 Pensacola, Fla.
40 Montgomery, Ala.
41 Albany, Ga.
42 Macon, Ga.
43 Columbus, Ga.–Ala.
44 Atlanta, Ga.
45 Birmingham, Ala.
46 Memphis, Tenn.–Ark.
47 Huntsville, Ala.
48 Chattanooga, Tenn.–Ga.
49 Nashville, Tenn.
50 Knoxville, Tenn.
51 Bristol, Va.–Tenn.
52 Huntington-Ashland, W.Va.–Ky.–Ohio
53 Lexington, Ky.
54 Louisville, Ky.–Ind.
55 Evansville, Ind.–Ky.
56 Terra Haute, Ind.
57 Springfield, Ill.
58 Champaign-Urbana, Ill.
59 Lafayette-West Lafayette, Ind.
60 Indianapolis, Ind.

61 Anderson, Ind.
62 Cincinnati, Ohio–Ky.–Ind.
63 Dayton, Ohio
64 Columbus, Ohio
65 Clarksburg, W. Va.
66 Pittsburgh, Pa.
67 Youngstown-Warren, Ohio
68 Cleveland, Ohio
69 Lima, Ohio
70 Toledo, Ohio
71 Detroit, Mich.
72 Saginaw, Mich.
73 Grand Rapids, Mich.
74 Lansing, Mich.
75 Fort Wayne, Ind.
76 South Bend, Ind.
77 Chicago, Ill.
78 Peoria, Ill.
79 Davenport-Rock Island-Moline, Iowa-Ill.
80 Cedar Rapids, Iowa
81 Dubuque, Iowa
82 Rockford, Ill.
83 Madison, Wis.
84 Milwaukee, Wis.
85 Appleton-Oshkosh, Wis.
86 Waussau, Wis.
87 Duluth-Superior, Minn.–Wis.
88 Eau Claire, Wis.
89 La Cross, Wis.
90 Rochester, Minn.

91 Minneapolis-St. Paul, Minn.
92 Grand Forks, N.D.
93 Minot, N.D.
94 Great Falls, Mont.
95 Billings, Mont.
96 Bismarck, N.D.
97 Fargo-Moorhead, N.D.–Minn.
98 Aberdeen, S.D.
99 Sioux Falls, S.D.
100 Rapid City, S.D.
101 Scottsbluff, Nebr.
102 Grand Island, Nebr.
103 Sioux City, Iowa-Nebr.
104 Fort Dodge, Iowa
105 Waterloo, Iowa
106 Des Moines, Iowa
107 Omaha, Nebr.-Iowa
108 Lincoln, Nebr.
109 Salina, Kans.
110 Wichita, Kans.
111 Kansas City, Mo.–Kans.
112 Columbia, Mo.
113 Quincy, Ill.
114 St. Louis, Mo.–Ill.
115 Paducah, Ky.
116 Springfield, Mo.
117 Little Rock-North Little Rock, Ark.
118 Fort Smith, Ark.–Okla.
119 Tulsa, Okla.
120 Oklahoma City, Okla.
121 Wichita Falls, Tex.
122 Amarillo, Tex.
123 Lubbock, Tex.
124 Odessa, Tex.
125 Abilene, Tex.
126 San Angelo, Tex.
127 Dallas, Tex.
128 Killeen-Temple, Tex.
129 Austin, Tex.
130 Tyler, Tex.
131 Texarkana, Tex.–Ark.
132 Shreveport, La.
133 Monroe, La.
134 Greenville, Miss.
135 Jackson, Miss.
136 Meridian, Miss.
137 Mobile, Ala.
138 New Orleans, La.
139 Lake Charles, La.

140 Beaumont-Port Arthur-Orange, Tex.
141 Houston, Tex.
142 San Antonio, Tex.
143 Corpus Christi, Tex.
144 McAllen-Pharr-Edinburg, Tex.
145 El Paso, Tex.
146 Albuquerque, N.M.
147 Colorado Springs, Col.
148 Denver, Col.
149 Grand Junction, Col.
150 Cheyenne, Wyo.
151 Salt Lake City, Utah
152 Idaho Falls, Idaho
153 Butte, Mont.
154 Spokane, Wash.
155 Seattle-Everett, Wash.
156 Yakima, Wash.
157 Portland, Ore.–Wash.
158 Eugene, Ore.
159 Boise City, Idaho
160 Reno, Nev.
161 Las Vegas, Nev.
162 Phoenix, Ariz.
163 Tucson, Ariz.
164 San Diego, Calif.
165 Los Angeles-Long Beach, Calif.
166 Fresno, Calif.
167 Stockton, Calif.
168 Sacramento, Calif.
169 Redding, Calif.
170 Eureka, Calif.
171 San Francisco-Oakland, Calif.
172 Anchorage, Alaska
173 Honolulu, Hawaii

to markets as a measure of interregional interdependence, and (6) the importance of simulation experiments. A more thorough discussion of these and other dimensions of MULTIREGION is available. (Olsen, *et al.*, 1977).

A REGIONAL ECONOMY VIEWED AS A LABOR MARKET

The economist's classic supply-demand representation of labor markets (Figure 10-2) leads one to expect both a price and a quantity response to any disequilibrium situation. Starting from an equilibrium (w_0, q_0) defined by the intersection of demand and supply schedules D_0 and S_0, an exogenous shift of the demand schedule to D_1 creates an excess demand ($q_a - q_0$) at the prevailing wage w_0. Under these circumstances and without the migration of jobs or people, market forces would tend to a new equilibrium (w_1, q_1) defined by the intersection of D_1 and S_0. The movement along S_0 represents a price-induced increase in labor participation and the movement along D_1 represents a price-induced substitution of relatively less expensive inputs for labor in the production process. With the migration of jobs and people allowed for, a less severe change in

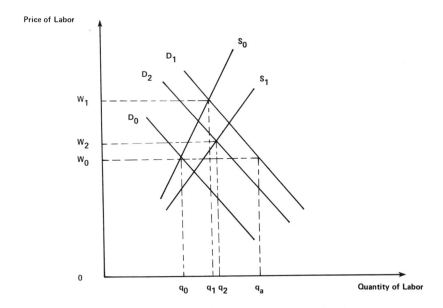

Figure 10-2. The Economist's Supply—Demand Representation of a Labor Market

price and quantity would result; D_1 shifts back to D_2 as the region becomes a less attractive location for industry and S_0 shifts out to S_1 as people are attracted by the region's tight labor market conditions. The location of the final equilibrium really depends on the sensitivity of regional labor demands and supplies to change in regional and interregional prices and socioeconomic conditions.

While this classic representation is relatively simple and therefore useful for many purposes, it remains incomplete as a guide for hypothesis testing or model building. At a minimum a more operational theory would need to recognize that labor market adjustments take place over time with the result that markets are frequently in disequilibrium; observed changes are usually less than desired changes. In addition, explicit recognition needs to be given to the fact that aggregate labor market processes are simply reflections of numerous microeconomic decisions by households and firms; separate decisions are usually made with respect to the birth, death, migration, and internal development of both people and jobs.

In the absence of a more comprehensive theoretical model and somewhat constrained by a lack of appropriate regional data, we have proceeded with a rather pragmatic view of a region as a labor market (Figure 10-3). Basically, a region's labor supply is seen to be affected by changes in mortality, fertility, migration, and labor force participation while its labor demand may be affected by changes in its attractiveness as a location for natural-resource-based industries, manufacturing, and local service industries. As a general rule these labor market concepts and sensitivities have been quantified by applying regression analysis techniques to existing Census of Population data aggregated to BEA economic areas (migration is the only exception; data for State Economic Areas were used). MULTIREGION is a computer program or model embodying these statistical representations of regional and interregional labor market equilibrating processes as adjusted through a series of simulation experiments. While still a bit more *ad hoc* than might be desired, the results do form a meaningful and operational representation of regional and interregional labor market processes—a firm basis for extrapolation from the past and present to future regional socioeconomic conditions and impacts.

THE COMPUTATIONAL SEQUENCE

A few characteristics of MULTIREGION deserve mention at this time because they significantly affect the computational sequence. First, MULTIREGION operates in five-year time steps (1970, 1975,

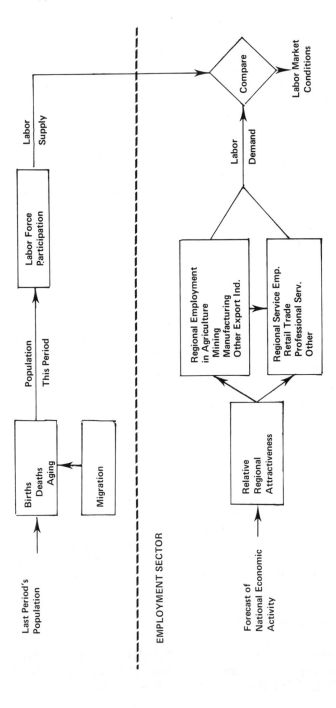

POPULATION SECTOR

EMPLOYMENT SECTOR

Figure 10–3. A Region's Economy as a Labor Market

1980, 1985, . . .), even though some labor supply and demand components adjust to regional socioeconomic conditions contemporaneously, or at least, with a lag of less than five years. As a consequence, a multistage (iterative) computation process is followed where last period values of some explanatory variables (e.g., labor market tightness) are used to produce first-stage estimates of regional labor supply and demand; the first-stage labor market conditions then are used to compute revised regional estimates. Second, MULTIREGION operates within the context of a given national economy so that across-region sums of employment, population and labor supply are forced to predetermined national totals (the shaded boxes in Figure 10−4). Third, interregional migration balances are imposed so that across-region sums of outmigrants and inmigrants are equal. Finally, MULTIREGION imposes some ceilings and floors to regional labor market conditions to prevent irrational results such as negative unemployment rates.

During any five-year time step, computations for each BEA economic area proceed as follows: (1) trial population values are computed where population "this period" is assumed to equal population "last period," plus births, minus deaths, plus inmigrants, minus outmigrants; (2) trial labor supply values are computed by multiplying the estimated population by labor participation rates; (3) trial labor demand values are computed as the sum of forecasted agriculture and mining employment, the region's share of forecasted national manufacturing employment, and local service employment; (4) trial labor market conditions (e.g., unemployment rates) are computed by bringing together trial labor supply and demand values; (and 5) final labor market conditions are computed by reiterating steps 1 through 4, a user-specified number of times. Finally, regional and interregional conditions are recompiled and the computations for the next five-year time step may begin.

THE POPULATION SECTOR

At this point the labor market equilibrating forces identified by our empirical analyses need to be highlighted. We begin with the components of the population or labor supply sector—mortality and fertility, migration, and labor force participation.

Mortality and Fertility

Because mortality and fertility are age- and sex-specific, the overall numbers of births and deaths in a region are quite sensitive to the age-sex composition of the population as a whole. We have found

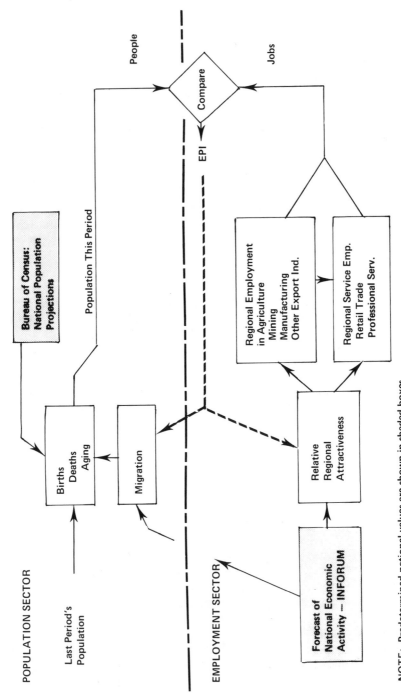

NOTE: Predetermined national values are shown in shaded boxes.

Figure 10–4.   MULTIREGION. The Interaction of People and Jobs

age- and sex-specific mortality and fertility rates for individual BEA areas vary consistently over time from corresponding national averages. While these regional deviations are greater for births than for deaths, both show evidence of a slow decrease over time. The stability of these regional deviations and their slow decrease over time provide a solid basis for projecting regional fertility and mortality trends *without* reference to labor market conditions.

Migration

Understanding the relationship of interregional population migration to changing regional socioeconomic conditions is of paramount importance. While most migration flows are selective of the younger, more educated, and more skilled elements of the population, the greatest need is to understand better how migration acts as a labor market equilibrating force. Our empirical results identify three important sources of this equilibrating role. First, when inmigration and outmigration relationships are taken together, tight local labor market conditions promote *net* inmigration; the effect is strongest for persons 20−29 years old and declines with increasing age. In this case, tight labor market conditions are defined as the difference between local and national labor market tightness. Labor market tightness is best measured in terms of a simple employment pressure index (EPI), the ratio of total employment plus Armed Forces personnel to the population of working age (aged 15−64); the higher the EPI, the tighter the labor market. Second, movers appear to exhibit a strong preference for regions with high interregional accessibility (not necessarily high population density), perhaps for the greater freedom of choice and lower risk they offer. Interregional accessibility is measured by a relative population potential variable, the share of the nation's population accessible to each BEA area by highway transport. Third, population density has a negative influence on inmigration and a positive influence on outmigration (except for 20−24 year olds). This seems to indicate that movers prefer, *ceterus paribus*, less densely-populated destinations with high interregional accessibility, a preference not inconsistent with increasing suburbanization and the growing suburb to suburb dominance of interregional migrations.

These results are significant for the estimation of regional futures with MULTIREGION in two ways. First, a tight regional labor market influences the estimation of *net* inmigration, both within and between five-year time steps. Second, increased interregional accessibility influences the estimation of *net* inmigration between five-year time steps. Together, these forces provide a substantial understanding of some contemporary dynamic regional processes. For example, as a region such as the Southeast experiences more than its proportional share of growth in interregional accessibility as a result of the completion of the Interstate Highway System (an exogenous perturbation), industry locates there in response to better market accessibility (to be discussed below); this results in a tightening of labor markets which increasingly and fairly promptly converts historically large net outmigration streams to net inmigration. This process is further reinforced, albeit with some delay, by the higher relative population potentials that result from growing regional populations that are more effectively tied together by the improved highway network.

Labor Force Participation

The responsiveness of labor force participation rates to changing socioeconomic conditions is probably not sufficiently appreciated. First, the positive impact of labor market tightness (again, best measured by EPI) on male and female labor force participation can be especially significant for discretionary workers (all age groups except males aged 25 to 64). Second, the opportunity for females to work (measured by the "femininity" of an area's industrial structure—the actual percent of employed persons that are female) has a very important positive influence on female labor force participation as well as a negative influence on male participation.

The significance of these results is the obvious flexibility of the regional labor supplies estimated with MULTIREGION. There are substantial changes in labor force participation as labor market tightness varies, and the response of female labor participation to the arrival of new female-intensive industries such as textiles and apparel can be so great that the unemployment rate may remain virtually unchanged. Both of these responses tend to make regional unemployment rates less than ideal targets for regional development planning and analysis (Kraft, *et al.*, 1971) and have led to the use of the EPI as our measure of labor market tightness. As a direct result of the use of EPI, labor force participation is carefully treated for the estimation of regional labor supplies, but it is of less consequence than the direct comparison of people and jobs (EPI) for the determination of regional and interregional socioeconomic growth and development.

THE EMPLOYMENT SECTOR

We now turn to the components of the employment or labor demand sector—natural-resource-based employment, manufacturing employment, and local service employment.

Natural-Resource-Based Employment

Included in this category are agriculture, forestry and fisheries, four categories of mining, and employment related to the use of major outdoor recreation resources such as the Great Smoky Mountains National Park in Tennessee or the Yellowstone National Park in Montana-Wyoming. Because most of these natural resources are not spatially ubiquitous but exist only in certain places, the regional activity levels of these industries can be considered a function of the aggregate demands for their products and the relative regional costs to the user of exploiting the resources at different geographical locations. Because the relative regional costs of exploiting these resources change very slowly, the activity levels of these sectors can be treated fairly exogenously. MULTIREGION employs a formal shift-and-share framework for this purpose. Regional employment levels in each natural-resource-based industry are computed at the beginning of each five-year time step and do not change until the next time step begins; this sector has *not* been related to labor market conditions.

Manufacturing Employment

Regional multiplier (or export base) models embody the argument that so much of the economic activity within small geographic areas is oriented toward serving markets outside the region that, in a very real sense, the activities of these export-oriented industries form the basis or foundation for the remaining local service industries. Within MULTIREGION, most manufacturing industries are considered to be export-oriented and regions are assumed to be competing against each other in a game called "industrial location."

Simple regional attractiveness models have been used to estimate the relative importance of regional characteristics such as (1) initial conditions, (2) interregional market accessibility, (3) market competition, (4) labor conditions, (5) natural and amenity resource availability, (6) financial resources and subsidies, and (7) the availability of intermediate inputs to the periodic outcomes of the industrial location game. The empirical results imply that the most important determinants of the present locations of manufacturing employment have been the past locations of employment (initial conditions) and interregional market accessibility; other regional characteristics such as labor conditions and financial subsidies do not appear to be very important at the BEA economic area level.

The importance of initial conditions reinforces the idea that inertia is a very powerful force; but, in addition, the fact that the positive association between present and past employment locations has been significantly less than one-to-one for most industries provides a measure of broad trends toward spatial dispersion. After adjusting for initial conditions, interregional market size—measured in terms of access by truck transportation to final demand, intermediate suppliers, intermediate demanders and others in the same industry—has been the most important determinant of locational change. These results are used in MULTIREGION to consider and measure interregional interindustry linkages and effects.

Within MULTIREGION, a region's future manufacturing employment in each of fourteen industry groups is estimated at the beginning of each five-year time step and is not altered until the next five-year time step. Thus, it is assumed that manufacturing location responds slowly to changing regional conditions. There may be substantial changes in the location of manufacturing employment over time, but they depend on each industry's trend toward spatial dispersion and changes in interregional market size. Because of this relatively slow response to changing conditions, MULTIREGION recompiles measures of interregional market size only at the end of each five-year time step.

Local Service Employment

This employment sector includes industries such as construction, transportation services, wholesale and retail trade, personal and professional services, and public administration. Nationally, service employment has been growing more rapidly than population or manufacturing employment. Regionally, there has been great variation among BEA areas in the amount of local service employment per capita but there also has been a general convergence of regions toward national per capita values.

Simple regional attractiveness models have been used to identify initial conditions and total regional employment growth as the major determinants of service employment location. Again, past employment location is the most important determinant of present location, reinforcing the importance of inertia but also capturing trends toward more spatial diffusion. Although local service industries are supposed to be spatially diffused by definition, there is significant evidence of further dispersion, perhaps attributable to a closer alignment over time of regional and national business and consumer tastes and/or a greater "taking in of one's own wash" by all regions. After adjusting for initial conditions, total employment growth is the most important determinant of locational change, which reinforces the notion that the size of regional "multiplier" effects depends on the size of the initial change.

In addition to the effects of initial conditions and total employment growth, about one-half of the local service industries exhibit a positive association with interregional market size, a negative association with population density, and a weak positive association with labor market tightness. While obviously of less importance than initial conditions and total employment growth, these relationships do have a role in reconciling the population and employment sectors.

Within MULTIREGION, regional service employment in each of sixteen industry groups is computed at the beginning of each five-year time step but after manufacturing and natural-resource-based employment. However, these service employment estimates are subject to revision within each time step as the population and employment sectors are reconciled.

RECONCILING THE POPULATION
AND EMPLOYMENT SECTORS

Table 10—1 summarizes the more important labor market equilibrating forces embedded in the population and employment sectors of MULTIREGION. By recalling the computational sequence, this information may be used to state more clearly the population and employment reconciliation process within a five-year time step (the short term), between five-year time steps (the medium term), and over a series of time steps (the long term). It will be recalled that a multistage (iterative) computation process is followed within each five-year time step: last period values of some explanatory variables are used to produce first-stage estimates that are recycled a number of times to ultimately compute final regional values. After each five-year time step all regional and interregional conditions are recompiled before the next time step is begun.

During the short term (one five-year time step), it is clear that migration and local service employment absorb the adjustments necessary to reconcile the population and employment sectors; their values are adjusted during the multistage computations of each five-year time step. While it is also true that labor force participation rates are adjusted at this point, they are of no importance to the reconciliation process because the employment pressure index is used to measure labor market tightness; they would have been very important had the unemployment rate been used. Labor force calculations are included only to provide labor supply information; they do not influence the major outputs (employment and population) of the model. In fact, the picture of a regional economy depicted in Figure 10—3 has been revised to recognize the reduced importance of labor supply (Figure 10—4).

Table 10–1. Labor Market Equilibrium Forces Embedded in Multiregion

	Influenced by	Contributes to the Reconciliation of Population Employment Sectors During		
		Short Term	Medium Term	Long Term
Population Sector				
Mortality and Fertility Rates	Trended deviations from the nation	*		
In- and Out-Migration Rates	Labor market tightness (EPI)		*	*
	Population density (P.DEN)		*	*
	Relative population potential (R.POT)		*	*
Labor Force Participation Rates	Labor market tightness (EPI)			
	Industry Mix			
Employment Sector				
Natural-Resource-Based Employment Shares	Exogenous shift and share analysis			
Manufacturing Employment Shares	Initial conditions			*
	Interregional market size		*	*
Local Service Employment Shares	Initial conditions		*	*
	Total regional employment growth (TEG)	*	*	*
	Labor market tightness (EPI)	*	*	*
	Population density (L.C.)		*	*
	Relative population potential (R.POT)			*

Note: Short term = within a five-year time step.
Medium term = two or three five-year time steps.
Long term = four or more five-year time steps.

During the medium term (2 or 3 five-year time steps), more components of each sector contribute to the reconciliation. Between five-year time steps migration, manufacturing employment, and service employment adjust to changing labor market conditions.

During the long term (4 or more five-year time steps), the age and sex specific fertility and mortality rates may remain exogenous but the absolute numbers of births and deaths in a region can vary enough because of underlying changes in population composition to contribute to the reconciliation of population and employment.

INTERREGIONAL INTERDEPENDENCE: ACCESS TO MARKETS

Interregional accessibility and interregional market size have had a prominent role in the empirical analyses of migration, manufacturing employment, and local service employment because they constitute a means of considering and measuring *inter*regional linkages and effects. Since the gradual completion of the Interstate Highway System has had a substantial and differential regional impact on the growth of market accessibility (Olsen and Westley, 1974), a major effort was devoted to the measurement of the time of truck transport between the metropolitan centers of pairs of BEA areas.

These computed truck operating times for 1950, 1960, and 1970, along with projections for 1980, when the Interstate System is expected to be complete, are used to define interregional market size for each BEA area according to the gravity and potential concepts of human interaction commonly used by regional scientists.

In particular, absolute and relative interregional market potentials are computed according to the formulas:

$$\text{Absolute potential} = POT_{ik} = \sum_{j=1}^{171} (MASS_{jk}/D_{ij}^{\lambda_k}) \text{ for}$$

$$D_{ij} \leq 8.3 \text{ hours}$$

$$\text{Relative potential} = R.POT_{ik} = Pot_{ik}/MASS_{us,k}$$

where

POT_{ik} = the market potential for commodity k in BEA area i;

$MASS_{jk}$ = a measure of mass appropriate to commodity k in BEA area j (e.g., population or employment in an industry associated with commodity k as a buyer or seller);

D_{ij} = *minimum* truck operating time between i and j (where $i = j$, $D_{ij} = 1/2 D_{ij}$ to the nearest BEA area); and

λ_k = distance decay coefficient that varies with the good being shipped.

It is important to note that the market potential in BEA area i varies directly with mass at area j and inversely with the time of truck transport between i and j. In general, a region becomes more attractive as a destination for migrants and as a location for industry when transportation improvements reduce interregional access times and population and employment grow in nearby regions. Because most regions are growing in attractiveness in this absolute sense, *relative* market potentials are used to argue that a region becomes more attractive only when its share of the total national market increases.

Within MULTIREGION, interregional market potentials are computed only at the end of each five-year time step for use as inputs to the determination of migration and manufacturing employment during the next five-year time step. Thus, interregional effects are assumed to occur slowly in part for computational efficiency but more importantly because empirical studies have identified substantial periods of adjustment to changes in interregional accessibility. MULTIREGION assumes that changes in interregional accessibility have substantial and cumulative effects on regional growth and development in the medium and long term but not in the short term.

SIMULATION EXPERIMENTS

It is almost impossible to overemphasize the importance of simulation experiments (validation exercises) to the ultimate success of a regional modeling project. In the face of an incomplete theory of regional change and frequently inappropriate regional data, econometric science can take us only so far. Successful regional model building remains as much art as science and much of the art appears to be concentrated in the later stages of the endeavor when scientifically derived empirical relationships must be "tuned" to adequately track reality over time.

In the case of MULTIREGION, the assembled empirical relationships have always discriminated well between growing and declining regions. But the rates of adjustment implied by these relationships have been too rapid. This has undoubtedly been due to a form of cross-section bias; relationships estimated from cross-section data tend to define long-term "desired" or "equilibrium" conditions. Our careful pooling of data from successive cross sections has not been sufficient to overcome this problem. As a result, when the model has been used to track historical regional growth (1960 to 1975), too rapid a rate of adjustment toward equilibrium conditions has prevailed. But these mistrackings of the model during simulation experiments have been an important source of information for tuning the model components to achieve more satisfactory rates of adjustment.

Since this experience is one that has been frequently encountered in regional economic modeling (Hamilton, et al., 1960; Harris, 1973; and Birch, et al., 1976), it is probably a condition to be usefully appreciated and explored rather than denied or concealed. In the present absence of clear decision rules for altering models in the light of results from simulation experiments, we have proceeded to make only the simplest of scalar and residual adjustments to the equations within MULTIREGION. With better decision rules, more complex adjustments to individual coefficients would appear appropriate.

CONCLUSIONS

In this chapter the major dimensions of MULTIREGION, a computer model of regional socioeconomic development, have been summarized in part for the results that have been obtained but also for the research methodology that has been used. We remain convinced that through the somewhat artful combination of econometric analyses and simulation experiments, substantial progress can be made toward understanding and anticipating regional and interregional socioeconomic tradeoffs and displacements.

REFERENCES

Alonso, W., "Balanced Growth: Definitions and Alternatives," September 1973. Paper prepared for Oak Ridge National Laboratory in cooperation with the U.S. Department of Housing and Urban Development.

Birch, D.L., P.M. Allaman, E.A. Martin, Inter-Area Migration Project: Second Interim Report. Joint Center for Urban Studies of MIT and Harvard University, March 1976.

Garnick, D.H., C.E. Trott, A. Olson, H. Hertzfeld, and V. Fahle, Toward Development of a National-Regional Impact Evaluation System and the Upper Licking Area Pilot Study, Staff Paper No. 18, Office of Business Economics, U.S. Department of Commerce, 1971.

Hamilton, H.R., S. Goldstone, J. Milliman, A. Pugh, III, E. Roberts, and A. Zellner, Systems Simulation for Regional Analysis: An Application to River-Basin Planning, Cambridge, MIT Press, 1969.

Harris, C.C., Jr., The Urban Economies, 1985: A Multiregional Multi-Industry Forecasting Model, Lexington, Mass., Lexington Books, 1973.

Kraft, G., A.R. Willens, J.B. Kaler, and J.R. Meyer, *"On the Definition of a Depressed Area,"* in J.F. Kain and J.R. Meyer (Eds.) *Essays in Regional Economics*, Cambridge, Mass., Harvard University Press, 1971.

Leven, C.L., J.B. Legler, and P. Shapiro, *An Analytical Framework for Regional Development Policy*, Cambridge, Mass., MIT Press, 1970.

Olsen, R.J. and G.W. Westley, *"Regional Differences in the Growth of Market Potentials, 1950–1970,"* *Regional Science Perspectives*, Vol. 4, pp. 99–111, 1974.

Olsen, R.J., G.W. Westley, D.P. Vogt, C.R. Kerley, D.J. Bjornstad, H.W. Herzog, L.G. Bray, S.T. Grady, and R.H. Nakosteen, *MULTIREGION: A Simulation—Forecasting Model of BEA Economic Area Population and Employment*, Oak Ridge National Laboratory. ORNL/RUS–25, 1977.

Chapter 11

On Interrelations Between Human Settlement Systems and Regional Socioeconomic Systems

Piotr Korcelli

INTRODUCTION

Much of the recent discussion of settlement system structure and change has focussed on the question of intraregional versus extraregional functions of cities (W. Stöhr, 1974). This dichotomy is reflected in controversies concerning place and nonplace urban realms (M.M. Webber, 1964), hierarchical and intermetropolitan innovation diffusion patterns (A. Pred, 1976), and the vertical and horizontal organization of national settlement systems (K. Dziewoński, 1975). From a broader perspective, this question also has been addressed within the growth pole and spatial diffusion theories. Still other theoretical approaches to the study of urban and regional systems emphasize either the intraregional or the extraregional dimension of urban functions. The first group includes central place theory and classical location theory in general, which pay considerable attention to the friction of distance and transportation costs and to the consequent spatial aspects of linkage patterns. The second group includes interregional trade and urban economic base theories, which emphasize intersectoral linkages. It also should be noted that the concept of territorial production complexes (A.G. Aganbegyan, M.K. Bandman, A.G. Granberg, 1976) is among the few to stress both sectoral and spatial aspects simultaneously.

Relations between city functions with intraregional and extraregional range can be projected onto a broader plane of relationships between urban and regional systems, since it is evident that the degree of correspondence between urban and regional systems depends on the nature and proportions of the two groups of functions under discussion. The identification of correspondence levels is important because of the role which socioeconomic regionalization plays in the study and planning of settlement systems at a national and a regional scale (B. Khorev, 1971).

This chapter reviews selected hypotheses and findings pertaining to regional and interregional dimensions of settlement systems and explores some of their planning implications. An examination of interrelations between the administrative hierarchy of Polish cities and the pattern of tertiary activities within the Polish national settlement system provides empirical illustrations of some of the issues discussed.

THE REGIONAL AND INTERREGIONAL NATURE OF SETTLEMENT SYSTEMS

The evolution of national settlement systems has been described and interpreted in two basic ways. The first approach starts from the central place model and leads to the concepts of metropolitan regions (O.D. Duncan et al., 1960), and urban fields (J. Friedmann and J. Miller, 1965). It may be called a regional approach since most, if not all, the functions considered relate to the regional dimension of settlement systems. More recent concepts of daily urban systems (B.J.L. Berry, 1973), metropolitan labor market areas (P. Hall et al., 1973) and functional urban regions (N. Hansen, 1976) also belong to this tradition. In each case the region is defined differently; terms such as hinterland, dominance zone, periphery, and labor shed reflect particular kinds of relations identified. The scope of functions considered varies from predominantly commercial in classical central place schemes to a more or less comprehensive mix in the case of metropolitan regions and urban fields. The daily urban system and functional urban region concepts are primarily concerned with daily human interactions, and especially with journey-to-work patterns.

The sequence of spatial patterns reflects changing proportions among individual economic activities as well as evolving costs of transportation—factors which result in a specific interplay of spatial concentration and deconcentration phenomena. When concentration forces prevail the result is a pattern of metropolitan dominance. The opposite tendency produces a shift towards urban fields where, due to a high level of spatial mobility and the growing role of quaternary and foot-loose activities, the comparative locational advantages of central and peripheral zones become reversed. Under planned-economy conditions, development tends towards the abolition of earlier differences between urban and rural (or central and peripheral) zones on a regional scale in favor of unified, or integrated, settlement systems (B.Khorev, 1972; D. Khodzaev and B. Khorev, 1973, 1976).

The second approach starts essentially from the same point as the first, but its emphasis is less on intraregional linkage patterns than on interregional scale of specialization and interaction. It is claimed that in the course of development of settlement systems, regional ties are gradually overshadowed by what could be called territorially discrete linkages. M.M. Webber's concept of nonplace urban realms has already been mentioned, but perhaps the most representative approach is the "large-city focussed model of city system development" proposed by A. Pred (1973, 1975).

Pred starts with the hypothesis that intermetropolitan linkages tend to be stronger than intraregional, horizontal links. He subscribes to the contention of J. Friedmann (1972, p. 97) that "for the same spatial system, any two core regions [large cities] of approximately the same level in the hierarchy will tend to have a greater and more balanced volume of mutual interaction, modified by distance, than either will have with individual lower-order cores."

The first tier of Pred's model portrays the process of circular and cumulative growth of large urban centers which reinforce their advantages after having acquired a dominant position at an early development stage. In the second tier matrices of interurban interactions are introduced which again indicate the dominance and persistence of those channels of goods, people and information flows which interconnect the large units in the city-system. Unfortunately, the direction in which the interaction matrices evolve is not determined endogenously in the model. Any shifts occurring in the rank-size patterns can only be accounted for by a probabilistic component in the model.

Several authors have attempted hypothetically to disaggregate a national settlement system into its basic components. L. Bourne (1975) has formulated a model of a national settlement system which is dominated by metropolitan centers and is characterized by a step-like size hierarchy; its main subsystems consist of urban regions (organized about a single metropolitan center) which also display internal hierarchical arrangements. Finally, the regional subsystems contain local urban systems, covering zones of daily contacts of residents of a given urban center. The model implicitly gives great weight to intraregional linkage patterns as opposed to interactions among the cores of individual urban regions.

The interregional linkage dimension is heavily emphasized by

K. Dziewoński (1971, 1975) who maintains that urban agglomerations (metropolitan areas) are oriented more towards one another than each is towards its surrounding region. Hence, urban agglomerations can be portrayed as forming a single subsystem in a national settlement system. The remaining subsystems in Dziewoński's typology are less significant from the point of view of major linkage channels and development patterns. They are, in fact, analogous to the regional and local subsystems identified by Bourne.

The regional-interregional dichotomy identified in the body of concepts pertaining to the structure of national settlement systems can be resolved by treating it as an empirical question, or by showing that the two approaches are complementary. These approaches will now be examined in turn.

A. Pred (1976) has cited at least eight studies whose findings indicate that interdependencies among cities situated in different regions are actually stronger and more important than those between close-by urban units, or between a regional capital and its subdominant centers. Pred himself has presented data on the spatial structure of multilocational business organizations in the United States which yield similar results. Without going into the details of his argument (it is not certain, for example, if the location of a firm's headquarters in a small town B necessarily suggests that this town exerts a control over a segment of the employment market in a large metropolis A in which a major subsidiary plant is situated), one may note that it is primarily directed against narrowly-conceived central place theory interpretations of innovation diffusion and growth transmission mechanisms which in any case are no longer popular in the academic community. On the other hand, it has been demonstrated that some spatial diffusion processes clearly conform to urban hierarchical structures (see, for example, Jui-Cheng-Huang and P. Gould, 1974).

In Poland, to give another example, the question of interregional versus extraregional functions of cities (and the related spatial linkage patterns) has been tackled in considerable detail in urban economic base studies. More recently, some projects based on interaction data between regions as well as between urban places have been undertaken. Again, some of the results confirm the hypothesis according to which interregional flows are dominant (and, therefore, one can speak of a subsystem composed of leading urban agglomerations within a national settlement system) while others point up the intensity of intraregional interactions. Thus, an analysis of commodity flows (Z. Chojnicki and T. Czyz, 1973) has shown no definite hierarchical patterns. As to movements of people, it has been estimated that about a quarter of all long-distance train journeys occur between Warsaw and four other major urban agglomerations: Gdańsk, Katowice, Poznań and Cracow. However, this does not necessarily imply a conclusion concerning the ascendency of inter-metropolitan linkages because the flow patterns in question may also have a hierarchical nature, and they reflect major tourism and recreation traffic routes. Z. Rykiel (1976) has demonstrated quite recently that in terms of their basic structural characteristics urban agglomerations in Poland conform to the features which are typical of the respective regions surrounding them. On this basis Rykiel advanced a hypothesis that urban agglomeration systems have more of a regional than an interregional character. His analysis unfortunately was limited mostly to stock data. A current follow-up study based on postal data should throw more light on this issue.

More research clearly is needed on interactions within settlement systems, both on a national and a regional scale. So far, the existing evidence concerning the relative importance of intra- and interregional linkages falls short of being conclusive. Static analyses of interactions can be expected to provide only limited evidence in favor of one or the other of the two main hypotheses discussed. A more effective approach would be to demonstrate temporal changes in the character of linkages (from regional to interregional or vice versa) for individual types of activities.

Conceptually, contradictions between the regional and interregional approaches to the study of settlement systems can be solved by simply assuming a complementarity between them. Intuitively, the spatial patterns of flows are functions of the activities concerned, in addition to being functions of the media involved. It is readily observed, for example, that commuting to work is local or regional in scale while the shipping of coal and tourist traffic are national or even international in scale. The complementarity hypothesis finds its analogy in the spatial diffusion theory which recognizes the existence of parallel mechanisms of intermetropolitan, hierarchical, and spatially continuous (the "neighbourhood effect") growth. Such a hypothesis is also implied by several concepts relating to settlement structure. G.M. Lappo's (1974) concept of urban agglomerations as nodal points in the growth of regional settlement systems belongs to this category.

The question of the relative importance of interregional versus regional linkage patterns may therefore be somewhat ill-posed. What is required is more systematic study of a wide array of interurban flow patterns and an attempt to identify types of interaction typical of a given spatial scale, economic development level or overall density pattern. It is noteworthy that the gravity model still remains the main tool in spatial interaction studies and that most of the research effort in this field, over the last decade or so, has been put into the improvement of formal properties of the model (see A.G. Wilson, 1974) rather than in testing basic interaction hypotheses (F. Cesario and T. Smith, 1975). It has been suggested, for example, that at least in central districts of large cities the type of behavior depicted by gravity formulas (as well as intervening opportunity formulas) does not in fact occur, and when it does it may be largely attributable to the spatial arrangement of trip destinations and infrastructure (see L. Curry, 1972).

When dealt with in a comparative framework, the question of regional versus interregional flow patterns is further complicated by the density and size factors mentioned earlier. Thus, commuting to work may represent an intermetropolitan type of flow in the case of Holland, while on the other extreme of the spatial scale, the inter-industry linkages may operate within individual regions, as in the territorial-production complexes of the Soviet Union.

In summation, then, the study of national and regional settlement systems has witnessed the development of two bodies of concepts, each emphasizing a different scale of spatial linkages. However, there is much evidence indicating that these two approaches are complementary rather than contradictory. Each points towards certain aspects of spatial interaction which, however, cannot be clearly separated. The division into hierarchical and specialized (or vertical and horizontal) patterns within settlement systems is apparently too gross since both the former and the latter are in fact composed of a number of more specific, mutually-overlapping patterns.

TYPES OF URBAN-REGIONAL INTERRELATIONS

Having presented some concepts related to the spatial structure of settlement systems it is possible now to turn to the question of regional systems and their interrelations with settlement systems. Regional systems are treated here as interdependent sets of territorially continuous units rather than in terms of spatial patterns of economic and social linkages in general. Following this assumption one can identify two types of regions: (a) those which by definition closely conform to the structure of settlement systems, e.g. nodal regions or functional urban regions; and (b) those which may or may not correspond to settlement systems, e.g. systems of political, administrative, planning, economic, cultural or ethnic regions.

Settlement systems are formed under given social and economic conditions; therefore their structure is, to a considerable degree, a reflection of the distribution of productive forces (see G.N. Fomin, 1976). This relationship, however, in fact has a feedback character (N.T. Agaphonov and S.B. Lavrov, 1976) because the settlement system exerts an influence on spatial economic development patterns (V. Gokhman, G. Lappo, I. Maergoiz and J. Mashbits, 1976). One can consider urban and economic regions as mutually adjusting spatial systems. Due to time lags and the impact of other factors the correlation between the two sets of regions can be expected to vary over space as well as over time. For example, K. Dziewoński (1976) has found that relationships between urban and industrial development in Poland are regionally differentiated, the northern part of the country exhibiting higher urbanization while the southern regions have a higher industrialization level.

As far as administrative or planning regions are concerned, the divergencies between urban and regional patterns may be quite pronounced, and their character is clearly dependent upon prevailing socioeconomic conditions. One of the factors making for the discrepancies observed is the continuous nature of settlement systems development as opposed to discrete changes in the structure of administrative and planning units. Perhaps the most rudimentary case is that of the extent of urbanized areas versus the administrative boundaries of cities. It has generated a voluminous literature and a number of definitions of urban agglomerations and metropolitan areas are used for statistical purposes. This is one aspect of a more general problem reported, for example, by A.C. Wood (1960) in his well-known book on the 1400 governments in the New York Metropolitan Region.

Large metropolitan areas are frequently representative of a situation in which the mutual adjustment of urban and administrative spatial divisions (and even statistical divisions) is very limited in scope. Some of the recent territorial administrative reforms in Europe represent another case. For example, the shift from a three-level to a two-level hierarchy of spatial administrative units in Poland, which took place between 1973 and 1975, can be said to follow some of the general patterns of settlement. As a result of the change, four of the upper-level units (voivodships) now correspond roughly to the extent of individual urban agglomerations. In addition, areas characterized by a bipolar structure of settlement have been split according to actual regional linkage patterns. The opposite impact direction can also be identified. For example, because of their function as voivodship capitals, several medium-size cities have succeeded in moving rapidly upward in the urban hierarchy (both in terms of size and economic importance) during the 1950–1975 period. It may also be expected that the new territorial division will tend to promote the formation of a pattern of city-regions corresponding to the pattern of the top-level administrative units.

The feedback relation between settlement systems, on the one hand, and socioeconomic regional systems, on the other can be examined by disaggregating the two kinds of spatial systems, with explicit account being taken of social, political and economic conditions. In this way one can establish certain types of interdependence. It is worthwhile to pursue this kind of research because it may: (1) give more insight into the role of external factors in the development of settlement systems; (2) promote recent trends toward the integration of urban and regional research (see, for example, H. Richardson, 1973); and finally (3) increase understanding of the effects of the implicit planning dimension on the settlement system and make them fit more closely with the explicit planning dimension.

A FEW REMARKS ON PLANNING IMPLICATIONS

The interregional-extraregional dichotomy in the range of interurban linkages and the relations between hierarchical and nonhierarchical (i.e. cross-hierarchical, or core-periphery) components in the settlement system bear on a number of planning questions at both the national and regional levels. Among these questions two have particular interest: the impact of sectoral planning on settlement systems and the role of settlement systems structure in regional development planning. Because the second question has been extensively treated within the growth pole framework (see N. Hansen, 1975; B.J.L. Berry, 1973) the discussion here will be limited largely to the first, which has been referred to as an implicit dimension in settlement planning and policy. In terms of theory this area has not developed far, although the recent work of J.R. Lasuén (1973) on interrelations between sectoral and spatial concentration, and of R. Domański (1975) on transformations of settlement systems indicate some interesting research paths. On the applied side this question has been dealt with in an integrated planning model (B. Winiarski, 1974) which, under planned-economy conditions, assumes an iterative procedure of adjusting sectoral decisions to spatial development goals.

One comprehensive planning approach aimed at the coordination of settlement systems and regional socioeconomic systems is the program to integrate the unified settlement systems concept with that of territorial-production complexes (E. Alayev, B. Khorev, 1976). Following this approach, settlement systems are arranged into three hierarchical levels, i.e. national, regional and local. It is primarily the second level which is defined in terms of inner sectoral linkages, while the third is based mostly on human activity patterns, mainly the place-of-residence to place-of-work relationships.

At a smaller spatial scale and with high population densities, the problem of the degree of closure of territorial planning units, i.e. the proportions between intraregional and interregional flows, is of growing importance. The "openness" of a region's economy is responsible for the fact that factor allocations made on a regional scale have a spatially relative nature, and the interdependencies between sectoral and regional patterns can be solved at the central level only (B. Winiarski, 1974). Such an approach implies that the whole country is treated in fact as one economic region. Thus a long-term plan of physical development at the national level, which has been worked out in Poland recently, emphasizes the interactions between some fifty cities and urban agglomerations (i.e. development centers at the national level) in addition to identifying a number of regional and local development centers. On the other hand, in the French regional-national planning model REGINA (R. Courbis, 1975), the smallest spatial units of reference were defined in terms of urban labor market areas and an attempt was made to coordinate the territorial disaggregation level with the spatial range of economic (interindustry flows) and social (migration) linkages. However, such an approach assumes very comprehensive knowledge of interactions within the urban system.

CASE STUDY OF THE URBAN HIERARCHY IN POLAND: ADMINISTRATIVE AND TERTIARY ACTIVITY PATTERNS

A current study is attempting to trace the changing position of administrative centers of different levels within the full set of urban places in Poland, in terms of comparative rates of growth, functional structure and patterns of spatial linkages. So far its scope has been limited to selected tertiary sector characteristics (see P. Korcelli and A. Potrykowska, 1976). The underlying objective pertains to the question of the extent to which a settlement system (or more specifically, some of its hierarchical components) is moulded by territorial administrative divisions. This represents one aspect of a broader problem of interdependence between settlement systems and regional systems of hierarchical organization. The matter is also of practical importance in view of the recent change in administrative divisions in Poland, including a shift from a three-level to a two-level structure. The study of the performance of administrative centers over the past decades should permit some predictions to be made concerning the evolution of the cities which have moved up in the administrative hierarchy, as well as that of cities which have lost their previous rank.

The initial hypotheses have been formulated as follows: (1) the pattern of tertiary functions in the settlement system conforms to the administrative pattern; and (2) the two patterns tend to grow more alike over time, i.e. the development of service activities is a positive function of the city administrative rank.

It should be noted that under planned-economy conditions the spatial organization of the tertiary sector is contained, to a certain extent, within the administrative framework, i.e. the range of a considerable group of functions, especially public services, follows administrative boundaries. To avoid the tautology, the activities selected in the analysis are other than public administration.

The degree of correspondence between tertiary sector and spatial administrative patterns in the settlement system, as postulated in the initial hypotheses, is conditioned by a number of distorting factors. These include (a) differing individual economic sector proportions among cities as well as over time; (b) variations in the spatial range of individual activities. Even those functions which are thought to have a typical central place character may form specialized clusters at the national level, e.g. retail and medical facilities in health resorts. One can assume that individual tertiary functions are to a varying degree nested within local, regional, and national systems; (c) economic base rules according to which the share of endogenous sectors expand with growing city size (E. Ullman and M. Dacey, 1960); (d) spatial variations in the level and patterns of consumption (service demand) as well as the patterns of service supply (E. Nowosielska, 1972); and (e) internal functional specialization of urban agglomerations (B.J.L. Berry, 1960) and the patterns of commuting to work. Some of the tertiary activities tend to be employment, rather than residential population, oriented.

There are basically three indirect ways of measuring tertiary sector activities on a comparative scale: (1) the economic base approach, which emphasizes the relative size of regionally oriented exogenous employment (M. Jerczyński, 1973); (2) the central place approach based on centrality indices (the number of functions or number of establishments per urban place) and, finally, (3) the metropolitan dominance concept, with its conventional per capita indices. The last approach has been adopted in the present study for a number of reasons.

The first option is conceptually possible but it would require an *a priori* definition of the spatial range for each function. Since the actual range is generally dependent on city size, the share of regionally-oriented exogenous employment as identified indirectly tends to be underestimated in the case of small places, but overestimated in the case of large cities which have a greater endogenous sector. This approach was ruled out on practical grounds because of the high level of employment data aggregation for smaller urban places. The second option was also out of the question for data reasons. In addition, it does not seem appropriate because when a large group of urban places are studied their arrangement according to centrality indices always follows (in terms of correlation values) the structure as measured by population size.

The data actually used consist of sixteen per capita indices pertaining to retail trade, catering, primary and secondary education, medical services, entertainment, hotels, etc., i.e. those activities which have been traditionally regarded as the principal generators of intra-regional and hierarchical linkage patterns. For medium-size and small towns the number of indices used was smaller because of data limitations.

The plotting of individual index values against city size yielded simple correlation coefficients that were astonishingly low; in fact most of the values fell within the ± 0.2 range. The high degree of dispersion does not permit conclusions to be drawn concerning the uniformity of tertiary-function development in cities of different size. Some regularities, however, could be identified. First, the r values had negative signs in 116 out of 136 cases, which is in accordance with the economic base rule which postulates a higher per capita service-functions supply in small as compared to large cities. Second, when administrative centers (343 units) were subtracted from the whole set of 891 urban places, higher negative r values or a shift from positive to negative values occurred in 61 out of 65 cases. This supports the initial hypothesis that administrative centers are characterized by higher per capita index values than the remaining urban places. However, the correlation coefficients did not indicate any clear temporal pattern of change.

Similar results were obtained by analyzing rank patterns of individual per capita indices as well as the distribution of the sum of ranks. The figures show that administrative centers are characterized by a higher concentration of service sector establishments than non-administrative centers within a given population size category. The administrative centers of lower orders have generally higher ranks than the centers of higher orders. For example, the median rank (sum of ranks) for provincial (voivodship) capitals is below the median for the whole set of 891 urban places, while the corresponding index for district (poviat) capitals is well above the median. The poviat centers accounted for two-thirds out of the top thirty urban places, when arranged according to the lowest sum of ranks.

A comparison of rank patterns for 1960, 1965, 1970 and 1973 showed no definite trend in the distribution of service sector activities by administrative status of cities. There was no indication of an adjustment of service patterns to the orders of urban administrative hierarchy nor any signs of spatial concentration in the service sector. The ranks of administrative centers, in terms of per capita indices of service functions, have even slightly declined over the period under investigation. This is attributed to the high rates of growth of these cities; tertiary functions have lagged somewhat behind rapidly expanding population and industrial employment.

Another observation is the high stability of the rank structure, which is mainly attributed to urban population rank-size patterns. The present data show that rank correlation coefficient values for individual tertiary sector indices tend to be not much lower than the corresponding values for urban population. (For example, the rank coefficients for 79 major cities arranged according to the number of doctors per 1000 inhabitants were 0.93, 0.93 and 0.92 for the three consecutive time periods; the corresponding population rank-size values were 0.92, 0.99 and 0.99.)

The findings, though they are partial and fail to take account of the distorting factors listed earlier, can be summed up as follows: First, the spatial pattern of administration and service sector functions in a settlement system are interdependent, although to a lower degree than expected. This conclusion is also supported by a recent factor analysis of Polish cities by A. Zagozdzon (1976). Second, to fully assess the impact of administrative divisions upon the existing settlement structure, a study should cover at least two or three decades. This again points to the resistence of historically-developed settlement patterns to external factors, and to their high stability.

CONCLUSIONS

The question of interrelations between settlement systems and regional socioeconomic systems is extremely broad and in fact is present in most, if not all, settlement concepts. It has been treated explicitly in the large body of work referring to the structure of settlement and the distribution of productive forces. It is latent in the recent discussion on intraregional versus interregional linkages among cities. Many aspects of this question, however, have not been studied in a comprehensive way. For example, although urban spatial interaction models also have been applied on a regional scale, their structure has remained basically the same. Also, these models have not been successfully combined with regional economic and spatial demographic models. From a different perspective, many approaches to regional analysis fail to take account of the structure of settlement systems. Despite the fact that "urban and regional" is often combined in a single phrase, there are many problems on the interface which have received little attention.

REFERENCES

Aganbegyan, A.G., Bandman, M.K. (1976), Simulation of the Formation of Territorial Production Complexes, 96–118 in *Soviet Geographic Studies*, USSR Academy of Sciences, National Committee of Soviet Geographers, Moscow.

Aganbegyan, A.G., Bandman, M.K., Granberg, A.G. (1976), Programmnocelovoy podkhod y matematicheskoe modelyrovanye perspectyv razvytya Sibirii (A Comprehensive Programming Approach to Mathematical Modelling of the Development of Siberia), 108–122 in *Sovremennye problemy geografii*, Nauka, Moscow.

Agaphonov, N.T., Lavrov, S.B. (1976), Some Interrelations of the Urbanization and the Forms of Social Organization of Production, in *Processes and Patterns of Urbanization*, Leningrad, National Committee of Soviet Geographers.

Alayev, E., Khorev, B. (1976), Formation of a Unified Settlement System in the USSR, 169–170 in *Soviet Geographical Studies*, USSR Academy of Sciences, National Committee of Soviet Geographers, Moscow.

Berry, B.J.L. (1960), The Impact of the Expanding Metropolitan Communities upon the Central Place Hierarchy, *Annals of the Association of American Geographers*, 49, 145–155.

Berry, B.J.L. (1973), *Growth Centers in American Urban System*, Vols. 1, 2, Ballinger, Cambridge, Mass.

Bourne, L.S. (1975), *Urban Systems. Strategies for Regulation*, Clarendon Press, Oxford.

Cesario, F.J., Smith, T.E. (1975), Directions for Future Research in Spatial Interaction Modelling, *Papers of the Regional Science Association*, 35, 57–72.

Chojnicki, Z., Czyż, T. (1973), Structural Changes in the Economic Regions in Poland: A Study by Factor Analysis of Commodity Flows, *Geographia Polonica*, 25, 31–48.

Courbis, R. (1975), Urban Analysis in the Regional-National Model REGINA of the French Economy, *Environment and Planning A*, 7, 863–878.

Curry, L. (1972), A Spatial Analysis of Gravity Flows, *Regional Studies*, 6, 131–147.

Domański, R. (1975), *Elements of the Theory of Processes in Urban Settlement Systems*, Paper presented at the Regional Science Conference, Budapest.

Duncan, O.D. et al. (1960), *Metropolis and Region*, Resources for the Future, Baltimore.

Dziewoński, K. (1971), *Program badań systemu osadniczego Polski* (Programmes of Studies on the Settlement System of Poland), Institute of Geography, P.Ac.Sc., Warszawa.

Dziewoński, K. (1975), The Place of Urban Agglomerations in the Settlement System of Poland, *Geographia Polonica*, *30*, 9–20.

Dziewoński, K. (1976), Changes in the Processes of Industrialization and Urbanization, *Geographia Polonica*, *33*, 39–58.

Fomin, G.N. (1976), Scientific Fundamentals and Ways of Realization of the General Scheme of Population Distribution in the USSR, *Geoforum*, *7*, 259–269.

Friedmann, J. (1972), A General Theory of Polarized Development, in N. Hansen, ed., *Growth Centers in Regional Economic Development*, Free Press, New York.

Friedmann, J., Miller, J. (1965), The Urban Field, *Journal of the American Institute of Planners*, *31*, 312–319.

Gokhman, V., Lappo, G., Maergoiz, J., Mashbits, J. (1976), Geographic Aspects of Urbanization and its Peculiarities in Countries with Different Social Systems, *Geoforum*, *7*, 271–283.

Hall, P. et al. (1973), *The Containment of Urban England, 1, 2*, Allen and Unwin, London.

Hansen, N. (1975), An Evaluation of Growth Center Theory and Practice, *Environment and Planning A*, *7*, 821–832.

Hansen, N. (1976), *Systems Approaches to Human Settlements*, RM–76–36, International Institute for Applied Systems Analysis, Laxenburg, Austria.

Jerczyński, M. (1973), *Zagadnienia specjalizacji bazy ekonomicznej w Polsce* (Problems of Specialization in the Economic Base of Polish Cities), in Studia nad struktura funkcjonalna miast, *Prace Geograficzne*, *97*, Warszawa.

Jui-Cheng-Huang, Gould, P. (1974), Diffusion in the Urban Hierarchy: The Case of Rotary Clubs, *Economic Geography*, *50*, 333–340.

Khodzaev, D.G., Khorev, B.S. (1976), A Single System of Settling (SSS) in the USSR and the Planning of the Development of Towns, *Geoforum*, *7*, 285–293.

Khodzaev, D.G., Khorev, B.S. (1973), The Concept of a Unified Settlement System and the Planned Control of the Growth of Towns in the USSR, *Geographia Polonica*, *27*, 43–51.

Khorev, B.S. (1971), *Problemy gorodov* (Problems of Cities), Mysl, Moscow.

Korcelli, P. (1976), *The Human Settlement Systems Study: Suggested Research Directions*, RM–76–38, International Institute for Applied Systems Analysis, Laxenburg, Austria.

Korcelli, P., Potrykowska, A. (1976), *Rozwój funkcji usługowych a hierarchia administracyjna miast w Polsce* (Urban Administrative Hierarchy and the Development of the Tertiary Sector), Committee for Space Economy and Regional Planning, P.Ac.Sc., Warszawa.

Lappo, G.M. (1976), Basic Characteristics and Problems of the Development of Urban Agglomerations, *Geographia Polonica, 37*, in print.

Lasuén, J.R. (1973), Urbanization and Development—the Temporal Interaction Between Geographical and Sectoral Clusters, *Urban Studies, 10*, 163–188.

Marshall, J.U. (1969), *The Location of Service Towns: An Approach to the Analysis of Central Place Systems*, Department of Geography, University of Toronto, University of Toronto Press.

Nowosielska, E. (1972), *Zróżnicowanie popytu i podaży usług w układzie wojewódzkim* (Spatial Variations in Service Demand and Supply by Voivodships), Committee for Space Economy and Regional Planning; P.Ac.Sc., *Biuletyn, 73*, Warszawa.

Pred, A. (1973), *The Growth and Development of Systems of Cities in Advanced Economies*, in Systems of Cities and Information Flows: *Two Essays, Lund Studies in Geography*, Ser. B., *38*.

Pred, A. (1975), On the Spatial Structure of Organizations and the Complexity of Metropolitan Interdependence, *Papers of the Regional Science Association, 35*, 115–142.

Pred, A. (1976), *The Interurban Transmission of Growth in Advanced Economies: Empirical Findings Versus Regional Planning Assumptions*, RR–76–4, International Institute for Applied Systems Analysis, Laxenburg, Austria.

Richardson, H.W. (1973), *Regional Growth Theory*, Macmillan, London.

Rykiel, Z. (1976), *Miejsce aglomeracji wielkomiejskich w przestrzeni społ eczno-gospodarczej Polski* (The Place of Urban Agglomerations in the Socio-Economic Space in Poland), Doctoral theses, Institute of Geography and Spatial Organization, P.Ac.Sc., Warszawa.

Stöhr, W. (1974), *Interurban Systems and Regional Economic Development* Association of American Geographers, Resource Paper No. 26, Washington, D.C.

Ullman, E., Dacey, M. (1960), The Minimum Requirements Approach to the Urban Economic Base, *Papers and Proceedings of the Regional Science Association, 6*, 175–194.

Webber, M.M. (1974), The Urban Place and the Non-Place Urban Realm, 79–153 in M.M. Webber, ed., *Explorations into Urban Structure*, University of Pennsylvania Press, Philadelphia.

Wilson, A.G. (1974), *Urban and Regional Models in Geography and Planning*, Wiley, London.

Winiarski, B. (1974), Regional Planning and Its Interdependencies with Planning on National Level, 207–226 in K. Secomski, ed. *Spatial Planning and Policy. Theoretical Foundations*, Polish Scientific Publishers, Warszawa.

Wood, R.C. (1960), *1400 Governments*, New York Metropolitan Region Study, Harvard University Press, Cambridge, Mass.

Zagożdżon, A. (1976), Regional and Subregional Centres in Poland. A General Characterization, *Geographia Polonica, 33*, 59–74.

❋ *Chapter 12*

Border Regions: A Critique of Spatial Theory and a European Case Study

Niles M. Hansen

INTRODUCTION

In Europe and North America increasing attention is being devoted to the special problems of border regions, which may be defined as subnational areas whose social and economic life is directly and significantly affected by proximity to an international frontier. This study critically summarizes the nature and significance of location theory and the growth pole literature with respect to border region issues and policies. The trinational Alsace-Baden-Basel area is considered in some detail because it has become a focal point for several trends or tendencies toward change which are being experienced in varying degree by border regions throughout Western Europe and elsewhere. These include increasing international economic integration, the revival of regional ethnic and linguistic communities, and pressures to decentralize political and economic decision-making processes within countries. The concluding section suggests a number of working hypotheses that could prove useful in further research on border region economies.

LOCATION THEORY

Border Region Disadvantages
Neither Christaller nor Lösch developed a systematic theory of border regions. Nevertheless, both scholars tended to regard them as disadvantaged areas because of international barriers to trade and the threat of military invasion.

In terms of Christaller's analysis, central place systems may be organized according to either of two nowfamiliar economic rationales, the market principle or the traffic principle. But it is especially relevant in the context of border regions that Christaller [7, pp. 77–80] also recognized a third system of spatial organization based on the "sociopolitical separation principle." This system arises when there are strong notions of community and of defense and protection. The determination of its exact laws lies in the domain of theoretical political geography, but Christaller [7, p. 80] held that the separation principle "has neither the authority nor the rationality of the economic principles, but it has the authority of stately and sovereign might."

Border regions may be fragile in Christaller's scheme because national frontiers artificially cut up spatially complementary regions. Christaller [7, pp. 95–96] further maintained that capital costs have great importance in the development of central places because they primarily determine the lower range limit of central goods, and particularly those with a high proportion of capital costs to total costs. In unstable border areas capital costs would contain a high risk premium and consequently goods would have to be sold at higher prices. This in turn would lead to a transfer of consumption to other central places. Central places on unstable borders will thus have relatively small complementary areas and limited development. Of course, cities may grow on national borders for defensive purposes but they may have only fractional hinterlands. Or cities that once had a large complementary region (e.g., Vienna before the First World War) may lose most of their market areas when drastic political boundary revisions take place (e.g., Vienna after the First World War). Although Christaller [7, p. 79] illustrated a possible system of central places according to the separation principle, the only general conclusion to be drawn when this principle is operative is that many more central places will be required to supply a region with central goods than would have been the case if the economic principles had been followed.

Lösch [21, pp. 199–200; see also pp. 445–451] also realized that border regions may have special problems because of conflicts between political and economic goals. The goals of economic landscapes are, in order of priority: prosperity, *Kultur*, power, and continuance. However, the political goals of the nation-state have exactly the reverse order. In this context Lösch noted a number of specific difficulties that arise in border regions because of political boundaries. First, tariffs separate economically complementary market areas; second, differences in language, customs and national character have the same effect as customs duties; third, public contracts and "official traffic" do not cross the border; and fourth, border areas are the most threatened in military terms.

In contrast to Christaller and Lösch, Giersch [13] developed a theory of location that was primarily intended to explain the consequences of political boundaries. Giersch argued that the lower the costs of transportation of a product and the greater the internal economies of large-scale production, the larger will be the market areas and the fewer the firms that will emerge. What is particularly significant is that the larger the market areas the fewer will be the entrepreneurs who choose a location near the frontier. There is a network of markets for every commodity but the whole system of networks tends to become denser in the center than at the extremities. When capital growth, internal and external economies (due to indivisibilities), and rent-lag are introduced into the model, the advantages of the favored location cumulate, an agglomeration center necessarily appears, and the spatial distribution of economic activities acquires a cone-like shape. Thus, in Europe, for example, political boundaries and national agglomeration have produced a form of international deglomeration. The European distribution of industries is broader than that of the United States, with its unitary market, but the resulting pattern has been unfavorable for European border regions.

Border Region Advantages

Despite the generally unfavorable picture, location theorists have recognized that border regions may have some advantages. Christaller [7, p. 46] noted that central places on stable political boundaries may benefit from the development of trading activity at the border, the storage of goods, and earnings derived from the collection of duties, even though they may have no, or almost no, complementary region. For some central goods, e.g., concerts and dining, the border may not be an impediment, in which case the complementary region has the ideal form of a circle that may extend far into the neighboring country.

Lösch [21, pp. 382–388] pointed out that border regions may benefit from transfrontier investments made in order to avoid customs duties. Thus, Swiss entrepreneurs had long established branches in German border regions for this reason, although lower wages may also have been a motive. Headquarters were maintained in Switzerland to save on taxes but branches could be readily managed from the home office, Swiss key personnel employed, and contact with Swiss financial backers maintained. Similarly, Lösch argued that many branch plants of U.S. firms would never have been established in Canadian border areas in the absence of a political frontier.

In terms of Giersch's analysis, international economic integration would weaken the international deglomeration effects of national agglomeration. Within a European Common Market, for example, particular regions would tend to gain economically because of their location near the industrial center. But it is difficult to speak here of border region advantages because the areas in question would in fact no longer be border regions.

GROWTH POLE THEORY

Growth pole theory emphasizes that international and interregional inequalities are an inevitable part of the development process. It maintains that analysis of sustained growth of total production should concentrate on the process by which various activities appear, grow in importance, and in some cases disappear, and it emphasizes that growth rates vary considerably from sector to sector. Entrepreneurial innovation is given a prominent place in explaining the origins of the growth process, which takes the form of a succession of dynamic sectors, or poles, through time. A particularly regional flavor has been given to the pole concept by emphasizing that growth is concentrated in various spatial loci as well as in certain leading industrial branches. A great deal of attention is given in this context to the importance of economies of scale and to larger considerations of external economies of agglomeration. In the past two decades a large theoretical literature has evolved around these notions and growth center policies (usually intended to induce growth in lagging regions) have been adopted by planning authorities all over the world, although the extent to which they have been influenced by growth pole theory has varied considerably (see, for example, Hansen [15], Kuklinski [20] and Moseley [23]).

An influential French literature maintains that the growth pole approach is instructive in the study of border regions. Much of this literature is concerned with the Franco-German-Swiss border area, and particularly with the French region of Alsace in relation to the contiguous German region of Baden and the neighboring Swiss metropole of Basel. The dominant theme is that Alsace is in a more or less threatened economic position vis-à-vis Baden and Basel.

Gendarme [12] argues that the main consequence of a political frontier is to check the spread effects (*effets de diffusion*) of a development pole. The latter will not have the same strength in inducing other activities that they would have had inside a national space. He calls particular attention to situations where "zones of underdevelopment" on one side of the border coexist with "zones of overdevelopment" on the other. This phenomenon, which he describes as an "incomplete development pole," is a result of such factors as customs barriers, failure to take advantage of complementary natural resources, a tendency for transportation routes to run parallel with borders rather than across them, and supply and demand problems with respect to labor market integration.

Gendarme recognizes that investments are made across a border in order to penetrate a foreign market and still maintain control of operations from a position of proximity in the country of origin. However, he regards such investments as exceptional in the total scheme of things; more significant is the tendency of countries to react negatively, for narrowly nationalist reasons, to foreign investments. Moreover, within nations capital mobility has worsened the economic situation in border regions. A "fortress mentality" has led to stagnation because industrialists refuse to invest in threatened areas, with the exception of activities related to national defense or when essential resources (iron ore, coal) are found there. For such reasons a region such as Alsace could be regarded as having experienced World War Two already in 1933. (Similarly, Lorraine's lack of investments in manufacturing activities related to the steel produced there can be attributed to the region's proximity to Germany. In fact, in the 1930s some plants originally located between the Maginot Line and the Siegfried Line were dismantled and reassembled in central France.)

Urban [29] also has examined the evolution of the Alsace-Baden-Basel area in terms of growth pole theory but, in contrast to Gendarme, stresses that the spread effects of growth poles override political boundaries, in this case allegedly to the detriment of Alsace. Boudeville [3] takes an intermediate position concerning the impact of a border on spread effects, but he [4, p. 232] argues nonetheless that a multinodal growth pole should be developed in southern Alsace "in order to balance Basel's dangerous polarization at the junction of the Rhine and the Swiss plateau."

A SUMMARY CRITIQUE OF
THE LOCATION AND GROWTH
POLE THEORIES IN A BORDER
REGION CONTEXT

Although many of the peculiarities of border regions have been clearly recognized by location theorists, it is difficult to derive policy implications from their models because they neglect the development process. Problems common to border regions—disparities in growth rates, commuting and migration of workers across frontiers, lack of coherence in social and economic infrastructure, differing planning contexts, etc.—are not amenable to solutions flowing directly from location theory because it has not been concerned with policy paths that could be followed in order to realize economically rational market structures.

Growth pole theory developed in part as a reaction against static location theory. However, because it provides few insights into border region problems that are not found already—at least implicitly—in the older literature, it is difficult to see what is to be gained by adopting its often imprecise jargon. Berry [2, p. 108] has argued that since the growth pole approach is "sadly deficient" in terms of theory it should be subsumed under the more general hierarchical diffusion model of regional development. According to this model, growth-inducing innovations are transmitted simultaneously from higher to lower order centers in the urban hierarchy and outward from urban centers into their surrounding hinterland areas in the form of radiating spread effects. But Pred [25] has convincingly demonstrated that these assumptions are mistaken; moreover, the disappointing record of growth center policies that have been implemented in many countries reinforces this position.

Although Alsace-Baden-Basel has been the principal border area examined in the growth pole literature and although it also has attracted the attention of location theorists, notably Lösch [21, pp. 383, 449], neither of these approaches has succeeded in formulating a satisfactory theory of border regions. It will be argued in the remainder of this chapter that this trinational area nevertheless provides insights that should be instructive in developing such a theory.

ALSACE-BADEN-BASEL

The Importance of Basel

The economy of Basel is characterized by an internationally important tertiary sector (banks, insurance companies, trade, transportation) and by an industrial sector oriented toward rapidly-growing, high-technology activities (chemistry, machine construction, graphic arts). Hoffmann-La Roche, Ciba-Geigy and Sandoz, the giants of Basel's chemical industry, ranked second, fifth, and seventh among the world's leading pharmaceutical companies in 1974. The three groups together have well over 200 production and processing plants outside Switzerland and nearly three times as many persons employed abroad as at headquarters [18, p. 13]. The dynamism of the local economy is supported by close collaboration between the University and industry, sustained scientific research efforts, and a marked capacity for technical and commercial innovation (see Urban [29]). Using 1965 data (still the most recent relevant data available at this writing), Gaudard [11, p. 657] remarks that "Basel had a per capita social product of Fr. 11,610 compared with the Swiss average of Fr. 8430, which placed it at the first rank in the Confederation. Geneva, with Fr. 10,165, came next. These two border cantons thus preceded Zurich (Fr. 9755), whose reputation for wealth is generally recognized."

Physical geography has limited Basel's territorial spheres of influence within Switzerland but its economic influence extends well into southern Alsace and Baden. However, it is noteworthy that along the entire Swiss frontier, Swiss cities exert influence on foreign territory whereas the converse situation is practically nonexistent. This suggests that the reasons for Basel's regional preeminence are to be found in large part in the more general context of Swiss development, and here the border has played a significant and positive role. In the sixteenth and seventeenth centuries Basel and Geneva welcomes thousands of religious and political refugees from France; their knowledge, initiative, and capital played an important part in local economic development. Down to the present day the Swiss border has provided security for people and, together with the stability of the Swiss franc and the discretion of Swiss bankers, security for capital. Moreover, Switzerland is crossed by a number of major international trade routes. Border cities have benefited from the development of service activities oriented toward international transit, as well as from the intensity of Swiss foreign trade, which accounts for about 2 percent of all global exports (see Gaudard [11]).

In view of these considerations Basel's importance cannot simply be explained by the city's position in a regional, national, or even international urban hierarchy. Rather, it is a result of complex historical, geographic, political and economic factors, both internal and external, which have operated in the context of a stable border situation. Moreover, the significance of this stability has been enhanced during periods of international instability elsewhere in Europe.

Alsace as a Border Region

Within the French national context Alsace is generally regarded as one of the more developed regions. The data presented in Table 12–1 support this view. For most of the economic indicators shown Alsace fares better than France as a whole. Alsace's somewhat lower values

Table 12–1. Selected Economic Indicators for France and Alsace

	France	Alsace	Rank of Alsace[1]
Gross Domestic Product Per Capita, 1970	15,400 F.	15,600 F.	4
Gross Disposable Income Per Capita, 1970	11,100 F.	10,600 F.	4
Percent of Population Residing in Urban-Industrial Zones, 1968	79.0	90.7	5
Residential and Tertiary Energy Consumption (KWH) Per Capita, 1973	1060	1005	7
Percent of Households with Refrigerator, 1974	88.5	92.6	1
Percent of Households with Washing Machine, 1974	68.7	75.8	3
Percent of Households with Television, 1974	82.4	85.1	3
Percent of Households with Automobile, 1974	62.7	67.0	5

Note: [1] Rank refers to the place of Alsace in the array of France's twenty-one planning program regions.

Source: Institut National de la Statistique et des Etudes Economiques, "Statistiques et indicateurs des régions françaises," *Les collections de l'INSEE*, série R, No. 19–20, November, 1975, pp. 20, 53, 264, 270.

for per capita gross disposable income and residential and tertiary energy consumption reflect the great weight of the Paris region. In the general setting of France's 21 program regions, the rank of Alsace is relatively high for every variable.

However, as the growth pole literature illustrates, Alsace is regarded as a weak region when compared with neighboring German and Swiss regions. One manifestation of this position is the flow of daily commuters who take advantage of higher wage levels across the Rhine. Their number increased from 8800 in 1952 to 14,500 in 1968 to 31,200 in 1974; the corresponding figures for international commuters as a proportion of employed Alsatian residents were 1.6 percent, 2.6 percent, and 5.4 percent, respectively. The census of 1975 indicated that Alsace had more international out-commuters than any other French region. In southern Alsace, these *frontaliers*, who nearly all worked in Switzerland, accounted for 6.4 percent of the employed residents. In more populous northern Alsace the comparable figure was 3.2 percent, though in fifteen communes the proportion working in the Federal Republic of Germany (FRG) was greater than 30 percent (see INSEE [17]). This fluidity, which is virtually a one-way street, is not without its problems. For example, early in 1966 wages on the German side of the border were 21 percent higher than on the French side; many Alsatian firms felt that as a result they were losing needed skilled workers to German firms. In contrast, during the 1966–67 recession many Alsatian workers in Germany were affected by layoffs (see Gendarme [12, p. 897]). The recession of the mid-1970s had a similar effect. The number of *frontaliers* going to both the FRG and Switzerland declined to 29,300 in 1975 and to 27,200 in March of 1976. However, it was expected that international commuting would resume its long-run upward movement when the cyclical situation improved, especially in view of the age structure of commuters. In 1975, 64 percent of the *frontaliers* were in the relatively mobile 20–35 age-group, whereas only 40 percent of the Alsatians working in Alsace were in this age-group (see INSEE [17, p. 33]).

A survey carried out in 1965 indicated that the four principal causes for international commuting from Alsace were, in order of importance: (1) higher wages in the FRG and Switzerland; (2) the threat of unemployment in Alsace; (3) insufficient transportation facilities in Alsace; and (4) better working conditions across the Rhine (see Urban [29, p. 619]). It should be noted that the devaluation of the French franc in relation to the German mark and the Swiss franc in the early 1970s increased the economic incentive for Alsatians to commute to work across the Rhine. In view of these considerations it is not uncommon to find complaints in France that the rapid growth of Baden and Basel represents a brake on the expansion of Alsace, because their growth deprives Alsace of skilled workers. But then one must ask why employment-inducing investments are not greater in Alsace. Productive investments in Alsace certainly were hindered for a long period by the fact that it was a border region on an unstable frontier. As a result of the Franco-Prussian War (1870), Alsace became a part of Germany just when its linkages with the rest of France were beginning to bring significant economic benefits. By the turn of the century, when the Alsatian economy was finally becoming integrated with that of Germany, the events that culminated in the First World War put a check on German investments in the region. In 1918 Alsace returned to France, but the fortress mentality of the interwar years and the Second World War itself were highly detrimental to the region's development. Traband [28, pp. 401–402] points out that "each regime brought its wave of investments but none had sufficient time to realize development potentials. This progression in spurts explains why Alsace has so many small and medium-size firms but few with more than a thousand workers."

Private investment in Alsace is no doubt inhibited by deficiencies in public infrastructure. In contrast to neighboring cities such as Karlsruhe and Basel, which contain numerous specialized services and corporate decision centers, the development of the tertiary sector in Alsace suffers from a lack of telecommunications facilities. The road network in Alsace badly needs improvement, whereas the regions across the Rhine are closely linked to an express highway system serving the industrial heartland of Europe. Moreover, banking and financial facilities are more numerous and more powerful in Baden and Basel than in Alsace. Despite these and similar problems, a study by Prud'homme [26] indicates that Alsace has been "clearly disfavored" by central government regional policy (see also INSEE [16, p. 342]).

In the past two decades a high proportion of new industrial plant locations in Alsace has been generated by foreign investments. Between the beginning of 1955 and the end of 1973, 204 plants in Alsace were either newly located by or purchased by foreign investors (see Table 12–2). Foreign investment accounted for nearly one-half of the new firms in the region during this period.

Firms which were primarily controlled (over 50 percent owner-

Table 12–2. New Industrial Firms and Industrial Employment in Alsace Attributable to French and Foreign Investments, 1955 Through 1973

Origin	Number of Firms	Percent of All New Firms	Number of Jobs	Percent of All New Jobs
1. French	214	51.2	37,877	57.6
2. Foreign				
F.R.G.	106	25.4	14,098	21.4
Switzerland	37	8.8	3,234	4.9
U.S.A.	16	3.8	5,016	7.6
Great Britain	3	0.7	886	1.4
Canada	2	0.5	730	1.1
Belgium	2	0.5	65	0.1
Other	3	0.7	357	0.5
Total	169	40.4	24,386	37.1
3. Mixed Franco-foreign	31	7.4	3,359	5.1
4. Mixed foreign	4	1.0	170	0.3
Grand total	418	100.0	65,792	100.0

Source: Derived from Association de Développement et d'Industrialisation de la Région Alsace, *Les Investissements étrangers en Alsace*, Strasbourg: ADIRA, 1974, p. 2.

ship) by foreign investors accounted for about 28,000 new jobs during the 1955−73 period. These jobs represented 42 percent of newly-created employment and nearly 11 percent of total employment in the region in 1973. In terms of new jobs created, the most important sources of foreign investment were the FRG (21.4 percent), the United States (7.6 percent) and Switzerland (4.9 percent). Foreign investment was especially significant in southern Alsace, accounting for 61 percent of new employment. In northern Alsace the corresponding figure was 30 percent; in this area the weight of large French firms such as Peugeot, Citroën, and Rhône-Poulenc dampened the role of foreign investment.

Foreign investments in Alsace have been largely responsible for the growth of the chemical and plastic materials sectors, and, more recently, the electrical equipment and electronics sectors. Their role has been fundamental in the diversification of regional industry. German investments have been made in a wide range of activities but their predominance is especially great in such traditional branches of Alsatian industry as textiles, leather products, and wood products. American and Swiss investments, on the other hand, have been highly concentrated in high-productivity plants in the electrical equipment, electronics, chemical and plastics sectors (see ADIRA [1]).

It is noteworthy that German and Swiss investors (as well as those in Belgium and Luxemburg) tend to view investments in France as an extension of their enterprises beyond national frontiers. They usually acquire stock in existing firms or buy them outright; the extensions are traditional whether viewed from a sectoral or a regional perspective and they often are made because of labor shortages at home. This contrasts with the behavior of investors from noncontiguous countries such as the United States, Great Britain, and the Netherlands; they tend to consider the whole of France, but the specific decision concerning where to locate is made in the context of an European network of production and an attempt is made to minimize production costs in the individual plant. Essentially, what one is dealing with here is the large, innovative multinational corporation more concerned with setting up new establishments than with geographic extensions of traditional activities (see DATAR [8, pp. 25−28]).

When both international commuting and foreign investments are taken into account it is apparent that the Alsatian economy is closely linked to those of her contiguous foreign neighbors. On the other hand, a study by DATAR [8] indicates that investments in Alsace from other, noncontiguous foreign countries, while far from negligible, do not set the region apart from other French regions in any significant way. If the Alsatian economy is less strong than those of Baden and Basel, Alsatians nonetheless benefit economically from their proximity to these areas. The notion that Alsace is threatened economically or politically by foreign neighbors is outdated. Indeed, the greatest economic threat appears to be neglect by Paris, which is reluctant to see Alsace become more thoroughly integrated into the Rhine axis extending from the North Sea to Switzerland. As many authorities point out, this space is the dynamic backbone of the European Community (see DATAR [10, p. 34], Juillard [19], Nonn [24, pp. 3–13], and Urban [29, pp. 623–629]).

As remarked earlier, Alsace has been disfavored by French regional policy; but there is an even more fundamental issue here, namely, that of national administrative structures and their impact on regional economic initiatives. In the FRG a great deal of autonomy is accorded the various states (*Länder*) and despite regional disparities there is a remarkable degree of geographic balance in the overall development of the country. (The relatively dispersed network of cities and industrial activities is a consequence of the fact that Germany was not a centralized state at the time of the first industrial revolution, but rather a loose confederation of autonomous states.) Income from taxation is divided among the central government, the states, and the municipalities. The last are free to dispose of their funds as they see fit; in addition, they benefit from easy access to financial markets. Management of local government is facilitated because their financial resources are known in advance. Decentralized decision-making also favors rapid adaptation to the requirements of social and economic development. The autonomy of local governments in Switzerland is even more pronounced (see DATAR [9, p. 126] and Urban [29, p. 623]). One of the principal obstacles to meaningful regional planning in France has been its vertical and hierarchical system of public administration; each ministry has its central administration in Paris and exterior services in the provinces. Despite recent reforms favoring decentralized decision-making, Maugué [22, p. 44] concludes that "it increasingly appears that a true regionalization is needed if Alsace is to be able to exploit her advantages. The Alsatian economy will never be able to compete with bordering Rhine regions until she can exercise—as the German states and the Swiss cantons—a high degree of autonomy of action, which will permit her to deal directly with her own economic problems."

IMPLICATIONS FOR BORDER
REGION ANALYSIS

The foregoing discussions suggest a number of working hypotheses that could prove useful in further research on border region economies.

First, both location theorists and growth pole theorists have tended to emphasize the fragile and threatened nature of border regions. This may correspond to reality in some instances, e.g., along the increasingly porous Iron Curtain, but within Western Europe the international political climate has changed to such an extent that it seems more reasonable to study border regions in the context of economic integration. (In a more modest way this also pertains to the situation with respect to the United States and Mexico.)

In Giersch's theory of location, centrally-located border regions would gain economically by international economic integration. The growth of the Rhine axis appears to support this position. However, the picture is more complex than Giersch's theory implies. A study by Robert [27, pp. 353–354] of the recent economic and demographic evolution of North-West Europe (Belgium, The Netherlands, France, the FRG, and Great Britain) indicates that the attractiveness of coastal areas has increased because of European dependence on energy and raw materials from other continents, the evolution of transportation technology and the increasing importance of sea transportation for exports of manufactured products and for imports of raw materials, and the construction of advanced facilities in port areas for transforming primary materials. Also, if enterprises outside an economic union locate plants within the union for fear of losing a market, this may give yet another advantage to peripheral maritime areas, e.g., Belgium and The Netherlands. The growth of border regions along the southern Rhine may be due not only to their central location within Western Europe, but also to the fact that they are linked by waterway to the North Sea. It may thus be hypothesized that economic integration will promote growth in centrally-located border regions but the extent of this growth will be conditioned by the degree of accessibility to rapidly-growing peripheral areas.

Location theorists were correct in maintaining that a political boundary causes numerous inefficiencies with respect to duplication of administrative services and of facilities for providing many central goods. However, as Christaller noted, a stable frontier can have advantages. For some goods and services a central place on a border has a hinterland corresponding to the market principle; and the border creates functions related to trade, storage and customs activities. It may be added that the increased factor mobility that accompanies greater economic integration creates enhanced employment opportunities for workers in a region such as Alsace (see also Burtenshaw [6]). It also contributes to the importance of the border as a functioning institution. A border is a line that unites as well as separates. Gordon [14, p. 490] finds that "the United States-Mexican border came first and then came the population. The population was not already there in the border cities from Brownsville to Tijuana." In view of these considerations, it may be hypothesized that a stable border, together with relatively unimpeded international labor and capital mobility will, on balance, be more advantageous than disadvantageous to a border region.

Finally, the "problems" of border regions often are more political than economic in nature. This was clearly recognized by the German location theorists, who held that rational spatial allocation is thwarted by nationalist political actions. On the other hand, some growth pole theorists have in effect promoted nationalism by their unsubstantiated assertions that "domination" from one side of a border, viz. Basel and Baden, is a "threat" to the other wise, viz. Alsace. Alsace is in fact one of the economically stronger French regions. It would be still stronger were it not for central government neglect and the failure to integrate the Alsatian economy more closely with that of other regions of the Rhine axis. Curiously, nationalism also has been invoked to argue that the economically weaker side of a frontier is a threat to the stronger side, because workers from the former depress wages in the latter when they seek employment there legally or illegally. In this view, the United States border with Mexico should be closed tightly. Briggs [5, p. 482], an advocate of this stance, maintains that "Nominally there may be a world community, but the welfare of most people is dependent upon the decisions of their own government. . . . Consequently, the study of political economy—as has always been the case—begins with existence of political borders." In other words, the worker on the stronger side should not be rewarded according to his efficiency but according to his ability to differentiate labor markets artificially. It is the workers in Baden and Basel who should raise the cry of an Alsatian threat if this position is valid. Such arguments shed little light on border region problems and opportunities because they do not suggest how the nature of these regions can be better understood. By contributing to the persistence of nationalist rhetoric they may in fact inhibit the improvement of economic well-being in border regions.

REFERENCES

1. Association de Développement et d'Industrialisation de la Région Alsace. *Les investissements étrangers en Alsace*, Strasbourg: ADIRA, 1974.

2. Berry, B.J.L. "Hierarchical Diffusion: The Basis of Developmental Filtering and Spread in a System of Growth Centers," in N.M. Hansen (Ed.), *Growth Centers in Regional Economic Development*, New York: The Free Press, 1972.

3. Boudeville, J. "Analyse économique des régions frontière," *Economies et sociétés*, 5 (1971), pp. 773–790.

4. ____. "Polarisation and Urbanisation," *Economie appliquée*, 38 (1975), pp. 215–241.

5. Briggs, V. "Illegal Aliens: The Need for a More Restrictive Border Policy," *Social Science Quarterly*, 56 (1975), pp. 477–484.

6. Burtenshaw, D. *Saar-Lorraine*, London: Oxford University Press, 1976.

7. Christaller, W. *Die zentralen Orte in Süddeutschland*, Jena: Gustav Fischer, 1933. Translated by C.W. Baskin as *Central Places in Southern Germany*, Englewood Cliffs, New Jersey: Prentice-Hall, 1966.

8. Délégation à l'Aménagement du Territoire et à l'Action Régionale. *Investissement étrangers et aménagement du territoire*, Paris: DATAR, 1974.

9. ____. *Scénarios européens*, Paris: DATAR, 1974.

10. ____. *Dynamique urbaine et projet régional*, Paris: DATAR, 1975.

11. Gaudard, G. "Le problème des régions frontière suisses," *Economies et sociétés*, 5 (1971), pp. 649–670.

12. Gendarme, R. "Les problèmes économiques des régions frontières européennes," *Revue économique*, 21 (1970), pp. 889–917.

13. Giersch, H. "Economic Union Between Nations and the Location of Industries," *Review of Economic Studies*, 17 (1949–50), pp. 87–97.

14. Gordon, W. "A Case for a Less Restrictive Border Policy," *Social Science Quarterly*, 56 (1975), pp. 485–491.

15. Hansen, N.M. "An Evaluation of Growth Centre Theory and Practice," *Environment and Planning*, 7 (1975), pp. 821–832.

16. Institut National de la Statistique et des Etudes Economiques. "Statistiques et indicateurs des régions francaises," *Les Collections de l'INSEE*, série R, No. 19–20, November, 1975.

17. ____. Direction Régionale de Strasbourg, "Les travailleurs frontaliers alsaciens en Allemagne ou en Suisse," *Chiffres pour l'Alsace*, 3 (1976), pp. 1–53.

18. *International Herald-Tribune*, May 10, 1976.

19. Juillard, E. "Esquisse de régions multinationales sur le Rhin entre Mannheim et Bâle," *Economies et sociétés*, 5 (1971), pp. 593–602.

20. Kuklinski, A.R. (Ed.). *Growth Poles and Growth Centres in Regional Planning*, Paris and The Hague: Mouton, 1972.

21. Lösch, A. *Die räumliche Ordnung der Wirtschaft*, Jena: Gustav Fischer, 1940. Translated by W.H. Woglom with the assistance of W.F. Stolper as *The Economics of Location*, New Haven: Yale University Press, 1954.

22. Maugué, P. "L'Alsace," in G. Héraud (Ed.), *Contre les Etats: les régions d'Europe*, Paris and Nice: Presses d'Europe, 1973.

23. Moseley, M.J. *Growth Centers in Spatial Planning*, Oxford: Pergamon Press, 1974.

24. Nonn, H. *L'Alsace*, Paris: Librairie Larousse, 1973.

25. Pred, A. *The Interurban Transmission of Growth in Advanced Economies: Empirical Findings versus Regional Planning Assumptions*, Laxenburg, Austria: International Institute for Applied Systems Analysis, RR−76−4, March 1976.

26. Prud'homme, R. "Regional Policy in France, 1962−1972," in N.M. Hansen (Ed.), *Public Policy and Regional Development*, Cambridge, Mass.: Ballinger, 1974.

27. Robert, J. "Prospective Study on Physical Planning and the Environment in the Megalopolis in Formation in North-West Europe," *Urban Ecology*, 1 (1976), pp. 331−411.

28. Traband, A. "De l'influence du Rhin-frontière sur l'organisation régionale," *Bulletin de la Faculté des Lettres de Strasbourg*, 47 (1969), pp. 389−402.

29. Urban, S. "L'intégration économique européenne et l'évolution régionale de part et d'autre du Rhin (Alsace, Bade, Bâle)," *Economies et sociétés*, 5 (1971), pp. 603−635.

Chapter 13

Quality of Life and Changes in Human Settlement Patterns

Peter Nijkamp

INTRODUCTION

The explicit concern of modern public policy and planning with postwar changes in human settlement patterns has evoked the need for adequate research into the spatial components of human behavior, particularly as far as residential and employment decisions are concerned. The way in which one views and explains settlement patterns may have important repercussions for physical planning, as far as it is based on urban and regional research concerning mobility patterns.

According to Tinbergen [1956] any policy-oriented research may be subdivided into two stages, viz. the *analytical* stage and the *political* stage. The analytical stage is related to the way in which the elements of a socioeconomic system are linked together (including the way in which instruments of public policy may affect the endogenous and behavioral variables of the system concerned). The political stage describes which measures have to be taken in order to achieve a set of prespecified goals of the socioeconomic system at hand. In other words, the analytical aspects aim at providing an understanding of the processes giving rise to a certain state of a socioeconomic system, whereas the political aspects focus on procedures and policies to realize a set of well-defined public programs.

Both stages will be considered in this chapter. In the *analytical* stage the problems of changes in settlement patterns and in mobility patterns will be placed in the broader framework of the postwar evolution in welfare and quality-of-life. First, a welfare-model for residential choices and resulting commuting behavior will be presented. On the basis of this approach an aggregate assignment model of mobility behavior (particularly for journey-from-home-to work decisions) will be derived. Particular attention will be paid to the analysis of quality-of-life indicators and to some statistical methods to deal with these indicators. Next, the notion of spatial spill-over effects will be introduced, since these effects play in our opinion a key role in the interwoven process of residential decisions and commuting behavior. On the basis of these notions, an interregional model of residential choice and commuting behavior will be constructed. Then an attempt will be made to develop a procedure (based on mixed entropy and behavioral assumptions) to disaggregate this interregional model at the interlocal level. The working of the model will be clarified by referring to some empirical results from the Netherlands.

The *political* stage of this study is concerned with a description of a set of proposals recently made in the Netherlands to arrive at a more integrated and coordinated physical planning, in which a better control of the evolution of settlement patterns ranks very highly. Ultimately, these policy proposals will be confronted with the analytical part of the study.

A UTILITY MODEL OF SPATIAL MOBILITY

Problems like settlement and land use planning within the context both of the region and locality can only be attacked in a satisfactory manner on the basis of adequate insight into mobility motives of the ·population. This implies that phenomena like congestion, industrial and residential location, and environmental quality are to be linked to spatial interactions accruing from distance behavior in a socio-economic system.

The pattern of human settlement has been characterized by a high degree of dynamics during the postwar period. Increased suburbanization demonstrates that mobility forms a key element of recent spatial developments. According to Masotti and Hadden [1972] this large-scale suburbanization might even be called an "urbanization of the suburbs." The increased mobility is most clearly reflected by the large rise in the average commuting radius (cf. Hansen [1976] and Lamb [1975]).

This increase in mobility can be explained from two factors, viz. changes in the *demand* structure of residential and recreational facilities and changes in the *supply* structure of recreational and environmental facilities (in general: utility systems; cf. Bökemann]1972]). The demand side is related to the general rise in economic welfare, which has induced a new set of priorities in the luxury sector (comfortable housing, recreation, sports and the like). The supply side is related to the general decline of many urban qualities due to the general production increase, congestion and pollution, and increased and large-scale urbanization. This discrepancy between demand and supply has led to a flight to the suburbs, in which a compromise could be found between the priorities for housing, recreation and accessibility to urban centers (with regard to job, cultural, and shopping facilities).

Generally speaking, the evolution of mobility of society and the associated changes in human settlement patterns can be explained from the residential attractiveness A_i^R of a residential place i and the labor attractiveness A_j^L of a labor place j. Attractiveness is defined here in a broad sense as an element that affects somebody's welfare position as far as it is related to his spatial behavior [1]. Therefore, the individual spatial welfare function w of a person can be defined as:

$$w = f(A_i^R, A_j^L) \qquad (13-1)$$

This welfare function of a person living in i and working in j satisfies the budget constraint:

$$t_{ij} A_j^L + p_i A_i^R \leq B , \qquad (13-2)$$

where B is the maximum total individual budget available for transportation expenditures and housing, and where t_{ij} and p_i represent the cost associated with bridging the distance between places i and j and the cost associated with housing, respectively.

In a figurative way, the spatial decision of an individual can be described as a compromise solution between alternative residential and labor places:

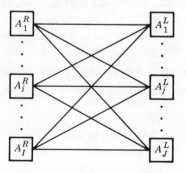

If an individual household has to make a choice in favor of a certain residential location, the following individual decision model may be hypothesized:

$$\max_{} w = \sum_{i,j} \gamma \, (A_i^R)^{\alpha_i} (A_j^L)^{\beta_j} \, \delta_{ij}$$
s.t.

$$\sum_{i,j} (t_{ij} \, A_j^L + p_i \, A_i^R) \, \delta_{ij} \leq B \qquad (13-3)$$

$$\sum_{i,j} \delta_{ij} = 1 \quad , \quad \delta_{ij} = 0, 1$$

If at the optimal residential locational decision the budget constraint is active, the following first-order conditions for maximizing behavior are valid:

$$\frac{\alpha_i \, A_j^L}{\beta_j \, A_i^R} = \frac{p_i}{t_{ij}} \qquad (13-4)$$

or:

$$\frac{A_j^L}{A_i^R} = \frac{\beta_j \, p_i}{\alpha_i \, t_{ij}} \quad , \qquad (13-5)$$

which implies that the compromise between residential attractiveness and labor attractiveness will be achieved at a point where the ratio of the attractiveness variables is proportional to the ratio of the preference elasticities of the attractiveness variables and inversely proportional to the ratio of their respective costs.

The spatial picture associated with the previous individual model can only be studied in a meaningful manner when these individual decisions are aggregated. The total aggregation of all individual decisions for a residential location in place i and a job in place j gives rise to a commuting flow between place i and j. On the basis of $(13-5)$ it can be derived that the volume of this commuting flow (denoted by v_{ij}) is a function of A_j^L, A_i^R, p_i and t_{ij}. In other words, the following aggregated commuting model may be hypothesized:

$$v_{ij} = \kappa \, (A_i^R)^{\epsilon} \, (A_j^L)^{\eta} \, p_i^{-\lambda} \, t_{ij}^{-\mu} \qquad (13-6)$$

By means of a time series or cross section analysis, this commuting model may be estimated and used as a spatial assignment model.

It is clear that a similar model can be constructed for migration flows, freight flows and shopping flows. In this way the evolution of mobility can be analyzed on the basis of spatial interactions between origins and destinations. The following section will be devoted to a more accurate and operational analysis of the attractiveness concepts.

A MULTIDIMENSIONAL ANALYSIS OF ATTRACTIVENESS

It was argued in the previous section that mobility can be considered as the result of discrepancies in spatial attractiveness variables. These attractiveness variables may include various elements. For example, the suburbanization process can be explained on the basis of the following factors (see also Nijkamp [1976]):

- the low residential attractiveness in many city centers due to the qualitative and quantitative shortage of dwellings caused by destruction from the war, rise in population and competition with respect to office buildings.
- the low environmental attractiveness in several cities due to congestion, pollution and lack of recreational areas.
- the high environmental attractiveness in suburbs and places around big centers due to the high-quality environmental conditions in more peripheral areas.
- the residential attractiveness of many suburbs due to the large housing programs being carried out there.
- the labor, cultural, educational and shopping attractiveness of big centers, so that a random scattering of population is prevented.
- the trip attractiveness due to both the accessibility of the central places with respect to surrounding areas and the rise in economic welfare compensating the higher transportation costs of commuting.

The foregoing remarks indicate that spatial interaction flows (like migration and commuting) are determined by tensions between the successive residential attractiveness indicators and the labor attractiveness indicators, apart from distance frictions. Given the fact that the individual income levels influence the mobility pattern (due to expenditures on housing and transportation), mobility patterns and settlement patterns may be closely related to specific socioeconomic groups.

Clearly, the various interactions in a spatial system arise from a multiplicity of differential attractiveness indicators. A useful analytical tool is to specify an *attractiveness profile* for each place or region separately. Such an attractiveness profile is a vector representation of a variety of elements determining human spatial behavior. These elements are related to both the labor characteristics of local production systems and to the residential and environmental characteristics of local settlement systems. The latter category includes in particular many quality-of-life indicators associated with the physical or natural environment of man.

The concept of an attractiveness profile was introduced *inter alia* in Nijkamp [1975a, 1976a, 1976b]. For example, the residential attractiveness of a place can be represented by means of the following vector a^R :

$$
a^R = \begin{bmatrix} a^R_1 \\ \cdot \\ \cdot \\ \cdot \\ \cdot \\ \cdot \\ \cdot \\ \cdot \\ \cdot \\ \cdot \\ a^R_N \end{bmatrix} = \begin{bmatrix} \text{availability of dwellings} \\ \text{quality of dwellings} \\ \text{size of recreation areas} \\ \text{availability of shops} \\ \text{cultural facilities} \\ \cdot \\ \cdot \\ \cdot \\ \cdot \\ \cdot \end{bmatrix} \qquad (13\text{--}7)
$$

All elements of the residential attractiveness profile can in principle be specified in measurable units. They are assumed to be measured according to the principle "the higher, the better." Therefore, for each place i separately a residential attractiveness profile a^R_i can be determined. The same holds true for the labor attractiveness profile a^L_j, which includes elements like wages and salaries, availability of jobs, degree of social stability, etc. The advantage of an attractiveness profile is the fact that such a vector representation is capable of specifying in an operational way the variety of urban characteristics.

One may hypothesize that a place will attract more residents to the degree that its attractiveness profile corresponds more closely to the needs and desires of people. In other words, a certain place i will be more attractive with respect to a place j to the extent that the differential attractiveness indicator of i with respect to j is higher.

The *differential* residential attractiveness indicator Δ_{ij}^{R} of i with respect to j can be defined as a generalized distance metric (the Minkowski p-metric) between the elements of a_i^R and a_j^R :

$$\Delta_{ij}^R = \left\{ \sum_{n=1}^N \left| \frac{a_{in}^R - a_{jn}^R}{a_n^{R\ \max}} \right|^p \right\}^{1/p} , \qquad (13-8)$$

where $a_n^{R\ \max}$ is equal to the maximum value of a_{in}^R over all places i, i.e.

$$a_n^{R\ \max} = \max_i\ a_{in}^R \qquad (13-9)$$

It is easily seen that the Euclidean metric and the rectangular ("city-block") metric are special cases of (13-8), viz. if $p = 2$ and $p = 1$, respectively. A similar indicator can be defined with respect to labor attractiveness.

Instead of a differential indicator one may also define a so-called *similarity* indicator s_{ij}^R :

$$s_{ij}^R = \frac{1}{1 + \Delta_{ij}^R} \qquad (13-10)$$

In case of a maximum discrepancy (i.e., $\Delta_{ij}^R \to \infty$), $s_{ij}^R = 0$. In case of a minimum discrepancy (i.e. $\Delta_{ij}^R = 0$), $s_{ij}^R = 1$.

The probability of commuting flows v_{ij} between place i and j is higher to the extent that the residential attractiveness of i exceeds that of j, and the labor attractiveness of j exceeds that of i. This can be illustrated by means of Figure 13-1A and 13-1B.

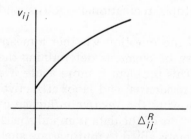

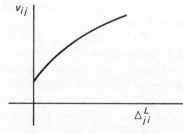

Figure 13-1A. Commuting Flows as a Function of the Differential Residential Attractiveness.

Figure 13-1B. Commuting Flows as a Function of the Differential Labor Attractiveness.

Furthermore, it is clear that distance friction will also play an important role in the degree of spatial interactions between place i and j, as can be illustrated by means of Figure 13–1C.

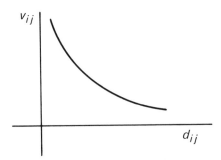

Figure 13–1C. Commuting Flows as a Function of Distance d_{ij}.

On the basis of the preceding notions of attractiveness frictions and distance frictions the evolution of settlement systems can in principle be analyzed and predicted. For example, the general model to be used now for commuting flows is:

$$v_{ij} = f(\Delta_{ij}^R, \ \Delta_{ij}^L, \ d_{ij}) \qquad (13–11)$$

or:

$$v_{ij} = \kappa (\Delta_{ij}^R)^\epsilon \ (\Delta_{ij}^L)^\eta \ d_{ij}^{-\beta} \qquad (13–12)$$

If the evolution of a settlement pattern is to be studied more accurately from the viewpoint of changes in quality-of-life (cf. Nijkamp [1976c]), the residential attractiveness factors can be split up into housing factors, environmental factors, recreational factors and sociocultural factors.

One of the intriguing problems is the question whether a meaningful delineation of the great variety of elements determining the attractiveness indicators is possible. This problem is more acute if a large set of variables associated with residential and labor attractiveness is to be considered without knowing the relative influence of each of these variables. Then a reduction of the data is an indispensable stage of the analysis. This problem is allied to multivariate analysis (like principal component methods) in which a set of variables is to be reduced to a limited number of variables. The advantage of principal component techniques is the fact that a limited number of (transformed) independent factors arises, whereas an apparent drawback is the fact that these new independent factors do not have a clear meaning.

In this respect a new technique, viz. *interdependence analysis*, seems to be worthwhile (see also Appendix A). Interdependence analysis serves to reduce a multidimensional data set to a subset composed of *original* variables (see Beale [1970] and Boyce et al. [1974]). Interdependence analysis is an optimal subset selection on the basis of statistical correlation techniques by means of which a limited subset of variables can be selected out of the original total set of variables. In this way the multidimensional data set is reduced to an optimum subset that reflects the original data to a maximum degree. The advantage of an interdependence analysis is the fact the optimum subset is composed of *original* variables and not of transformed variables (like in a principal component analysis). The basic idea of an interdependence analysis rests upon a recursive correlation analysis between successive subsets of the original data set. Then the aim of this analysis is to find by means of multiple correlation coefficients a subset of original variables which are associated with the total data set to an optimum degree (in terms of correlation coefficients).

In our case of a set of attractiveness indicators over a set of places i ($i = 1, \ldots, I$) the following multidimensional datamatrix arises:

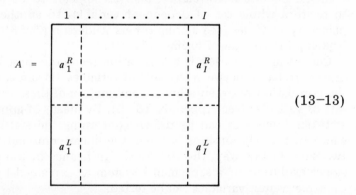

$$\tag{13-13}$$

The great variety of characteristics present in the rows of A can now be reduced to a desired number in a meaningful way by means of an interdependence analysis.

In the preceding analysis particular attention has been paid to the effect of structural local attractiveness characteristics upon spatial mobility arising from commuting patterns (see (13-11)). This analysis can be generalized in a straightforward way by also taking into account phenomena like recreation flows, migration flows and growth of population in a settlements system. For example, the net migration m_i to a place i can be assumed to be a function of the residential attractiveness A_i^R and the labor attractiveness A_i^L (cf. (13−6)):

$$m_i = \kappa (A_i^R)^\epsilon (A_i^L)^\eta \qquad (13-14)$$

Given the multidimensional nature of residential and labor attractiveness, these variables can be measured as the generalized distance with respect to the origin by means of the Minkowski p-metric [2]:

$$A_i^R = \left\{ \sum_{n=1}^N \left| \frac{a_{in}^R}{a_n^{R\ \max}} \right|^p \right\}^{1/p} \qquad (13-15)$$

In this way the evolution of a system of settlements can be described and analyzed from the viewpoint of a great variety of residential and labor attractiveness indicators. The evolution of such a system can be described in terms of net migration flows, net commuting flows, net recreation flows etc. Now the question arises as to whether all these variables characterizing the development of a settlement pattern can be linked simultaneously to the attractiveness phenomena. *Canonical correlation analysis* appears to be a useful tool to relate a whole set of dependent variables to another set of explanatory variables (see among others Anderson [1958], Bartels and Nijkamp [1976], and Dhrymes [1970]).

Canonical correlation is a correlation technique based on a maximum correlation between two sets of variables. Its aim is to maximize the correlation between a linear combination of these two successive sets of variables (see Appendix 13−B). By means of appropriate test statistics inferences can be drawn concerning the statistical significance of the relationships between the linear combinations of these two sets. In this way, the statistical significance of the multidimensional evolution of a settlements system as explained by a large set of attractiveness variables can be tested.

The over-all conclusion is that interdependence analysis and canonical correlation analysis are powerful tools in analyzing multidimensional data.

SPATIAL SPILL-OVER EFFECTS
AND SETTLEMENT PATTERNS

In the preceding section no attention was paid to spatial spill-over effects in spatial interactions. In general, the growth of places (in other words, relative attractiveness) is co-determined by the attractiveness of surrounding places. This contiguity effect is particularly important for residential location decisions (and so for migration and commuting behavior).

The foregoing remarks imply that the attractiveness A_i^R or A_i^L of a place i (see (13–15)) is co-determined by the attractiveness of surrounding places. Therefore, the total attractiveness A_i^{-R} is composed of an *internal* attractiveness A_i^R and the *external* attractiveness $\hat{A}_i^R$, i.e.,

$$A_i^{-R} = \sigma_i A_i^R + (1 - \sigma_i)\hat{A}_i^R , \qquad (13-16)$$

where σ_i is a relative weight and where $\hat{A}_i^R$ is a weighted attractiveness indicator on the basis of the weighted attractiveness of regions contiguous to region i:

$$\hat{A}_i^R = \sum_{j_i} w_{j_i} A_{j_i}^{-R} , \qquad (13-17)$$

where the lower index j_i refers to all regions j contiguous to region i, and where the weights w_{j_i} may be related to the size s_{j_i} and the distance d_{ij_i} as follows:

$$w_{j_i} = \frac{\dfrac{s_{j_i}}{d_{ij_i}}}{\displaystyle\sum_{j_i} \dfrac{s_{j_i}}{d_{ij_i}}} \qquad (13-18)$$

Substitution of (13–17) into (13–16) yields the following result:

$$A_i^{-R} = \sigma_i A_i^R + (1 - \sigma_i) \sum_{j_i} w_{j_i} A_{j_i}^{-R} , \qquad (13-19)$$

or in vector notation:

$$A^{-R} = \hat{\sigma} A^R + (I - \hat{\sigma}) W A^{-R} , \qquad (13-20)$$

where A^{-R} and A^R are $(I \times 1)$ vectors including the elements A_i^{-R} and A_i^R, respectively; $\hat{\sigma}$ a diagonal matrix with the elements σ_i on the main diagonal; and W a connectivity matrix with the contiguity weights w_{j_i} as elements. The total attractiveness vector A^{-R} can now be written as a multiplier expression:

$$A^{-R} = \{I - (I - \hat{\sigma}) W\}^{-1} \hat{\sigma} A^R \quad , \quad (13-21)$$

provided $\{I - (I - \hat{\sigma})W\}^{-1}$ is nonsingular. The latter matrix multiplier calculates both the *direct* and *indirect* attractiveness indicators of a region. An application of this multiplier concept is contained in Nijkamp [1976b, 1976c].

The foregoing spill-over adjustments can be introduced into the behavioral models (13–11) and (13–14), viz. by calculating the total attractiveness elements on the basis of the above-mentioned spatial spill-over effects. This implies, for example, that the commuting model can be re-specified as:

$$v_{ij} = f(A_i^{-R}, A_j^{-R}, A_i^{-L}, A_j^{-L}, d_{ij}) \quad (13-22)$$

A next adjustment deals with the *temporal* adjustment process of spatial interactions. One may assume that the spatial interactions satisfy a certain time-varying adjustment process, so that the spatial interactions in a certain time period t are co-determined by the interactions from the previous time period. This implies in case of model (13–22):

$$v_{ij,t} = f(A_{i,t}^{-R}, A_{j,t}^{-R}, A_{i,t}^{-L}, A_{j,t}^{-L}, d_{ij,t}, v_{ij,t-1}) \quad (13-23)$$

The relationships for net immigration of each place can be dealt with in an analogous manner (cf. (13–14)):

$$m_{i,t} = f(A_{i,t}^{-R}, A_{i,t}^{-L}, m_{i,t-1}) \quad , \quad (13-24)$$

which also represents a distributed lag structure.

If the additional assumption is made that the flows from a previous period to region i may determine the flows in a later period to a contiguous region, a complicated problem of *spatial and temporal autocorrelation* arises. An analysis of this problem as well as a solution method with numerical applications is contained in Hordijk and Nijkamp [1977].

The foregoing models are based on the assumption that the development of a settlement system is influenced to a considerable degree by the attractiveness of all places in this system, both as far as the quality-of-life is concerned and the situation in the labor market. By means of the multidimensional indicators an operational approach to the changes and spatial interactions in a settlement pattern is possible. By means of regression techniques these models can be estimated in principle, provided sufficient information concerning the attractiveness and the spatial interactions is available (time series and cross-section data). The following section will be devoted to situations in which insufficient information is available.

DISAGGREGATION OF SPATIAL INTERACTION MODELS

In the foregoing sections the assumption was made that sufficient information was available to estimate or to calibrate the relationships describing the spatial interactions in a settlement system. Empirical investigations demonstrate, however, that the mobility patterns associated with quality-of-life characteristics are very hard to gauge at a detailed level. Insight into detailed mobility patterns is, however, a necessary condition for predictions of future developments and for effective spatial policies.

It frequently occurs that observations are only available on a more global level of mobility patterns (for example, on an interregional level), whereas on an interlocal level no information is available at all. Now the question arises as to whether information on *interregional* mobility patterns and on the residential and labor attractiveness of all places within such an interregional system can be used to estimate the *interlocal* mobility patterns and the development of all places in this system of settlements.

For example, assume a system composed of P regions. Then the total number of interregional flows (migration, commuting, etc.) is equal to $P(P-1)$. Assume that each region contains Q places. Then the total number of interlocal flows is equal to $PQ(PQ-1)$. If the $P(P-1)$ interregional flows are known, the question arises whether the $PQ(PQ-1)$ interlocal flows can be estimated on the basis of the interregional flows (see Figure 13-2).

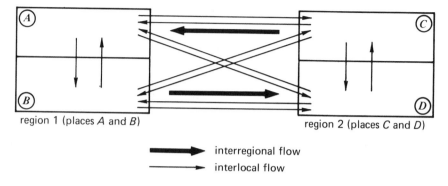

region 1 (places A and B)   region 2 (places C and D)

➡ interregional flow

→ interlocal flow

Figure 13-2. Interregional and Interlocal Flows

The first way to attack this problem is to use the behavioral models mentioned above. This implies that interlocal mobility patterns are estimated on the basis of information on local attractiveness characteristics, given the interregional flows. This in turn implies that the following relationship has to be estimated (cf. (13-22)):

$$v_{ij}^{ps} = f(A_i^{-R,p}, A_j^{-R,s}, A_i^{-L,p}, A_j^{-L,s}, d_{ij}^{ps}) , \qquad (13-25)$$

where v_{ij}^{ps} is the volume of interaction (migration, commuting, etc.) from place i in region p to place j in region s. The remaining variables can be interpreted in a similar manner.

The foregoing model can be estimated by means of least squares procedures, given a set of observations on $v_{ij}^{ps}, A_i^{-R,p}, A_j^{-R,s}, A_i^{-L,s}, A_j^{-L,s}, d_{ij}^{ps}$ (either as time series or as a cross-section). However, detailed data on inter*local* flows are only rarely available, so that v_{ij}^{ps} is frequently unknown. The only information available concerns the inter*regional* flows v^{ps} $(p,s = 1, \ldots, P; p \neq s)$. This implies the following additivity conditions for the interlocal flows between place i in region p and place j in region s:

$$v^{ps} = \sum_{i \epsilon p} \sum_{j \epsilon s} v_{ij}^{ps} , \qquad (13-26)$$

where the symbol 'ϵ' denotes "belongs to." Therefore, the parameters of (13-25) have to be estimated subject to the additivity conditions $(13-26)$. This implies that the parameters of an inter*local* mobility pattern and of the structure of a settlement system have to be estimated on the basis of inter*regional* flows and *local* attractiveness characteristics.

The basic problem is now to disaggregate the interregional structure to an interlocal structure, taking account of the fact that observations on v_{ij}^{ps} are not available. The abundant amount of degrees of freedom with respect to the estimation of interlocal mobility patterns can be solved as follows. Substitution of $(13-25)$ into $(13-26)$ yields the following result:

$$(13-27)$$

$$v^{ps} = \sum_{i \epsilon p} \sum_{j \epsilon s} (A_i^{-R,p}, A_j^{-R,s}, A_i^{-L,p}, A_j^{-L,s}, d_{ij}^{ps})$$

This is an equation with observable and known variables both on the left side and on the right side. By means of least squares techniques the parameters associated with the explanatory variables can be estimated in principle. Once these parameters have been estimated, they may be substituted into $(13-25)$ to gauge the interlocal mobility patterns.

It should be noted that the test statistics associated with the latter least squares methods are only relevant for the inter*regional* pattern, so that the reliability of the estimated inter*local* pattern cannot be tested. Therefore, it might be useful to integrate this behavioral approach with an alternative approach which is rather popular in spatial interaction modelling, viz. *entropy analysis* (cf. Wilson [1970]).

Entropy assumptions can be considered as the foundation for the use of the well-known gravity models in various spatial analyses. The entropy hypothesis provides the means to calculate the most probable configuration of a spatial system. This entropy is not only a mechanistic, physical concept; it can also be interpreted by means of behavioral hypotheses about minimum cost behavior (see, for a broader exposition, Nijkamp [1975b]).

The entropy model related to the foregoing disaggregation of inter*regional* mobility patterns to inter*local* mobility patterns can be written as:

$$\max w = - \sum_{i \epsilon p} \sum_{j \epsilon s} \sum_{p=1}^{P} \sum_{\substack{s=1 \\ p \neq s}}^{P} (v_{ij}^{rs} \; \ln \; v_{ij}^{rs} - v_{ij}^{rs})$$

$$\sum_{i \epsilon p} \sum_{j \epsilon s} v_{ij}^{ps} = v^{ps} \quad , \quad \forall \, p,s \qquad (13-28)$$

$$\sum_{i \epsilon p} \sum_{j \epsilon s} \sum_{p=1}^{P} \sum_{\substack{s=1 \\ p \neq s}}^{P} v_{ij}^{ps} \ d_{ij}^{ps} = T \quad ,$$

where T is the total distance budget within the interregional system. The solution of the latter entropy model can be calculated as follows:

$$v_{ij}^{ps} = C_{ps} \ v^{ps} \ \exp \ (-\beta \ d_{ij}^{ps}) \quad , \qquad (13-29)$$

where C_{ps} is equal to:

$$C_{ps} = \{ \sum_{i \epsilon p} \sum_{j \epsilon s} \exp \ (-\beta \ d_{ij}^{ps})\}^{-1} \qquad (13-30)$$

This model can be calibrated by means of the usual recursive solution procedures for entropy models.

It is clear that in general the results of the entropy model will differ from those obtained by means of the above-mentioned behavioral model. Therefore, the question arises as to whether the entropy model and the behavioral model can be integrated in a meaningful way so as to benefit from the advantages of both models.

Two alternative approaches are, in principle, available to arrive at an integration of the behavioral and the entropy model.

The first approach starts off from the results of the behavioral model (13–25), assessed by means of the auxiliary system (13–27). The estimated interlocal flows v_{ij}^{rs} are then used as observations in the entropy equation (13–29), so that the parameters of the entropy equation (C_{ps} and β) can be estimated by means of least-squares techniques. Next, the values of v_{ij}^{ps} can be calculated according to (13–29). These values can be substituted into (13–25) to estimate the parameters of the attractiveness variables (subject to the additivity condition (13–26)). The calculated interlocal mobility pattern can again be substituted into (13–30), etc. This recursive procedure will be terminated as soon as the successive steps show only a negligible difference with respect to the preceding step.

A drawback of this first approach is the fact that the entropy idea is not used in an appropriate way. The basic idea of an entropy model is to estimate simultaneously the spatial interactions as well as the associated parameters. In the previous approach, however, the spatial interactions are introduced as observed data from the behavioral model, so that less efficient use is made of the entropy model.

Therefore, an alternative approach may be considered in which the results of the behavioral model are used as *prior* information in the entropy model. It is well-known that entropy can be conceived of as the expected information content of a certain message (cf. Theil [1967]). In a more general setting, entropy is associated with the degree of uncertainty in choice situations with many alternatives. A decline in the degree of uncertainty will lead to a reduction of the entropy in the system at hand. Thus, additional information will decrease the entropy and increase the degree of certainty. In other words, additional (prior) information about the mobility patterns in a spatial interaction system may lead to more reliable estimates of these patterns.

This Bayesian notion of prior information (cf. Raiffa and Schlaifer [1961]) can be introduced into entropy models by making a distinction between *prior* probabilities and *posterior* probabilities. The probability of a spatial flow π_{ij}^{ps} is equal to:

$$\pi_{ij}^{ps} = \frac{v_{ij}^{ps}}{v} \quad , \tag{13-31}$$

where v is the total volume of flows. If the prior probability of a flow is calculated according to the behavioral model (13-25), it will be denoted by $\hat{\pi}_{ij}^{ps}$. This prior probability can be used in the entropy to calculate the ultimate probabilities of the spatial mobility pattern (see, for a broader exposition, also Hobson and Cheng [1973] and Kullback [1959]). This ultimate probability is the *conditional* probability that a certain mobility pattern arises, given the prior probability from the behavioral model.

The average conditional entropy (see also Nijkamp [1976a], Nijkamp and Paelinck [1974] and Theil [1967]) of a mobility pattern is equal to:

$$w = - \sum_{i \in p} \sum_{j \in s} \sum_{\substack{p=1 \\ p \neq s}}^{P} \sum_{s=1}^{P} \pi_{ij}^{ps} \, ln \, (\pi_{ij}^{ps} / \hat{\pi}_{ij}^{ps}) \tag{13-32}$$

It is easily seen that $w = 0$ when the prior probability $\hat{\pi}_{ij}^{ps}$ is equal to the posterior probability π_{ij}^{ps}. The ultimate result of the spatial interaction pattern associated with an average conditional entropy is:

$$v_{ij}^{ps} = v \, \hat{\pi}_{ij}^{ps} \, C_{ps} \, v^{ps} exp \, (- \beta \, d_{ij}^{ps}) \tag{13-33}$$

After the calibration of (13—33), the results can again be substituted into (13—25), etc. By means of the integration of the foregoing two models the advantages of a behavioral model can be linked to those of a gravity model. Applications of this analysis can be found in Nijkamp [1976a].

It also is clear that the other variables of a settlement system (like net migration) can be dealt with in a similar way. Given the structure of such a model, the results may be used to predict the mobility pattern in a scenario-analysis for the future. In this way, the method may be useful to gauge the interlocal mobility pattern associated with alternative spatial policies concerning residential and labor patterns. Changes in the physical infrastructure (leading to adjusted values of the distance variables) can also be analyzed in a similar way. In conclusion, the foregoing approach may be useful in analyzing in a detailed way mobility patterns and changes in settlement systems due to shifts in attractiveness and quality-of-life.

The foregoing multicriteria attractiveness analysis has been applied to several mobility problems in the Netherlands (migration, commuting, recreation and tourism). The residential and environmental quality indicators appeared to provide a significant explanation for the level and the direction of spatial flow variables. This implies that in principle the spatial interaction pattern associated with a broad set of attractiveness indicators can be gauged. The next question is, obviously, how this information can be used in planning practice.

Therefore, the next section will be devoted to some policy issues related to attractiveness, quality-of-life and settlement patterns in the Netherlands.

PHYSICAL PLANNING AND URBAN ATTRACTIVENESS

The quality-of-life appears to have undergone a significant decline in the western urbanized and industrialized countries, as witnessed by high levels of pollution, a decline in the quantity of natural areas due to road-building and house-building, congestion in recreation areas, congestion in city centers, decline in the quality of urban life, and similar phenomena.

Many planning agencies are confronted with the issue of how to develop integrated and balanced physical planning. It is important to note that effective spatial planning requires detailed insight into the motives of people and into human behavior. Knowledge of the determinants of human behavior is a prerequisite for a significant improvement of urban living conditions and for a reduction of the flight to the suburbs and to rural areas.

In recent years the need for urban renovation policies has frequently been emphasized. Such renovation is not primarily oriented to a demolition of older urban areas; its aim is rather to maintain and revive the positive social, economic and psychological elements of an older urban area. Therefore, many efforts are made to improve dwellings, to create small-scale urban recreation areas, to extend the variety of residential areas, to improve the accessibility of these areas, to provide sufficient public facilities and urban amenities, and to maintain specific urban characteristics.

The approach presented in the previous sections has already indicated the importance of a variety of attractiveness elements determining human behavior. Clearly, physical and spatial planning and policies have to take into account this analytical information: insight into the motives and evolutions of mobility patterns is a necessary condition to make planning successful.

In the Netherlands a very important government document has recently been published, viz. the Verstedelijkingsnota [1976] (urbanization report), which contains a series of proposed spatial policies and measures concerning the dispersion of population, urban reconstruction, suburbanization, rural development, etc. It is a unique report in the sense that the Dutch government attempts to implement a new spatial policy on the basis of a scientific investigation of all current spatial developments (for a brief review see also Witsen [1976]).

This urbanization report starts with the statement that, due to the energy and environmental crises, the period of unlimited growth and of unlimited future perspectives has gone. Instead of huge physical and spatial developments, a moderate view of urban and rural development is taken: modest land use, protection of ecologically valuable areas, reconstruction of urban areas, and so forth.

Further urbanization in the Netherlands should only take place in a very limited number of growth centers; otherwise the mobility pattern would affect the whole spatial pattern and environmental conditions. The center of the Dutch Rimcity has to be protected against urbanization, and urban sprawl to areas adjacent to the Rimcity has to be reduced (except in growth centers).

The contrast between rural and urban areas has to be maintained by means of a more appropriate mobility pattern with respect to residential, labor and recreational areas. The proposed reduction of mobility implies that the average commuting time should not exceed 30 minutes.

The general idea of this urbanization report is that a spatial differentiation can only be preserved if the city, as the nucleus of a spatial system, is able to carry out its tasks in an adequate way. Thus, the maintenance or the creation of a rich variety of *urban* functions is emphasized; the urban environment receives a high positive valuation in the report. In addition, the maintenance or the creation of varied *rural* areas is emphasized, *inter alia*, by proposing an institutional and organizational planning framework in terms of small-scale urban regions. Finally, infrastructure facilities for private transport (like roads) will no longer follow the uncontrolled trend of the increased mobility. In this way, the physical and spatial policy hopes to arrive at a closed residential-labor balance (in which commuting flows do not dominate the linkages between urban regions).

It is clear that the foregoing proposals for a better integration of residential, job, and recreational decisions imply that attractiveness indicators are of crucial importance in analyzing human behavior. In particular, the report's emphasis on residential and environmental attractiveness is in line with the multicriteria analysis proposed here. Unfortunately, the report does not take into account labor attractiveness (at least not in an adequate way), although it is clear on the basis of the preceding sections that this also is "one side of the mobility coin," co-determining the spatial pattern of society. But, in a period of an economic recession it is very hard to use an employment policy in the framework of physical planning.

The urbanization report was not based on formal mathematical models, so it is rather hard to make predictions about future spatial developments. These were studied in the report by means of a set of scenario-analyses, but it is clear that more reliable and testable inferences concerning future mobility patterns and the effects of the proposed physical and spatial policies can only be drawn if integrated formal models are used. This emphasizes once more our initial contention that analytical studies should be a prerequisite for political decisions.

APPENDIX 13–A.
INTERDEPENDENCE ANALYSIS

In case of a multidimensional datamatrix (cf. (13–12)) the question arises as to whether an optimum selection of a subset of original variables can be made. Interdependence analysis is a statistical correlation technique by means of which a whole set of variables can be replaced by a smaller subset which reflects the original set to an optimum degree.

Suppose a total set composed of N variables. Then the interdependence analysis attempts to select in an optimum manner J variables $(J < N)$ out of these N variables. The criterion for selecting these variables is based on a successive examination of each possible subset of J variables by means of regression analysis. The remaining $(N - J)$ variables are considered as the successive dependent variables in a regression equation containing the J variables as the explanatory variables. This gives rise to $N - J$ regression equations for each subset of J variables, while each regression equation gives rise to a certain squared multiple correlation coefficient R^2. It is evident that the total number of possible subsets of J variables is equal to $\binom{N}{J}$. The optimal subset composed of J variables is then based on the criterion that this subset should give rise to the maximum value of $R^2_{\min}$ over all $\binom{N}{J}$ subsets, where $R^2_{\min}$ is equal to the minimum value of R^2 over all successive $N - J$ regression equations. In other words, the criterion for an optimum subset selection of J variables out of N variables is:

$$\max_{k = 1, \ldots, \binom{N}{J}} \left\{ \min_{l = 1, \ldots, (N-J)} R^2_{kl} \right\} \quad , \quad (13A–1)$$

where R^2_{kl} is the (squared) multiple correlation coefficient associated with the lth regression equation from the kth subset.

It is clear that an exhaustive examination of all possible combinations is very time-consuming, so that an efficient algorithm has to be developed in order to arrive at an optimum subset. Examples of these algorithms are contained, for example, in Boyce et al. [1974] and Wiersma [1976]. These heuristic algorithms are based on statistical properties of the successive correlation coefficients, so that by means of threshold values several nonoptimal subsets can be eliminated *a priori*.

APPENDIX 13–B. CANONICAL CORRELATION ANALYSIS

Canonical correlation describes the linkages between two sets of variables. Suppose M standardized observations on two sets of variables x and y, where x and y are a $(K \times 1)$ and a $(L \times 1)$ vector of random variables, respectively, and $(K \leq L)$. The elements x and y are assumed to be normally distributed. Furthermore, the following assumption may be made:

$$Ex = 0; \quad Ey = 0; \quad Exx' = R_{11}; \quad Exy' = R_{12}; \quad (13B–1)$$

$$Eyx' = R'_{12}; \quad Eyy' = R_{22}$$

with

$$R = \begin{bmatrix} R_{11} & | & R_{12} \\ \text{---} & + & \text{---} \\ R'_{12} & | & R_{22} \end{bmatrix}$$
(13B–2)

Consider now the linear combination c_1^x and c_1^y of x and y, respectively:

$$c_1^x = \varphi'_1 \, x$$
(13B–3)

and:

$$c_1^y = \mu'_1 \, y$$
(13B–4)

If c_1^x and c_1^y should have a maximum mutual correlation, the following condition should be imposed:

(13B–5)

$$\max_{\varphi_1, \mu_1} \quad (\varphi'_1 \, R_{12} \, \mu_1) \, \{(\varphi'_1 \, R_{11} \, \varphi_1) \, (\mu'_1 \, R_{22} \, \mu_1)\}^{-\frac{1}{2}}$$

A unique solution can be derived when the following additional conditions are imposed:

$$\begin{cases} \text{var } c_1^x = \varphi'_1 \, R_{11} \, \varphi_1 = 1 \\ \text{var } c_1^y = \mu'_1 \, R_{22} \, \mu_1 = 1 \end{cases}$$
(13B–6)

If λ_{11} and λ_{12} represent the Lagrange multiplier associated with the two conditions from (13B–6), it can be shown that (cf. Anderson [1958] and Dhrymes [1970]):

$$\lambda_{11} = \lambda_{12} = \lambda_1 = \varphi'_1 \, R_{12} \, \mu_1 \, ,$$
(13B–7)

while φ_1 and μ_1 are the solution of:

$$\begin{bmatrix} -\lambda \, R_{11} & R_{12} \\ R'_{12} & -\lambda \, R_{22} \end{bmatrix} \begin{bmatrix} \varphi_1 \\ \mu_1 \end{bmatrix} = \begin{bmatrix} 0 \end{bmatrix}$$
(13B–8)

A nonzero solution requires that the discriminant of the matrix is equal to zero:

$$
\begin{vmatrix}
-\lambda\,R_{11} & R_{12} \\
R'_{12} & -\lambda\,R_{22}
\end{vmatrix} = 0 \quad , \qquad (13\text{B}-9)
$$

which leads in principle to $K + L$ roots. Now λ_1 is to be selected as the largest root (with corresponding solutions φ_1 and μ_1). The second set of solutions can be derived in a similar way by imposing the additional condition that the solutions φ_1 and μ_1 from the first stage are uncorrelated with those from the second stage, etc. In this recursive way all canonical variables φ_1, φ_2, ... and μ_1, μ_2, ... can be calculated. Next, the number of significant linear relationships can be determined by means of approximate χ^2 test-statistics (see also Bartlett [1941]).

NOTES TO CHAPTER 13

1. For the moment, attractiveness is conceived of as a unidimensional variable. A set of adjustments will be presented later. It is clear that residential attractiveness is closely related to the quality of life.

2. The measurement of a multidimensional phenomenon by means of its distance to the origin is suggested, among others, by Paelinck and Nijkamp [1976].

REFERENCES

Anderson, T.W., *An Introduction to Multivariate Statistical Analysis.* New York, Wiley, 1958.

Bartels, C.P.A., and P. Nijkamp, "An Empirical Welfare Approach to Regional Income Distribution." *Socio-Economic Planning Sciences, 10* (1976) 117−128.

Bartlett, M.S., "The Statistical Significance of Canonical Correlation." *Biometrika, 32* (1941), 29−38.

Beale, E.M.L., "Selecting an Optimum Subset." *Integer and Nonlinear Programming,* edited by J. Abadie. Amsterdam, North-Holland Publishing Co., 1970, 451−462.

Bökemann, D., "Utility Systems as Determinants of Settlement Patterns." *Recent Developments in Regional Science,* edited by R. Funck. London, Pion, 1972, 80−101.

Boyce, D.E., A. Fahri and R. Weischedel, *Optimal Subset Selection, Multiple Regression, Interdependence and Optimal Network Algorithms.* Berlin, Springer Verlag, 1974.

Dhrymes, P.J., *Econometrics, Statistical Foundations and Applications.* New York, Harper & Row, 1970.

Hansen, N.M., "Systems Approaches to Human Settlements." Laxenburg, International Institute for Applied Systems Analysis, RM−76−3, 1976.

Hobson, A., and B.K. Cheng, "A Comparison of the Shannon and Kullback Information Measures." *Journal of Statistical Physics, 7* (1973), 301−310.

Hordijk, L., and P. Nijkamp, "Dynamic Models of Spatial Auto-correlation." *Environment and Planning,* 9 (1977), 505–519.

Kullback, S., *Statistics and Information.* New York, Wiley, 1959.

Lamb, R., "Metropolitan Impacts on Rural America." Chicago, University of Chicago, Dept. of Geography, Research Paper No. 162, 1975.

Masotti, L.H., and J.K. Hadden (eds.), *The Urbanization of the Suburbs.* Beverly Hills, Sage Publications, 1972.

Nijkamp, P., "Urbane and Suburbane Leefbaarheidsperikelen." *Stedelijk Perspektief,* edited by P. Nijkamp and C. Verhage. Leiden, Stenfert Kroese, 1975a, 1–36.

Nijkamp, P., "Reflections on Gravity and Entropy Models." *Regional Science and Urban Economics,* 5, 3 (1975b), 203–255.

Nijkamp, P., "Spatial Mobility and Settlement Patterns: An Application of a Behavioural Entropy." Laxenburg, International Institute for Applied Systems Analysis, RM–76–45, 1976a.

Nijkamp, P., "An Impact Analysis of Environmental Attraction Profiles and Spatial Mobility." *Alternative Frameworks of Analysis,* edited by D. Massey and P.W.J. Batey, London, Pion, 1976b, 87–107.

Nijkamp, P., "Socio-Economic and Environmental Indicators as Determinants of Interregional Migration Flows." *Social Indicators Research,* 3, 1 (1976c), 101–110.

Nijkamp, P., "Environmental Attraction Forces and Regional Tourist Effects." *Analytical Systems of Tourism,* edited by C.E. Gearing and W.A. Swart, 1976d (forthcoming).

Nijkamp, P., and J.H.P. Paelinck, "A Dual Interpretation and Generalization of Entropy Maximization Models in Regional Science." *Papers of the Regional Science Association,* 33 (1974), 13–31.

Paelinck, J.H.P., and P. Nijkamp, *Operational Theory and Method in Regional Economics.* Farnborough, Saxon House, 1976 (jointly with D.C. Heath, Lexington).

Raiffa, H., and R. Schlaifer, *Applied Statistical Decision Theory.* Cambridge, Graduate School of Business Administration, Harvard University, 1961.

Swain, H., and M. Logan, "Urban Systems: a Policy Perspective." *Environment and Planning,* 7 (1975), 743–756.

Theil, H., *Economics and Information Theory.* Amsterdam, North-Holland Publishing Co., 1967.

Tinbergen, J., *Economic Policy; Principles and Design.* Amsterdam, North-Holland Publishing Co., 1956.

Verstedelijkingsnota, The Hague, Staatsuitgeverij, 1976.

Wiersma, J.S., "Optimale Deelverzamelingen Selektie?". Amsterdam, Dept. of Economics, Free University, 1976 (mimeographed).

Wilson, A.G., *Entropy in Urban and Regional Modelling.* London, Pion, 1970.

Witsen, J., "Some General Aspects of the Urbanisation Report." Paper presented at the Seminar on 'Planning Education,' Instituut voor Planologie, Utrecht, 1976 (mimeographed).

Index

About the Editor

Niles M. Hansen is Professor of Economics at the University of Texas at Austin. From 1975 to 1977 he was on leave to carry out research on human settlement systems at the International Institute for Applied Systems Analysis, Laxenburg, Austria. His recent publications include (ed.) *Public Policy and Regional Economic Development: The Experience of Nine Western Countries* and *Improving Access to Economic Opportunity: Nonmetropolitan Labor Markets in an Urban Society.*

About the Contributors

Brian J.L. Berry is Williams Professor of City and Regional Planning at Harvard University. He also is Chairman of the Ph.D. program in Urban Planning and Director of The Laboratory for Computer Graphics and Spatial Analysis. Among his recent books are: *The Geography of Economic Systems, The Changing Shape of Metropolitan America, Urbanization and Counter-Urbanization,* and *Contemporary Urban Ecology.*

Thomas Falk is Doctor of Economics and member of the Faculty at the Stockholm School of Economics. He is the author of *Urban Sweden: Changes in the Distribution of Population—the 1960s in Focus.* During 1977—78 he is Visiting Associate Professor of Geography at Pennsylvania State University.

Walter B. Stöhr is Professor of Regional Planning and Director, Interdisciplinary Institute for Urban and Regional Studies (IIR), University of Economics (Wirtschaftsuniversität), Vienna, Austria. He was previously Professor of Regional Planning at McMaster University, Canada, and for five years acted as Senior Regional Advisor to the Ford Foundation in Santiago, Chile. He has been a consultant to various international agencies and is the author of *Regional Development: Experiences and Prospects in Latin America, Interurban Systems and Regional Economic Development,* and various papers in professional journals.

Franz Tödtling is Research Associate at the Interdisciplinary Institute for Urban and Regional Studies (IIR), University of Economics (Wirtschaftsuniversität), Vienna, Austria. He previously worked for the Vienna Institute for Business Location and has been engaged in studies on locational problems of economic activities in an urban context. At present he is involved in comparative studies of national regional policies, especially questions of evaluation of the impact of regional policy instruments.

Heinz Lüdemann is Director of the Institute for Geography and Geoecology of the Academy of Sciences of the German Democratic Republic, in Leipzig.

Joachim Heinzmann is Head of the Secretariat of the Institute for Geography and Geoecology of the Academy of Sciences of the German Democratic Republic, in Leipzig.

Kazimierz Dziewoński is Professor of Economic Geography at the Institute of Geography and Spatial Organization of the Polish Academy of Sciences. He has taught at Liverpool University, the Polish School of Architecture, Wrocław and Warsaw Universities, the University of Pennsylvania (Department of Regional Science) and elsewhere. From 1946 to 1959 he held a number of major positions in Polish central planning institutions. His major research interests include locational theory, economic regionalization and urban geography. Since 1976 he has been a full member of the Polish Academy of Sciences.

Koichi Mera is Professor of Socio-Economic Planning at the University of Tsukuba in Japan and is the author of *Income Distribution and Regional Development*. Previously he taught at Harvard University and worked at the World Bank. He has contributed numerous papers on regional and urban economics to professional journals and he has served several international and national organizations as a consultant on regional development and related issues.

Alan G. Gilbert is Lecturer in the Economic Geography of Latin America at University College and the Institute of Latin American Studies, London. He has been a consultant to the Colombian, Peruvian and Venezuelan governments. He is the author of *Latin American Development: A Geographical Perspective*, has written various articles on urban and regional development in Latin America and has edited *Development Planning and Spatial Structure*.

William Alonso is Richard Saltonstall Professor of Population Policy and Director of the Center for Population Studies at Harvard University. He is the author of *Location and Land Use, Regional Development and Planning* and *Regional Planning* (the latter two edited with J.R.P. Friedmann).

Richard J. Olsen is a Senior Research Associate with Charles River Associates, Inc., Cambridge, Massachusetts. He was formerly Head, Regional and Urban Studies Section, Energy Division, Oak Ridge National Laboratory and has taught at the Universities of Tennessee and Massachusetts. He has authored a number of papers and reports on regional economics and is a member of the editorial board of *The Review of Regional Studies*.

Piotr Korcelli is Associate Professor and Head of the Urban and Population Studies Department at the Institute of Geography and Spatial Organization, Polish Academy of Sciences, Warsaw. He is the author of *The Evolution of the Spatial Structure of Metropolitan Areas in California* and *The Theory of Intra-urban Structure*.

Peter Nijkamp is Professor of Regional and Environmental Economics at the Free University, Amsterdam. He was educated in econometrics and regional economics and has published articles and books on programming models, entropy problems, environmental and urban problems, and regional planning. His recently published books include *Operational Theory and Method in Regional Economics* (together with Jean H.P. Paelinck), *Multi-Criteria Analysis and Regional Decision-Making* (together with Ad van Delft), and *Theory and Application of Environmental Economics*.

Date D

eturned

APR 2 5 1993